EMERGING ADULTHOOD AND HIGHER EDUCATION

This important book introduces Arnett's emerging adulthood theory to scholars and practitioners in higher education and student affairs, illuminating how recent social, cultural, and economic changes have altered the pathway to adulthood. Chapters in this edited collection explore how this theory fits alongside current student development theory, the implications for how college students learn and develop, and how emerging adulthood theory is uniquely suited to address challenges facing higher education today. *Emerging Adulthood and Higher Education* provides important recommendations for administrators, counselors, and student affairs personnel to provide effective programs and services to facilitate their emerging adults' journeys through this formative stage of life.

Joseph L. Murray is Associate Professor of Education and Director of the Graduate Program in College Student Personnel at Bucknell University, USA.

Jeffrey Jensen Arnett is Research Professor of Psychology at Clark University, USA. He is also the Founding President and Executive Director of the Society for the Study of Emerging Adulthood (www.ssea.org).

EMERGING ADULTHOOD AND HIGHER EDUCATION

A New Student Development Paradigm

Edited by Joseph L. Murray and Jeffrey Jensen Arnett

Routledge
Taylor & Francis Group

NEW YORK AND LONDON

First published 2019
by Routledge
711 Third Avenue, New York, NY 10017

and by Routledge
2 Park Square, Milton Park, Abingdon, Oxon, OX14 4RN

Routledge is an imprint of the Taylor & Francis Group, an informa business

Library of Congress Cataloging-in-Publication Data
A catalog record for this title has been requested

ISBN: 978-1-138-65412-9 (hbk)
ISBN: 978-1-138-65413-6 (pbk)
ISBN: 978-1-315-62340-5 (ebk)

Typeset in Bembo
by codeMantra

CONTENTS

PREFACE

As we write these words, it has been almost 12 years to the day since Jeff visited Bucknell University, at Joe's invitation, to share his groundbreaking research on emerging adulthood, a period from the late teens through the twenties, which he characterized as neither adolescence nor young adulthood but a new life stage that has arisen in recent decades, with distinctive features of its own. A casual conversation on a walk between meetings on campus would ultimately lead to the publication of this book.

It was March 2006, and Jeff had returned to the U.S. for a brief stay, before resuming his research in Denmark, where he was studying emerging adulthood with the support of a Fulbright Fellowship. He had recently published the first edition of his book, *Emerging Adulthood: The Winding Road from the Late Teens through the Twenties* (Arnett, 2004), which had begun to draw media attention beyond his more established audience of academics specializing in adolescent psychology. At the time, Joe was teaching in the Education Department at Bucknell and had recently launched a fledgling master's degree program in college student personnel, his primary area of specialization. Joe had recently incorporated readings on Jeff's work into a course on learning and development in post-secondary education, and was struck by the degree to which the readings had resonated on a personal level with the emerging adults enrolled in the course. Indeed, it was largely at their urging that he invited Jeff to campus for a speaking engagement that would include a dinner with a very enthusiastic group of emerging adults preparing for careers in student affairs.

Joe, too, recognized the significance of Jeff's work to the student affairs profession, especially at a time when the rapid pace of social and technological change had prompted ongoing conversations about the future of higher education and the ways in which it might need to adapt to the demands of a changing clientele. Jeff's theory of emerging adulthood seemed tailor-made for incorporation into both the literature of student affairs and professional preparation programs in the field, yet even amidst the attention that it had begun to garner in academia and in the popular news media, it had generated little to no comparable "buzz" within student affairs or even higher education generally. As we speculated about the more limited attention to emerging adulthood theory in higher education, it became clear to us that a need existed for a concise reference work on the topic specifically for student affairs professionals and others engaged with emerging adults in college and university settings. We also agreed on the spot to take on the project ourselves, as soon as our plates would clear.

Over the decade that followed, neither of our plates cleared, especially Jeff's. To the contrary, interest in his theory of emerging adulthood continued to grow. By 2013, the Society for the Study of Emerging Adulthood (SSEA) was established, along with its flagship journal, *Emerging Adulthood*. Two years later, the second edition of *Emerging Adulthood: The Winding Road from the Late Teens through the Twenties* (Arnett, 2015) was released, followed soon thereafter by the inaugural edition of *The Oxford Handbook of Emerging Adulthood* (Arnett, 2016). Even amidst all this activity, the void in the student affairs literature that we had identified years earlier remained.

In 2015, the time was right for us to take our idea to Routledge, where editor Heather Jarrow urged us to seek out recognized authorities within student affairs and higher education to author key chapters, noting that their credibility within the field would be critical to the receptivity that we would find among our intended readership. To our good fortune, we were able to assemble an all-star lineup of contributing authors with unimpeachable credentials pertaining to their respective topics. We are pleased to share their work with you and hope that it will inspire robust dialogue within higher education and student affairs, regarding the role of colleges and universities in facilitating emerging adults' journeys through this formative stage of life.

Overview

This book comprises 13 chapters, which together introduce emerging adulthood theory to scholars and practitioners in higher education and student affairs, examine characteristics of the emerging adult life stage as it is experienced by students and young alumni of collegiate institutions, and explore implications of a longer pathway to adulthood for administrative and student affairs practice. In the first of these chapters, we orient the reader to the book's content, situating Jeff's theory of emerging adulthood within an evolving body of foundational literature on higher education and student affairs. In the following chapter, Jeff presents an overview of his theory, highlighting the societal conditions that have lengthened the transition to adulthood and introducing the essential features of emerging adulthood. Joe then reviews the theoretical literature on psychosocial development in college, noting a trend toward integration of disciplinary perspectives and growing emphasis on social identity development.

In the fourth chapter, Rosemary Perez and Lisa Landreman examine social identity development in greater depth, with attention to the relevance of diversity to experiences of emerging adulthood. In the next chapter, Joe presents an overview of generational theory and profiles of the two most recent cohorts of emerging adults to enter higher education (Millennials and Generation Z). In the first of three chapters focused on specific aspects of emerging adulthood, Lisa Severy examines issues pertaining to career development. Aimee Adams and Bruce Sharkin then explore social and emotional problems in emerging adulthood, differentiated based on their externalizing versus internalizing nature. Richard Mullendore, Christina Daniel, and Michael Toney then discuss the relationship between emerging adults and their parents and how normative changes in the quality of these relationships have changed the experience of going away to college.

In the ninth chapter, the focus of the book shifts more directly to the practical implications of emerging adulthood theory, as Jarrett Warshaw and James Hearn discuss the use of Strategic Enrollment Management (SEM) to promote equity in recruitment, retention, and academic support for diverse student populations. Carney Strange then presents a model for creating campus environments for emerging adults, based on the previous work of Sharon Daloz Parks (2011), as well as his own work with James Banning (Strange & Banning, 2015). From there, Maureen Wilson and Patrick Love offer guidance to student affairs professionals on promoting emerging adults' growth in autonomy at three stages of their relationship with the institution. Expanding on this theme, Shelby Radcliffe calls upon student affairs and alumni relations professionals to join forces in support of alumni in their continued journeys through emerging adulthood. In the book's final chapter, we provide a synthesis of major themes raised by the contributing authors and offer further recommendations for research and practice.

References

Arnett, J. J. (2004). *Emerging adulthood: The winding road from the late teens through the twenties*. New York, NY: Oxford.

Arnett, J. J. (2015). *Emerging adulthood: The winding road from the late teens through the twenties* (2nd ed.). New York, NY: Oxford.

Arnett, J. J. (Ed.). (2016). *The Oxford handbook of emerging adulthood*. New York, NY: Oxford.

Parks, S. D. (2011). *Big questions, worthy dreams: Mentoring emerging adults in their search for meaning, purpose, and faith* (2nd ed.). San Francisco, CA: Jossey-Bass.

Strange, C., & Banning, J. (2015). *Designing for learning: Creating campus environments for student success*. San Francisco, CA: Jossey-Bass.

ACKNOWLEDGMENTS

While this book traces its origin to a conversation between two people, it took the work of many more to bring it to fruition. First and foremost, we extend our gratitude to the chapter authors for their diligent and thoughtful analyses of their respective topics. We are also grateful to the book's editor, Heather Jarrow, whose support for the project was key to getting the green light from Routledge and whose expert advice helped ensure that the finished product would not disappoint. We also appreciate the feedback that we received from the reviewers of our initial proposal, which helped us fine-tune our vision for the book in ways that align closely with the needs and interests of our anticipated readership.

Whereas much of Joe's work on the book was completed while on sabbatical during the 2016–2017 academic year, he would also like to thank the members of Bucknell's Faculty Development Committee for their approval of his proposal. He is also grateful to his family for their support and encouragement throughout the process. This would include his brothers, Jim and John Murray, his sisters-in-law, Karen Lynn and Taya Murray, and especially his sister and brother-in-law, Mary and Bill Martin, who generously made their lakeside cottage available to him as an ideal writer's retreat. Finally, he would like to thank Jeff for lending his expertise and good judgment to the production of the book. Jeff thanks Joe for his affable diligence throughout the process of editing the book, which made the experience a pleasure.

1

INTRODUCTION

Joseph L. Murray and Jeffrey Jensen Arnett

The primary goal of this book is to explore ways that the theory of emerging adulthood can be applied to student affairs. The theory of emerging adulthood, first proposed about 20 years ago (Arnett, 2000), has become highly influential as a framework for understanding development from age 18 to 29. An entire field of study has been spawned by the theory, including a thriving new Society for the Study of Emerging Adulthood (SSEA; see www.ssea.org). The theory underscores the changes over recent decades in how ages 18–29 are experienced, and consequently, has important implications for understanding the worlds that today's students come from prior to entering college as well as the futures for which students are preparing themselves, through the rest of their twenties and beyond. However, thus far, the application of emerging adulthood theory to student affairs has been limited despite the manifest relevance of the theory to development among students, most of whom fall into the 18–29 age range. The chapters in this book represent a variety of approaches to making fruitful use of the theory of emerging adulthood in promoting more effective student affairs practice. In this chapter, we provide an overview of the history and present status of the student affairs profession.

A review of the historical and contemporary literature of the student affairs profession reveals that both its stated philosophy and the theoretical principles that inform its practice have evolved through a process that has been both additive and integrative. The profession itself traces its origins to the late 19th and early 20th centuries, a time when the faculty role was broadened to include a growing emphasis on research, even as on-campus residency remained a critical element of the undergraduate experience. As administrative functions necessarily grew, the student affairs profession quickly came into its own (Cohen & Kisker, 2010). From its inception, the profession has placed its primary focus on education of the whole student. However, the prevailing orientation toward student affairs practice has undergone continuous revision, in response to both advances in relevant disciplinary knowledge and the changing demands of the times (Dungy & Gordon, 2011).

Three Eras of Student Affairs Practice

The history of the student affairs profession, as reflected in the philosophical literature of the field, has generally been portrayed as a sequence of three major eras, each characterized by a corresponding orientation toward professional practice: (1) *student services*, (2) *student development*, and (3) *student learning* (Carpenter, Dean, & Haber-Curran, 2016; Sherman, 2014). The service orientation of the earliest student affairs practitioners was articulated in the American Council on Education's (1937/1994) *Student Personnel Point of View*, which specified 23 essential student affairs functions, such as "orienting the student to his [sic] educational environment" and "providing a diagnostic service to help the student discover his [sic] abilities, aptitudes, and objectives" (p. 69). A more enduring legacy of this landmark document, however, was its call for education of the whole student, as an intellectual, emotional, physical, social, vocational, moral, and spiritual being, whose skills, aptitudes, values, resources, and aesthetic sensibilities all fell within the purview of collegiate institutions.

The shift from student services to student development reflected the growing influence of theoretical perspectives on student affairs practice. The prevailing philosophy of the student development era was perhaps best captured in the Council of Student Personnel Associations in Higher Education's (COSPA, 1975/1994) *Student Development Services in Post-Secondary Education*. In the closing decades of the 20th century, the COSPA document called upon practitioners to assume the role of student development specialists, drawing upon relevant theories to address individual, group, and organizational issues on their campuses. A series of subsequent statements, issued by various professional associations around the turn of the millennium, ushered in the third era by calling upon student affairs professionals to form partnerships with faculty and academic administrators to create seamless campus environments for student learning, broadly conceived to include both academics and personal development (American Association for Higher Education, American College Personnel Association, & National Association of Student Personnel Administrators, 1998; American College Personnel Association, 1996; National Association of Student Personnel Administrators & American College Personnel Association, 2004).

Standards for Preparation and Practice

With the establishment of a commonly held professional philosophy that incorporates a commitment to holistic learning, informed by relevant theories, the student affairs field has since turned its attention to articulation of uniform standards of professional preparation and practice. A major step toward accomplishment of this goal came when the American College Personnel Association (ACPA, 2007) published a statement of professional competencies and corresponding benchmarks for mastery at the basic, intermediate, and advanced levels. Within this statement, eight general areas of competency were identified: (1) *advising and helping*; (2) *assessment, evaluation, and research*; (3) *ethics*; (4) *legal foundations*; (5) *leadership, administration, and management*; (6) *pluralism and inclusion*; (7) *student learning and development*; and (8) *teaching*. Three years later, the Association partnered with the National Association of Student Personnel Administrators (NASPA) to issue a joint statement of ten professional competency areas with corresponding benchmarks at each of the original levels: (1) *advising and helping*; (2) *assessment, evaluation, and research*; (3) *equity, diversity, and inclusion*; (4) *ethical professional practice*; (5) *history, philosophy, and values*; (6) *human and organizational resources*; (7) *law, policy, and governance*; (8) *leadership*; (9) *personal foundations*; and (10) *student learning and development* (ACPA & NASPA, 2010).

While the aforementioned competency statements address general areas of expertise that are commonly shared across the student affairs profession, they offer little or no elaboration on application to specific functional areas within the field. In contrast, the Council for the Advancement of Standards in Higher Education (CAS), which was founded in 1979 as the Council for the Advancement of Standards in Student Services/Development Programs, offers detailed standards and guidelines for the provision of programs and services in 43 areas of practice, developed in conjunction with professional associations specializing in the respective areas (Wells, 2015).

Another distinctive feature of the CAS standards is the articulation of essential elements of master's degree programs designed to prepare individuals for entry into the student affairs field. In addition to addressing administrative and pedagogical matters, the document offers guidance on the content of curricula, thereby lending clarity to the shared body of knowledge that constitutes content expertise within the field. The subject matter of the curriculum is divided into two broad categories: (1) *foundational studies*, which orient the individual to the history and philosophy of higher education and student affairs and (2) *professional studies*, which directly inform student affairs practice. Within the broad category of professional studies, the document specifies five topic areas that must be addressed: (1) "student learning and development theories"; (2) "student characteristics and the effects of college on students"; (3) "individual and group strategies"; (4) "organization and administration of student affairs"; and (5) "assessment, evaluation, and research" (Wells, 2015, p. 348).

An Evolving Body of Knowledge

The substantive knowledge of the student affairs field, as described above, is by its nature a "moving target," as both the theories that inform professional practice and the underlying body of research remain in a state of flux. Adoption of a student learning agenda has prompted interest in developmental and pedagogical theories more traditionally associated with educational psychology (Silverman & Casazza, 2000) and adult and continuing education (Hamrick, Evans, & Schuh, 2002). Meanwhile, perspectives on cognitive and psychosocial development in college, and indeed, the concurrent processes of learning and development, have grown more integrative (Baxter Magolda, 2004; Kegan, 1994). A growing body of research on the effects of higher education on students (Feldman & Newcomb, 1969/1994; Mayhew et al., 2016; Pascarella & Terenzini, 1991, 2005) offers ever more nuanced understandings of the environmental conditions that are most conducive to learning and development in college. With its deepening embrace of both qualitative (Jones, Torres, & Arminio, 2014) and quantitative (Sriram, 2017) research, the student affairs field has likewise grown increasingly sophisticated and inclusive in its methods of inquiry. Disciplinary boundaries have also been transcended, as student affairs scholars and practitioners have turned to the literature of such widely varied fields as counseling psychology (Harper & Wilson, 2010; Reynolds, 2009), management (Bryan, 1996; Ellis, 2010; Varlotta & Jones, 2010), organizational studies (Kuk, Banning, & Amey, 2010; Manning, 2013), and neuroscience (Bresciani Ludvik, 2016) to inform their work.

Perhaps nowhere is the dynamic nature of the knowledge base of the profession more apparent than in the study of student characteristics, where profiles of one generation make way for those of another on an ongoing basis (Coomes & DeBard, 2004; DeCoster & Mable, 1981; Seemiller & Grace, 2016). A growing body of national data from surveys such as the *Cooperative Institutional Research Program (CIRP) Freshman Survey* (Higher Education Research Institute, 2017) and the *National Survey of Student Engagement (NSSE)* (Center for Postsecondary Research, Indiana University School of Education, 2017), have allowed even the most subtle shifts in student characteristics and attitudes to be tracked over time. As more has become known about such changes, generational theory has taken its place alongside developmental theory, as a foundation for research and practice, with findings from each branch of theory lending texture to those of the other. Studies of generational change lend themselves well to application of an interdisciplinary approach, as the relevant literature incorporates perspectives drawn from such fields as history (Strauss & Howe, 1991), sociology (Edmunds & Turner, 2002), psychology (Twenge, 2006, 2017), economics (Koulopoulos & Keldsen, 2014), and political science (Bessant, 2014).

Arnett's Theory of Emerging Adulthood

With the changes evident in the traditional aged college student population over time, it is reasonable to question prior assumptions regarding developmental change in college, as it manifests itself across generations reared under very different circumstances. Arnett (2015), a developmental psychologist, posits that social, cultural, and economic changes over the latter half of the 20th century have resulted in an elongation of the pathway to adulthood, especially within the most economically developed nations, such that the period from approximately 18 to 29 years of age now constitutes a distinct life stage that is neither adolescence nor adulthood. Arnett has labeled this period *emerging adulthood*, reflecting the fact that it is characterized—though not wholly defined—by its transitional nature. He cites four specific societal changes that have given rise to this phenomenon: (1) the Technology Revolution, (2) the Sexual Revolution, (3) the Women's Movement, and (4) the Youth Movement. He further identifies five features of emerging adulthood that differentiate it from previous conceptions of the designated period of life: (1) identity explorations, (2) instability, (3) self-focus, (4) feeling in-between, and (5) possibilities/optimism.

Within the field of adolescent development, traditionally the epicenter of research on the transition into adulthood, Arnett's (2015) theory of emerging adulthood has reframed conceptions of the transition itself. Although the principal publishing venues of researchers specializing in adolescent development and emerging adulthood would suggest strong scholarly affinities between the two groups (Swanson, 2016), the distinction between their areas of focus is also widely acknowledged in the relevant literature, where references to "adolescence and emerging adulthood" abound (e.g., Booth, Crouter, & Snyder, 2016; Thompson, Hammen, & Brennan, 2016; Wong, Branje, VanderValk, Hawk, & Meeus, 2010). Additionally, leading authors on emerging adulthood have been found to traverse across areas of scholarship and to collaborate frequently with specialists in other areas, leading one researcher to conclude that "emerging adulthood study has become increasingly interdisciplinary" (Swanson, 2016, p. 397).

While Arnett's (2015) work has drawn comparatively little attention within the fields of higher education and student affairs, the growing body of research that it has inspired is directly applicable to administrative and student affairs practice within college and university settings. Since it was first introduced (Arnett, 2000), the theory has informed numerous studies on such topics as relationships and sexuality (Claxton & van Dulmen, 2013; Fincham & Cui, 2011; Morgan, 2013; Shulman & Connolly, 2013), religion and spirituality (Barry & Abo-Zena, 2014; Smith & Snell, 2009), work and career development (Konstam, 2015; Marshall & Butler, 2016), and mental health issues (Schulenberg & Zarrett, 2006; Tanner, 2016). Additionally, a series of polls conducted annually from 2012 through 2015, under the sponsorship of Clark University (2017), has yielded national datasets pertaining to the characteristics and experiences of both student and nonstudent emerging adults. Thus, more widespread engagement of higher education and student affairs scholars in the study of emerging adulthood could potentially advance understanding of both college student development and emerging adulthood generally.

Bridging the Divide between Theory and Practice

Just as researchers in higher education and student affairs stand to benefit from a deeper understanding of the emerging adult life stage, so too do campus-based practitioners. However, the informational needs of the two populations differ somewhat, insofar as the interests of academic researchers often remain at the theoretical level, while working professionals must ultimately concern themselves with the application of theory to practice. This challenge centers on the concept of *transfer*, defined very generally as "prior learning affecting new learning or performance" (Marini & Genereux, 2010, p. 15). In a professional education context, transfer is what accounts for the difference between mere understanding of theoretical constructs and use of this knowledge to improve performance. In one of the most widely used models for assessment of employee training, Kirkpatrick (1998) identified four levels of outcome, ordered in step-by-step progression toward increasingly complex aims: (1) *reaction*, which is concerned with participants' satisfaction with training; (2) *learning*, which relates to trainees' mastery of instructional content; (3) *behavior*, which involves an actual change in how participants conduct themselves on the job; and (4) *results*, meaning the benefits that accrue to the organization as a consequence of improved performance. Under this model, the transition from level 2 to level 3 marks the point of transfer and is necessary to attainment of level 4.

Researchers have drawn distinctions between several forms of transfer, typically framed in terms of three dichotomies: (1) *positive versus negative*, (2) *near versus far*, and (3) *general versus specific*. The contrast between positive and negative transfer relates to the alignment of changes in behavior with the goals of learning. If participants' behavior changes in the desired way, positive transfer is said to have occurred. The concept of nearness of transfer relates to the degree of similarity between the tasks and contexts associated with learning versus application. When skills learned in one set of circumstances are successfully applied in very different circumstances, far transfer is said to have occurred. Finally, specificity relates to the narrowness of circumstances in which transfer occurs. If skills learned in employee training are successfully applied to a wide range of problems encountered on the job, general transfer is said to have occurred (Bouzguenda, 2014). Although both far and general transfer are seen as highly desirable, researchers have had greater success in verifying positive transfer when the tasks and conditions of learning and application have been more similar (Macaulay, 2000). Research suggests, further, that expert problem-solving, in particular, tends to be domain-specific (Glaser & Chi, 2009). An implication of this finding is that skilled problem-solving can be advanced through *conditionalized knowledge*, meaning "knowledge that becomes associated with the conditions and constraints of its use" (Glaser, 1984, p. 99).

Closely related to transfer is the concept of *meaningful learning*, in which the learner relates new knowledge to prior knowledge in ways that are "substantive" and "nonarbitrary" (Ausubel, 1963, p. 18). Meaningful learning contrasts with *rote learning*, in which new information is retained solely through arbitrary associations (Ausubel, 1963). Meaningful learning is conceptually grounded in *schema theory*, which holds that individuals mentally organize knowledge in networks of related information, known as *schemata*. In its singular form, "a schema is conceived of as a modifiable information structure that represents generic concepts stored in memory" (Glaser, 1984, p. 100). As new information is integrated into existing schemata, meaningful learning occurs. The distinction between rote and meaningful learning is central to the cultivation of higher order thinking skills, based on Bloom's (1956) taxonomy for the cognitive domain, which organizes educational outcomes in six progressive categories, based on their complexity: (1) *knowledge*, (2) *comprehension*, (3) *application*, (4) *analysis*, (5) *synthesis*, and (6) *evaluation*. Whereas the distinction between rote and meaningful learning mirrors the contrast drawn between knowledge and comprehension, it holds implications for both application to practice and the scholarly activities of analysis, synthesis, and evaluation.

This book fills a void in the existing literature on emerging adulthood by introducing Arnett's (2000, 2015) work to a student affairs and higher education readership, drawing upon the power of meaningful learning and conditionalized knowledge to promote transfer. Beginning with an introductory overview of emerging adulthood, meaningful learning is immediately promoted through references to Arnett's own research on college student and alumni populations, and is further reinforced through links to more familiar theories of psychosocial development, social identity formation, and generational change. Building upon this foundation, recognized student affairs scholars examine in greater depth the challenges of career development, social and psychological adjustment, and relationships with parents in emerging adulthood, thereby facilitating transfer to real-world situations encountered in higher education on a daily basis. Focusing more directly on implications for administrative and student affairs practice, other leading contributors to the literature of the field address the topics of optimizing enrollment, retention, and student success; designing campus learning environments; providing student affairs programs and services; and working with young alumni. The volume closes with an integrative summary of key points and an agenda for further examination of emerging adulthood and higher education, with attention to the interests of scholars and practitioners alike.

References

American Association for Higher Education (AAHE), American College Personnel Association (ACPA), & National Association of Student Personnel Administrators (NASPA). (1998). *Powerful partnerships: A shared responsibility for learning.* Washington, DC: Author.
American College Personnel Association (ACPA). (1996). The student learning imperative: Implications for student affairs. *Journal of College Student Development, 37,* 118–122.

American College Personnel Association (ACPA). (2007). *Professional competencies: A report of the Steering Committee on Professional Competencies*. Washington, DC: Author.

American College Personnel Association (ACPA) & National Association of Student Personnel Administrators (NASPA). (2010). *Professional competency areas for student affairs practitioners*. Washington, DC: Author.

American Council on Education (ACA). (1994). The student personnel point of view. In A. L. Rentz (Ed.), *Student affairs: A profession's heritage* (2nd ed., pp. 66–77). Lanham, MD: University Press of America. (Original work published 1937.).

Arnett, J. J. (2000). Emerging adulthood: A theory of development from the late teens through the twenties. *American Psychologist, 55,* 469–480.

Arnett, J. J. (2015). *Emerging adulthood: The winding road from the late teens through the twenties* (2nd ed.). New York, NY: Oxford.

Ausubel, D. P. (1963). *The psychology of meaningful verbal learning: An introduction to school learning*. New York, NY: Grune & Stratton.

Barry, C. M., & Abo-Zena, M. M. (Eds.). (2014). *Emerging adults' religiousness and spirituality: Meaning-making in an age of transition*. New York, NY: Oxford.

Baxter Magolda, M. B. (2004). Self-authorship as the common goal of 21st-century education. In M. Baxter Magolda & P. M. King (Eds.), *Learning partnerships: Theory and models of practice to educate for self-authorship* (pp. 1–35). Sterling, VA: Stylus.

Bessant, J. (2014). *Democracy bytes: New media, new politics, and generational change*. New York, NY: Palgrave Macmillan.

Bloom, B. S. (Ed.). (1956). *Taxonomy of educational objectives: The classification of educational goals (Handbook 1: Cognitive domain)*. New York, NY: McKay.

Booth, A., Crouter, A. C., & Snyder, A. (Eds.). (2016). *Romance and sex in adolescence and emerging adulthood: Risks and opportunities*. New York, NY: Routledge.

Bouzguenda, K. (2014). Enablers and inhibitors of learning transfer from theory to practice. In K. Schneider (Ed.), *Transfer of learning in organizations* (pp. 23–44). New York, NY: Springer.

Bresciani Ludvik, M. J. (Ed.). (2016). *The neuroscience of learning and development: Enhancing creativity, compassion, critical thinking, and peace in higher education*. Sterling, VA: Stylus.

Bryan, W. A. (Ed.). (1996). *Total quality management: Applying its principles to student affairs*. New Directions for Student Services, n. 76. San Francisco, CA: Jossey-Bass.

Carpenter, S. L., Dean, S., & Haber-Curran, P. (2016). The philosophical heritage of student affairs. In N. Zhang (Ed.), *Rentz's student affairs practice in higher education* (5th ed., pp. 3–27). Springfield, IL: Thomas.

Center for Postsecondary Research, Indiana University School of Education. (2017). *About NSSE*. Retrieved July 10, 2017 from http://nsse.indiana.edu/html/about.cfm

Clark University. (2017). *About the Clark University poll*. Retrieved July 13, 2017 from www2.clarku.edu/clark-poll-emerging-adults/

Claxton, S. E., & van Dulmen, M. H. M. (2013). Casual sexual relationships and experiences in emerging adulthood. *Emerging Adulthood, 1*(2), 138–150.

Cohen, A. M., & Kisker, C. B. (2010). *The shaping of American higher education: Emergence and growth of the contemporary system* (2nd ed.). San Francisco, CA: Jossey-Bass.

Coomes, M. D., & DeBard, R. (Eds.). (2004). *Serving the millennial generation*. New Directions for Student Services, n. 106. San Francisco, CA: Jossey-Bass.

Council of Student Personnel Associations in Higher Education (COSPA). (1994). Student development services in post-secondary education. In A. L. Rentz (Ed.), *Student affairs: A profession's heritage* (2nd ed., pp. 428–437). Lanham, MD: University Press of America. (Original work published 1975.).

DeCoster, D. A., & Mable, P. (Eds.). (1981). *Understanding today's students*. New Directions for Student Services, n. 16. San Francisco, CA: Jossey-Bass.

Dungy, G., & Gordon, S. A. (2011). The development of student affairs. In J. H. Schuh, S. R. Jones & S. R. Harper (Eds.), *Student services: A handbook for the profession* (5th ed., pp. 61–79). San Francisco, CA: Jossey-Bass.

Edmunds, J., & Turner, B. S. (2002). *Generations, culture and society*. Philadelphia, PA: Open University Press.

Ellis, S. E. (Ed.). (2010). *Strategic planning in student affairs*. New Directions for Student Services, n. 132. San Francisco, CA: Jossey-Bass.

Feldman, K. A., & Newcomb, T. M. (1994). *The impact of college on students*. New Brunswick, NJ: Transaction. (Original work published 1969).

Fincham, F. D., & Cui, M. (Eds.). (2011). *Romantic relationships in emerging adulthood*. New York, NY: Cambridge.

Glaser, R. (1984). Education and thinking: The role of knowledge. *American Psychologist, 39*(2), 93–104.

Glaser, R., & Chi, M. T. H. (2009). Overview. In M. T. H. Chi, R. Glaser, & M. J. Farr (Eds.), *The nature of expertise* (pp. xv–xxvii). New York, NY: Psychology Press.

Hamrick, F. A., Evans, N. J., & Schuh, J. H. (2002). *Foundations of student affairs practice: How philosophy, theory, and research strengthen educational outcomes*. San Francisco, CA: Jossey-Bass.

Harper, R., & Wilson, N. L. (Eds.). (2010). *More than listening: A casebook for using counseling skills in student affairs work*. Washington, DC: NASPA.

Higher Education Research Institute. (2017). *CIRP freshman survey*. Retrieved July 10, 2017 from https://heri.ucla.edu/cirp-freshman-survey/

Jones, S. R., Torres, V., & Arminio, J. (2014). *Negotiating the complexities of qualitative research in higher education: Fundamental elements and issues* (2nd ed.). New York, NY: Routledge.

Kegan, R. (1994). *In over our heads: The mental demands of modern life*. Cambridge, MA: Harvard University Press.

Kirkpatrick, D. L. (1998). *Evaluating training programs: The four levels* (2nd ed.). San Francisco, CA: Berrett-Koehler.

Konstam, V. (2015). *Emerging and young adulthood* (2nd ed.). New York, NY: Springer.

Koulopoulos, T., & Keldsen, D. (2014). *The Gen Z effect: The six forces shaping the future of business*. Brookline, MA: Bibliomotion.

Kuk, L., Banning, J. H., & Amey, M. J. (2010). *Positioning student affairs for sustainable change: Achieving organizational effectiveness through multiple perspectives*. Sterling, VA: Stylus.

Macaulay, C. (2000). Transfer of learning. In V. E. Cree & C. Macaulay (Eds.), *Transfer of learning in professional and vocational education* (pp. 1–26). New York, NY: Routledge.

Manning, K. (2013). *Organizational theory in higher education*. New York, NY: Routledge.

Marini, A., & Genereux, R. (2010). The challenge of teaching for transfer. In A. McKeough, J. Lupart, & A. Marini (Eds.), *Teaching for transfer: Fostering generalization in learning* (pp. 13–50). New York, NY: Routledge.

Marshall, E. A., & Butler, K. (2016). School-to-work transition in emerging adulthood. In J. J. Arnett (Ed.), *The Oxford handbook of emerging adulthood* (pp. 316–333). New York, NY: Oxford.

Mayhew, M. J., Rockenbach, A. N., Bowman, N. A., Seifert, T. A., Wolniak, G. C., Pascarella E. T., & Terenzini, P. T. (2016). *How college affects students, volume 3: 21st century evidence that higher education works*. San Francisco, CA: Jossey-Bass.

Morgan, E. M. (2013). Contemporary issues in sexual orientation and identity development in emerging adulthood. *Emerging Adulthood, 1*(1), 52–66.

National Association of Student Personnel Administrators (NASPA) & American College Personnel Association (ACPA). (2004). *Learning reconsidered: A campus-wide focus on the student experience.* Washington, DC: Author.

Pascarella, E. T., & Terenzini, P. T. (1991). *How college affects students: Findings and insights from twenty years of research.* San Francisco, CA: Jossey-Bass.

Pascarella, E. T., & Terenzini, P. T. (2005). *How college affects students, volume 2: A third decade of research.* San Francisco, CA: Jossey-Bass.

Reynolds, A. L. (2009). *Helping college students: Developing essential support skills for student affairs practice.* San Francisco, CA: Jossey-Bass.

Schulenberg, J. E., & Zarrett, N. R. (2006). Mental health during emerging adulthood: Continuity and discontinuity in courses, causes, and functions. In J. J. Arnett & J. L. Tanner (Eds.), *Emerging adults in America: Coming of age in the 21st Century* (pp. 135–172). Washington, DC: American Psychological Association.

Seemiller, C., & Grace, M. (2016). *Generation Z goes to college.* San Francisco, CA: Jossey-Bass.

Sherman, G. L. (2014). *Refocusing the self in higher education: A phenomenological perspective.* New York, NY: Routledge.

Shulman, S., & Connolly, J. (2013). The challenge of romantic relationships in emerging adulthood: Reconceptualization of the field. *Emerging Adulthood, 1*(1), 27–39.

Silverman, S. L., & Casazza, M. E. (2000). *Learning & development: Making connections to enhance teaching.* San Francisco, CA: Jossey-Bass.

Smith, C., & Snell, P. (2009). *Souls in transition: The religious and spiritual lives of emerging adults.* New York, NY: Oxford.

Sriram, R. (2017). *Student affairs by the numbers: Quantitative research and statistics for professionals.* Sterling, VA: Stylus.

Strauss, W., & Howe, N. (1991). *Generations: The history of America's future, 1584 to 2069.* New York, NY: Morrow.

Swanson, J. A. (2016). Trends in literature about emerging adulthood: Review of empirical studies. *Emerging Adulthood, 4*, 391–402.

Tanner, J. L. (2016). Mental health in emerging adulthood. In J. J. Arnett (Ed.), *The Oxford handbook of emerging adulthood* (pp. 499–520). New York, NY: Oxford.

Thompson, S. M., Hammen, C., & Brennan, P. A. (2016). The impact of asynchronous pubertal development on depressive symptoms in adolescence and emerging adulthood among females. *Journal of Youth and Adolescence, 45*(3), 494–501.

Twenge, J. M. (2006). *Generation me: Why today's young Americans are more confident, assertive, entitled—and more miserable than ever before.* New York, NY: Free Press.

Twenge, J. M. (2017). *iGen: Why today's super-connected kids are growing up less rebellious, more tolerant, less happy—and completely unprepared for adulthood (and what it means for the rest of us).* New York, NY: Atria.

Varlotta, L. E., & Jones, B. C. (Eds.). (2010). *Student affairs budgeting and financial management in the midst of fiscal crisis.* New Directions for Student Services, n. 129. San Francisco, CA: Jossey-Bass.

Wells, J. B. (Ed.). (2015). *CAS professional standards for higher education* (9th ed.). Washington, DC: Council for the Advancement of Standards in Higher Education.

Wong, T. M. L., Branje, S. J. T., VanderValk, I. E., Hawk, S. T., & Meeus, W. H. J. (2010). The role of siblings in identity development in adolescence and emerging adulthood. *Journal of Adolescence, 33*, 673–682.

2

CONCEPTUAL FOUNDATIONS OF EMERGING ADULTHOOD

Jeffrey Jensen Arnett

Since it was first proposed about 20 years ago, emerging adulthood theory has been widely used in many fields. According to Google Scholar, the original article outlining the theory (Arnett, 2000) had been cited over 10,000 times as of January, 2018. In light of the growing interest in the topic, it would seem the time is right for a book that explores ways that emerging adulthood theory can be applied to student affairs and student development on college campuses. This would seem to be a potentially fruitful application, as emerging adulthood theory pertains to ages 18–29, the age range into which most students fall and which is the focus of most student programs and services.

In this chapter, as background for the chapters to come, I provide a summary of the theory. I begin with the historical context of the rise of emerging adulthood as a new life stage. Then I specify five distinctive features of emerging adulthood and suggest some ways that the features can be applied to student life. I focus here on the American experience, as this was the original focus of the theory and is the focus of this book.

The Rise of EA: Four Revolutions

The theory of emerging adulthood (EA) was proposed in order to recognize that demographic changes had taken place in the age period 18–29 that were so profound that they had changed utterly the normative experience of the age period. Consequently, I believed, a new life stage concept would be helpful for drawing attention to those demographic changes and encouraging researchers to investigate the features that were now distinctive to ages 18–29.

One of those key demographic changes was the rise in college participation. Until the middle of the 20th century, tertiary education was mainly for the elite. In 1900, only 4% of 18–21 year-olds attended college, and by 1940, that proportion had risen only to 16% (Arnett, 2015). However, the percent-age rose steadily through the second half of the 20th century, surging among young women after 1960, until college had become an experience shared by the majority of emerging adults in the early 21st century (National Center for Education Statistics, 2018). Today, of the nearly 70% who obtain some tertiary education, about half attend four-year colleges and universities and about half attend two-year colleges or vocational training programs.

The second area of dramatic demographic change regarding the age period 18–29 was the rise in the typical ages of entering marriage and parenthood. In 1960, the median age of marriage in the United States was just 20.3 for women and 22.8 for men (Arnett, 2015). By 2017, the median age of marriage was 27.4 for women and 29.5 for men, a seven-year rise for both sexes in the span of just five decades—and still rising every year (United States Census Bureau, 2018). Age of entering parenthood followed a similar pattern, although far more children are born outside of marriage now (about 40% as of 2017) than was true in 1960.

Longer education and later ages of marriage and parenthood created a space between the late teens and the late twenties for the new life stage of emerging adulthood. But these demographic changes were not direct causes of the rise of the new life stage. Rather, they were reflections of other vast changes taking place in modern societies. Four revolutionary changes took place in the 1960s and 1970s that laid the foundation for the new life stage of emerging adulthood: the Technology Revolution, the Sexual Revolution, the Women's Movement, and the Youth Movement (Arnett, 2015).

The Technology Revolution that is relevant here is not personal comput-ers and smartphones but the manufacturing technologies that transformed the American economy. Because of extraordinary advances in technology, machines became able to perform most of the manufacturing jobs that were once the main source of employment in developed countries. As a consequence of this revolution, the United States and other developed countries have shifted from a manufacturing economy to a *knowledge economy* requiring information and tech-nology skills (Carnevale, Smith, & Strohl, 2013). In the early 20th century, most work entailed *making things* in factory-based manufacturing jobs. By the early 21st century, most work involved *using information* in service-based work such as business, finance, insurance, education, and health (McGill & Bell, 2010).

It is this economic shift that has mainly driven the increase in college enroll-ment over the past 50 years. The new knowledge economy emphasizes infor-mation and technology, and therefore, requires tertiary education and training for most jobs, especially for the jobs with the highest pay and status. Conse-quently, a majority of young Americans now continue their education beyond high school.

A second change was the Sexual Revolution. Beginning in the 1960s, the ease and availability of "the Pill" and other effective contraceptive methods led directly to the Sexual Revolution that began in the late 1960s, including less stringent standards of sexual morality. It became widely (if somewhat grudgingly) accepted that young people no longer had to enter marriage in order to have a regular sexual relationship. On college campuses, strict rules that young men could not enter women's residence halls and a young man and young woman could not be together in a student's room with the door closed gradually faded. Today there is widespread tolerance for sexual relations between young people in their late teens and twenties, including on college campuses.

The third revolution that shaped the lives of today's emerging adults was the Women's Movement. As a consequence of the Women's Movement, young women's options expanded in ways that make an early entry into adult obligations less desirable for them now compared to 50 years ago. The young women of 1960 were under a great deal of social pressure to find a husband by around age 20. Remaining single was simply not a viable social status for a woman after her early twenties. Relatively few women attended college, and those who did were often there for the purpose of obtaining their "m-r-s" degree (in the joke of the day)—that is, for the purpose of finding a husband. The range of occupations open to young women was severely restricted—secretary, waitress, teacher, nurse, perhaps a few others. Even these occupations were supposed to be temporary for young women, a brief pause on the way to finding a husband and having children. Having no other real options, and facing social limbo if they remained unmarried for long, their focus on marriage and children—the sooner the better—was acute.

For the young women of the 21st century, all this has changed. At every level of education, from elementary school through graduate school, females now surpass males. Fifty-six percent of the undergraduates in America's colleges and universities are women, according to the most recent figures (National Center for Education Statistics, 2018). Young women's occupational possibilities are now virtually unlimited, and although men still dominate in engineering and some sciences, women are equal to men in obtaining law, business, and medical degrees. With so many options open to them, and with so little pressure on them to marry by their early twenties, the lives of young American women today have changed almost beyond recognition from what they were 50 years ago. Correspondingly, the lives of young men have changed, because most no longer seek a dependent wife and mother but a partner who will also have a career. Now both men and women must coordinate their educational and career goals and ambitions as they navigate toward them in their twenties.

The fourth revolution of the 1960s and 1970s was the Youth Movement, which denigrated adulthood and exalted being, acting, and feeling young. "Never trust anyone over 30" and "I hope I die before I get old" are phrases that remain familiar to anyone who was around during that era. As a consequence of the Youth Movement, there has been a profound change in how young people view the meaning and value of becoming an adult and entering adult roles of spouse, parent, and employee. Young people of the 1950s were eager to enter adulthood and "settle down" (Modell, 1989). Perhaps because they grew up during the upheavals of the Great Depression and World War II, achieving the stability of a secure job, marriage, home, and children seemed like a great achievement to them. Also, because many of them planned to have three, four, or even five or more children, they had good reason to get started early in order to have all the children they wanted and space them out at reasonable intervals.

The young people of today, in contrast, see adulthood and its obligations in quite a different light. In their late teens and early twenties, most of them are wary of commitments to marriage, home, and children. Most of them do want to take on all of these adult roles, and most of them will have done so by the time they reach age 30. It is just that, in their late teens and early twenties, they ponder these obligations and think, "yes, but *not yet*." Adulthood and its commitments offer security and stability, but also represent a closing of doors—the end of independence, the end of spontaneity, the end of a sense of wide-open possibility.

For students, this change means that more of them than in the past are reluctant to enter a permanent occupational commitment fresh out of college. Many of them prefer to have a year or more of continued freedom and exploration after graduating, even if it means taking a low-level service job—restaurant work, retail sales, delivery services—that has nothing to do with what they studied in college. A 2017 survey by Accenture (2017) reported that 54% of recent grads considered themselves underemployed. Other estimates are similar. This is often interpreted as indicating that they cannot find a job commensurate with their education, and this is surely true in some cases. But keep in mind it includes many emerging adults who are not looking for a long-term job right after college, either because they plan to obtain further education, or because they are still not sure what they want to do, or because they simply want to enjoy the freedom of emerging adulthood a bit longer before taking on the enduring responsibilities of adult life. What looks from the outside like floundering may actually be continued exploration (Krahn, Howard, & Galambos, 2012).

What is Emerging Adulthood? Five Features

Emerging adulthood lasts from roughly age 18, when most young people finish secondary school, to age 29, when most people have moved toward making the commitments that structure adult life: marriage (or a long-term partnership), parenthood, and a long-term job. Thus, emerging adulthood includes the "college years," i.e., the years when people are most likely to be students at a residential college or university. But if this is truly a new life stage, it must be distinguishable from other life stages not just as an age range but because of what is typically occurring during those years. Infancy has crawling and babbling, early childhood has walking and talking, middle childhood has beginning formal schooling, and adolescence has puberty and secondary school. So, what are the distinguishing features of emerging adulthood? What makes it distinct from the adolescence that precedes it and the young adulthood that follows it? In the original theory (Arnett, 2004), based on a decade of research, I proposed five main features:

1. *identity explorations:* trying out various life options in education, work, love, and worldviews;
2. *instability*, in education, work, love, and place of residence;
3. *self-focus,* as obligations to others reach a lifespan low point;
4. *feeling in-between,* neither adolescent nor adult; and
5. *possibilities/optimism,* when hopes flourish and there is a crucial opportunity to change directions.

Let's look at each of these features in turn, and consider how each is applicable to the college context.

Identity Explorations

Above all, emerging adulthood is the time when young people explore the available options for their lives in a variety of areas, especially education, work, and love. In the course of these explorations, emerging adults develop an *identity,* that is, they clarify their sense of who they are and what they want out of life. The late teens and early-to-mid-twenties offer the best opportunity for such identity explorations. Emerging adults have become more independent of their parents than they were as adolescents and most of them have left home, but they have not yet entered the stable, enduring commitments typical of adult life, such as a long-term job, marriage, and parenthood. During this interval of years when they are neither beholden to their parents nor committed to an assortment of adult roles, they have an exceptional opportunity to try out different ways of living and different possible choices for education, work, and love.

Of course, it is adolescence rather than emerging adulthood that has typically been associated with identity formation. Decades ago, Erikson (1950) proposed identity vs. role confusion as the central crisis of the adolescent stage of life, and in the decades since he articulated this idea, the focus of research on identity has been on adolescence. However, Erikson also commented on the "prolonged adolescence" typical of industrialized societies, and the *psychosocial moratorium* granted to young people in such societies, "during which the young adult through free role experimentation may find a niche in some section of his [sic] society" (Erikson, 1968, p. 150).

Decades later, this observation applies to many more young people than when he first wrote it. If adolescence is the period from age 10 to 18 and emerging adulthood is the period from (roughly) age 18 to 29, most identity exploration takes place in emerging adulthood rather than adolescence. Research has shown that identity achievement has rarely been reached by the end of high school and that identity development continues through the late teens and the twenties (Schwartz, Zamboanga, Luyckx, Meca, & Ritchie, 2013).

In many ways, the American college is expressly designed for the identity explorations that are at the heart of emerging adulthood. Students have two years to try different courses before they commit to a major. Even after they choose a major, they can switch to another major if they find something they like better. As they try out different courses and different majors, they are introduced to a variety of different ideas that help them develop (and perhaps change) their worldviews. Meanwhile, as they are exploring possible directions for their work future and possible ways of looking at the world, there are hundreds, probably thousands, of other emerging adults around them every day, having experiences similar to their own, few of them married, all of them with a considerable amount of unstructured time—the perfect setting for explorations in love. A residential college is a social island set off from the rest of society, a temporary safe haven where emerging adults can explore identity possibilities in love, work, and worldviews with many of the responsibilities of adult life kept at bay.

Not all emerging adults are interested in exploring identity options during their college years. Some know from an early age what kind of work they want to do, and they enter college already firmly established on a path toward their career goal. For them, no period of exploration is necessary in their first year or two of college to allow them to find the kind of work that best fits with their identity. The purpose of college is to obtain the skills and the credentials that will enable them to do the work they know they are cut out to do. But they are the exception, not the rule.

The importance of identity explorations as part of the college experience can be seen in students' accounts of what they learned in college that was most important. Although preparation for a vocation is one obvious part of what they learn, in this literature, their main response centers on what they have experienced in terms of *personal growth,* i.e., identity issues (Pascarella & Terenzini, 2005). The importance of identity issues during college has long been recognized in theory and research on college students (e.g., Chickering & Reisser, 1993; Jones & Abes, 2011; Marcia, 1993). More recently, the college context has been recognized as important for developing aspects of identity such as ethnicity and sexual orientation. This area will be detailed extensively in Chapters 3 and 4.

In general, the late teens and early twenties, the years that are the heart of emerging adulthood, are the main years of educational explorations for most people. Few people are still bouncing from one possible path to another by the time they reach their late twenties. In both love and work, most people make a transition in their late twenties from the explorations of emerging adulthood to the more settled choices of young adulthood. They may obtain more education later in their twenties or beyond, but it is likely to be in the field they have already chosen.

Instability

The identity explorations of emerging adults and their shifting choices in education, work, and love make this life stage exceptionally full and intense but also exceptionally unstable. Emerging adults know they are supposed to have a Plan with a capital "P," that is, some kind of idea about the route they will be taking from adolescence to adulthood, and most of them come up with one. However, for almost all of them, their Plan is subject to numerous revisions during the emerging adult years. These revisions are a natural consequence of their identity explorations. They enter college and choose a major, then discover the major is not as interesting as it seemed—time to revise the Plan. Or they enter college and find themselves unable to focus on their studies, and their grades sink accordingly—time to revise the Plan. Or they go to work after high school but discover after a year or two that they need more education if they ever expect to make decent money—time to revise the Plan. Or they move in with a boyfriend or girlfriend and start to think of the Plan as founded on their future together, only to discover that they have no future together—time to revise the Plan.

With each revision in the Plan, they learn something about themselves and take a step toward clarifying the kind of future they want. But even if they succeed in doing so, that does not mean the instability of emerging adulthood is easy. Over half (52%) of 18–29 year-olds in a national survey agreed that "I often feel anxious," and about one-third agreed that "I often feel depressed" (Arnett & Schwab, 2012); the instability of emerging adulthood is arguably a contributor to their widespread anxieties and depressed moods.

Instability is a standard part of the American college experience. Although 70% of American emerging adults enter college following high school, this does not mean that all of them follow a direct path to a college degree four years later. Quite the contrary. For most emerging adults, entering college means embarking on a winding educational path that may or may not lead to a degree. Only 57% of students who enter a four-year college or university have graduated six years later (National Center for Education Statistics, 2018). Among 25–29 year-olds, just 30% have obtained a bachelor's degree. Even for emerging adults who do get a bachelor's degree, for most of them, it takes five or six years to get their "four-year degree."

There are many reasons why students often sputter in their educational progress once they enter college. With some emerging adults, it is clear that they were not ready for college when they entered. They did not really know why they were there, they were not committed to it, and consequently, they floundered. They may have come to college simply out of inertia, because it seemed like the thing to do, or because all of their friends were going and their parents expected them to go too. Some enter college because of their parents' wishes rather than their own, and fail as an act of defiance. Some enter college and find they lack the self-discipline to get themselves to class and do their course work. They may enjoy the freedom of being away from home so much that they are easily distracted by the pleasures of the moment, which usually do not include studying. This is a common sentiment among emerging adults in their mid-twenties, that they were too immature at age 18 or 19 to apply themselves to educational goals in college, and consequently, their early college years were wasted (Arnett, 2015). They got caught up in what one education critic Sperber (2000) calls the "beer and circus" of college life—the parties, the drinking, the social life, the sports events.

Although alcohol use has diminished in the current generation of college students compared to previous generations, it remains prevalent and continues to be a major contributor to educational instability in emerging adulthood. College students drink more than emerging adults who are not college students, and in national studies, nearly half of college students in their late teens and early twenties reported *binge drinking* (five or more alcoholic drinks in a row for men, four in a row for women) at least once in the past two weeks (Johnston, O'Malley, Bachman, & Schulenberg, 2012).

Self-Focus

There is no time of life that is more self-focused than emerging adulthood. Children and adolescents are self-focused in their own way, but they always have parents and teachers to answer to, and usually siblings as well. Nearly all of them live at home with at least one parent. There are household rules and standards to follow, and if they break them, they risk the wrath of other family members ("Who left their dishes on the table?!"). Parents keep track, at least to some extent, of where they are and what they are doing. Although adolescents typically grow more independent than they were as children, they remain part of a family system that requires responses from them on a daily basis. In addition, nearly all of them attend school, whether they like it or not (and many do not), where teachers set the standards and monitor their behavior and performance.

By age 30, a new web of other-focused commitments and obligations is well-established, for most people. At that age, the majority of Americans has married and had at least one child: a new household, then, with new rules and standards; a spouse, instead of parents and siblings, with whom they must coordinate activities and negotiate household duties and requirements; and a child, to be loved and provided for, who needs time and attention. By age 30, most Americans also have the first job that they will remain in for at least five years (Yates, 2005); an employer, then, in a job and a field they are committed to and want to succeed in, who holds them to standards of progress and achievement.

It is only in between, during emerging adulthood, that there are few ties that entail daily obligations and commitments to others. Most young Americans leave home at age 18 or 19, and moving out means that daily life is much more self-focused. There are daily decisions to make that can only be made by you, from what to have for dinner to when (or whether) to come home at night. Larger decisions, too, are mostly self-focused, including the big educational decisions such as whether to go to college, which college to attend, and what to study in college. Parents have an influence on these decisions, too, especially in American ethnic groups that have a more traditional view of parental authority, but overall, the individualism of American life means that these decisions are generally viewed as decisions for emerging adults themselves to make.

There is no doubt that attending a residential college or university tends to be a self-focused life. Students spend most of each day focused on their self-development, specifically, on obtaining the knowledge and skills that will prepare them for the knowledge economy, by attending classes and doing homework. They select daily from a number of leisure options, from sports to student organizations to partying, that they enjoy most. Many students also work, and their employment is also mostly self-focused, as it is motivated mainly by the need to support themselves and to gain money toward paying for the cost of their education.

Baxter Magolda (Baxter Magolda & Taylor, 2015) has written insightfully on how the college experience can promote an aspect of self-focus she calls *self-authorship*. Her concept of self-authorship is strongly related to identity development, in that self-authorship entails combining personal characteristics, experiences, and meaning-making capacities to construct a unique adult identity. In addition, based on her longitudinal research of college students, she emphasizes that self-authorship also involves examining critically the worldview developed during childhood on the basis of parental socialization, and crafting a more individualized worldview based on internal criteria. She views the college experience as a setting that is potentially fruitful for promoting emerging adults' self-authorship, and proposes ways that colleges can do this more effectively.

As the self-authorship concept indicates, self-focus in emerging adulthood is developmentally appropriate in the modern American context. To be self-focused is not necessarily to be selfish, and to say that emerging adulthood is a self-focused time is not meant pejoratively. There is nothing wrong about being self-focused during emerging adulthood; it is normal, healthy, and temporary. By focusing on themselves emerging adults develop skills at daily living, gain a better understanding of who they are and what they want from life, and begin to build a foundation for their adult lives. The goal of their self-focusing is self-sufficiency, learning to stand alone as a self-sufficient person, but they do not see self-sufficiency as a permanent state. Rather, they view it as a necessary step before committing themselves to enduring relationships with others, in love and work (Arnett, 2015).

Feeling In-Between

The identity explorations, instability, and self-focus of emerging adulthood give it the quality of an in-between period—between adolescence, when most people live in their parents' home and are required to attend secondary school, and young adulthood, when most people have entered marriage and parenthood and have settled into a stable occupational path. In between the restrictions of adolescence and the responsibilities of adulthood lie the identity explorations, instability, and self-focus of emerging adulthood.

It feels this way to most emerging adults, too—like an age in-between, neither adolescent nor adult, on the way to adulthood but not there yet. When asked whether they feel they have reached adulthood, their responses are often ambiguous, with one foot in "yes" and the other in "no." In 20 years of research on emerging adulthood, this is perhaps the most researched question: "Do you feel that you have reached adulthood?" Consistently, the most common response is neither yes nor no, but the in-between response: "in some ways yes, in some ways no" (Nelson & Luster, 2015). This in-between response has been found in a majority of American college students (Arnett, 1994; Reifman, Arnett, & Colwell, 2007), and in a majority of emerging adults across many countries, from China to the Czech Republic (Nelson & Luster, 2015).

The reason why so many emerging adults feel in-between is evident from the criteria they consider to be most important for becoming an adult. Their top criteria are gradual, so their feeling of becoming an adult is gradual, too. In a variety of regions of the United States, in a variety of ethnic groups, across social classes, in college and non-college samples, in studies using both questionnaires and interviews, people consistently state these as the top three criteria for adulthood (Nelson & Luster, 2015):

1. Accept responsibility for yourself.
2. Make independent decisions.
3. Become financially independent.

The Big Three criteria are gradual, incremental, rather than all-at-once. Consequently, although emerging adults begin to feel adult by the time they reach age 18 or 19, most do not feel completely adult until years later, some time in their mid-to-late twenties. By then, they have become confident that they have reached a point where they accept responsibility, make their own decisions, and are financially independent. While they are in the process of developing those qualities they feel in-between adolescence and full adulthood. The Big Three have been found to be prevalent not only in the United States but around the world (Arnett, 2015).

Residential colleges and universities are in many ways constructed to acknowledge, reflect, and support the in-between status of emerging adults.

For the first year or two most live in a residence hall with other students, where adults take care of daily duties such as preparing the meals, paying the electric and water bills, and cleaning the common living areas. Consequently, they live in a state of "semi-autonomy" (Goldscheider & Goldscheider, 1999), with more autonomy than they had as adolescents but not yet as much autonomy and responsibility as they will have later in adulthood. Their semi-autonomy is emblematic of their in-between state as emerging adults, on the way to adulthood but not there yet.

Possibilities/Optimism

Emerging adulthood is the age of possibilities, when many different futures remain possible, when little about a person's direction in life has been decided for certain. It tends to be an age of high hopes and great expectations, in part because few of their dreams have been tested in the fires of real life. Although, as noted earlier, the present may be fraught with anxiety, the future looks bright. In a national survey, 83% of 18–29-year-olds agreed that "At this time of my life, it still seems like anything is possible" (Arnett & Schwab, 2012). Emerging adults look to the future and envision a well-paying, satisfying job, a loving, lifelong marriage, and happy children who are above average. Most also envision obtaining at least a four-year college degree, although fewer than half of them will attain that goal by age 30.

Another aspect of emerging adulthood that makes it the age of possibilities is that it offers the potential for changing dramatically the direction of one's life (Arnett, 2015). A simple but crucial feature of emerging adulthood in this respect is that typically emerging adults have left their family of origin but are not yet committed to a new network of relationships and obligations. This is especially important for young people who have grown up in difficult conditions. A chaotic or unhappy family is difficult to rise above for children and adolescents, because they return to that family environment every day and the family's problems are often reflected in problems of their own. If the parents fight a lot, they have to listen to it. If the parents live in poverty, the children live in poverty, too, most likely in dangerous neighborhoods with inferior schools. If a parent is addicted to alcohol or other drugs, the disruptions from the parent's addiction rip through the rest of the family as well. However, with emerging adulthood and departure from the family home, an unparalleled opportunity begins for young people to transform their lives. For those who have come from a troubled family, this is their chance to try to straighten the parts of themselves that have become twisted.

It may be this aspect of the possibilities/optimism feature in emerging adulthood that has the most important implications for student affairs and student development programs. Many scholars have recognized that going to college can represent a chance to turn a life in a dramatically more positive direction

(Baxter Magolda & Taylor, 2015; McAdams, Josselson, & Lieblich, 2001; Parks, 2011). College can be an important turning point for emerging adults who have substantial potential and motivation to succeed but have so far been stifled by an unhealthy and unhelpful environment in their family and community. These circumstances present an opportunity for programs to assist vulnerable students with high potential, especially during the college transition. Because they enter college with many liabilities from their background, possibly including mental health issues, without assistance, these students may be among those most likely to drop out during the first year or two of college.

Even for those who have come from families they regard as relatively happy and healthy, emerging adulthood is an opportunity to transform themselves so that they are not merely made in their parents' images but have made independent decisions about what kind of person they wish to be and how they wish to live. During emerging adulthood, they have an exceptionally wide scope for making their own decisions. Eventually, virtually all emerging adults will enter new, long-term obligations in love and work, and once they do, their new obligations will set them on paths that resist change and that may continue for the rest of their lives. But for now, while emerging adulthood lasts, they have a chance to change their lives in profound ways.

Regardless of their family background, all emerging adults carry their family influences with them when they leave home, and the extent to which they can change what they have become by the end of adolescence is not unlimited. Still, more than any other period of life, emerging adulthood presents the possibility of change. For this limited window of time, seven, perhaps ten years, the fulfillment of all their hopes seems possible, because for most people the range of their choices for how to live is greater than it has ever been before and greater than it will ever be again. The higher education they receive—or fail to receive—during this period is a crucial factor in determining whether their possibilities will be actualized.

Conclusion: Student Affairs and Emerging Adult Development

The "college years" are also the main years of emerging adulthood, and this chapter has described ways that the theory of emerging adulthood can be fruitfully applied to college students' development. Emerging adulthood theory provides potentially helpful insights for student affairs, but it also places the college years into a larger developmental context and underscores how that context has changed in recent decades. Fifty years ago, the attainment of a college degree was followed for most people by a swift entry into adult life: a stable job, marriage, and parenthood. Today, it is normative for college graduation to be followed by an extended period of change and instability that lasts through most of the rest of the twenties. On average, it takes college graduates three years in the labor market before they find a stable job that will last at least five years (Yates, 2005). Most will not marry and become parents until around age 30 or later (Arnett, 2015). Their timing of marriage and parenthood tends to be even later than for their non-college peers.

This means that the future for which student affairs programs are helping to prepare students is different than in the past, which means that student affairs programs can be most effective if they change, too. The aims of these programs may be affected by recognizing that the college years are often just the beginning of the emerging adult odyssey. Identity explorations, instability, self-focus, feeling in-between, and possibilities/optimism are all features that do not expire on graduation day but are likely to continue to be important through most of the twenties. Student affairs programs can help provide students with the personal assets needed to navigate the often challenging years of emerging adulthood yet to come.

References

Accenture. (2017). *Gen Z rising*. Retrieved from www.accenture.com/us-en/insight-gen-z-rising

Arnett, J. J. (1994). Are college students adults? Their conceptions of the transition to adulthood. *Journal of Adult Development, 1*, 154–168.

Arnett, J. J. (2000). Emerging adulthood: A theory of development from the late teens through the twenties. *American Psychologist, 55*, 469–480.

Arnett, J. J. (2004). *Emerging adulthood: The winding road from the late teens through the twenties (1st edition)*. New York, NY: Oxford University Press.

Arnett, J. J. (2015). *Emerging adulthood: The winding road from the late teens through the twenties (2nd edition)*. New York, NY: Oxford University Press.

Arnett, J. J., & Schwab, J. (2012). *The Clark University poll of emerging adults: Thriving, struggling, and hopeful*. Worcester, MA: Clark University. Retrieved from www.clarku.edu/clark-poll-emerging-adults/

Baxter Magolda, M., & Taylor, K. B. (2015). Developing self-authorship in college to navigate Emerging adulthood. In J. J. Arnett (Ed.), *Oxford handbook of emerging adulthood*. New York, NY: Oxford University Press.

Carnevale, A. P., Smith, N., & Strohl, J. (2013). *Recovery: Job growth and education requirements through 2020*. Washington, DC: Georgetown University Center on Education and the Work Force.

Chickering, A. W., & Reisser, L. (1993). *Education and identity* (2nd ed.). San Francisco, CA: Jossey-Bass.

Erikson, E. H. (1950). *Childhood and society*. New York, NY: Norton.

Erikson, E. H. (1968). *Identity: Youth and crisis*. New York, NY: Norton.

Goldscheider, F., & Goldscheider, C. (1999). *The changing transition to adulthood*. Thousand Oaks, CA: Sage.

Johnston, L. D., O'Malley, P. M., Bachman, J. G., & Schulenberg, J. E. (2012). Monitoring the Future national survey results on drug use 1975–2012. Ann Arbor, MI: Institute for Social Research.

Jones, S. R., & Abes, E. S. (2011). The nature and uses of theory. In J. H. Schuh, S. R. Jones, & S. R. Harper (Eds.), *Student services: A handbook for the profession* (5th ed., pp. 149–167). San Francisco, CA: Jossey-Bass.

Krahn, H. J., Howard, A. J., & Galambos, N. (2012). Exploring or floundering? The meaning of employment and educational fluctuations in emerging adulthood. *Youth & Society, 44*, 1–22. DOI: 10.1177/0044118X12459061

McGill, B., & Bell, P. (2010, Winter). The big picture. *National Journal,* pp. 14–15. Retrievedfromhttps://www.allstate.com/resources/allstate/attachments/heartland-monitor/heartland_vii_editorial_supplement.pdf

Marcia, J. E. (1993). The status of the statuses: Research review. In J. E. Marcia, A. S. Waterman, D. R. Matteson, S. L. Archer, & J. L. Orlofsky (Eds.), *Ego identity: A handbook for psychosocial research* (pp. 22–41). New York, NY: Springer-Verlag.

McAdams, D. P., Josselson, R. E., & Lieblich, A. E. (2001). *Turns in the road: Narrative studies of lives in transition.* Washington, DC: American Psychological Association.

Modell, J. (1989). *Into one's own: From youth to adulthood in the United States, 1920–1975.* Berkeley, CA: University of California Press.

National Center for Education Statistics (NCES). (2018). *The condition of education, 2018.* Washington, DC: U.S. Department of Education. Retrieved from https://nces.ed.gov/pubs2018/2018144.pdf

Nelson, L. J., & Luster, S. (2015). Conceptions of adulthood. In J. J. Arnett (Ed.), *Oxford handbook of emerging adulthood.* New York, NY: Oxford University Press.

Parks, S. D. (2011). *Big questions, worthy dreams: Mentoring emerging adults in their search for meaning, purpose, and faith.* New York, NY: Wiley.

Pascarella, E. T., & Terenzini, P. T. (2005). *How college affects students: A third decade of research, Volume 2.* Indianapolis, IN: Jossey-Bass.

Reifman, A., Arnett, J. J., & Colwell, M. J. (2007). Emerging adulthood: Theory, assessment, and application. *Journal of Youth Development, 1*, 1–12.

Schwartz, S. J., Zamboanga, B. L., Luyckx, K., Meca, A., & Ritchie, R. A. (2013). Identity in emerging adulthood: Reviewing the field and looking forward. *Emerging Adulthood, 1*(2), 96–113.

Sperber, M. (2000). *Beer and circus: How big-time college sports is crippling undergraduate education.* New York, NY: Henry Holt.

United States Census Bureau. (2018). Historical marital status tables. Retrieved from www.census.gov/data/tables/time-series/demo/families/marital.html

Yates, J. A. (2005). The transition from school to work: Education and work experiences. *Monthly Labor Review, 128*(2), 21–32.

3

EMERGING ADULTHOOD AND PSYCHOSOCIAL DEVELOPMENT IN COLLEGE

Joseph L. Murray

As documented in the opening chapter of this book, the evolution of the student affairs profession can be charted across three general eras, each marked by a distinct goal orientation: (1) *student services*, (2) *student development*, and (3) *student learning* (Carpenter, Dean, & Haber-Curran, 2016; Sherman, 2014). A major factor in the ascendency of the student development perspective was the growing influence of theories pertaining to both cognitive and psychosocial development (Rentz, 1994). Even with the adoption of a student learning agenda, the traditional focus on psychosocial development, in particular, has remained central to the profession's foundational literature, in part due to the field's historical ties to the counseling profession (Renn & Reason, 2013). In this chapter, key theories of psychosocial development in college will be reviewed, beginning with Erikson's (1968) seminal stage theory, which established the centrality of identity development to the transition into adulthood, and progressing through the works of several contemporary scholars, which have highlighted human variation in the process of identity formation, the influence of environmental factors on the developmental process, and the interplay of various facets of change as they occur within the individual.

The Life Stage Perspective

Within the literature of student affairs, a distinction has traditionally been drawn between two major branches of developmental theory: (1) *cognitive-structural* theories, which are concerned with "*how* people think, reason, and make meaning of their experiences" (Patton, Renn, Guido, & Quaye, 2016, p. 284) and (2) *psychosocial* theories, which focus on "the *content* of development; that is, the important issues people face as their lives progress, such as how to define themselves, their relationships with others, and what to do with their lives" (p. 283).

While both branches of theory have incorporated developmental stages, the nature of these stages and the processes of transition from one to the next differ across the two theoretical realms. Within cognitive-structural theories, stages are hierarchically ordered and characterized by progressively more complex ways of thinking. Within psychosocial theories, stages are chronologically ordered and characterized by major issues associated with particular periods of life. Historically, this distinction has tended to carry an implicit assumption of universality in the application of cognitive-structural theories, in contrast to a prevailing recognition that patterns of psychosocial development are influenced by social and cultural factors, which can vary according to time and place (Knefelkamp, Widick, & Parker, 1978).

In what is arguably the most influential of the psychosocial theories, Erikson (1968) identified eight developmental stages spanning the entire life cycle, each characterized by a different developmental crisis. According to Erikson's theory, each crisis emerges at a point of natural ascendancy resulting from a convergence of social and biological factors, consistent with what he termed the *epigenetic principle*. Each stage carries the potential for either an adaptive or maladaptive resolution of its defining crisis, reflected in the dichotomous labels used by Erikson to designate the respective stages: (1) *basic trust versus basic mistrust* (infancy), (2) *autonomy versus shame and doubt* (early childhood), (3) *initiative versus guilt* (play age), (4) *industry versus inferiority* (school age), (5) *identity versus confusion* (adolescence), (6) *intimacy versus isolation* (young adulthood), (7) *generativity versus stagnation* (adulthood), and (8) *integrity versus despair* (old age).

Identity Development in College

Although Erikson (1968) situated identity formation—the process of self-reflection through which an individual establishes an enduring sense of self—within the context of adolescent psychosocial development, it has drawn similarly prominent attention within the literature on psychosocial development in college. One apparent factor in this application of Erikson's theory is the prevalence of research on identity development in which participant samples have been comprised entirely of college students. Marcia (1993) cited three apparent reasons for the emergence of this body of research: (1) "most researchers work in university settings", (2) "the age of identity resolution, around 18–22, is the age of most college students", and (3) "college is a definable social institution within which identity formation may be expected to take place" (p. 34). Speaking more directly to this last point, Jones and Abes (2013) observed that "put simply, an understanding of identity is necessary if one is to understand college students and their experiences in higher education contexts" (p. 19), an observation borne out in numerous studies of college outcomes (Mayhew et al., 2016; Pascarella & Terenzini, 1991, 2005).

Marcia's Ego-Identity Statuses

In introducing an extensive review of research on identity development from the late 1960s through the 1980s, Pascarella and Terenzini (1991) observed that "a substantial portion of the identity development research has been based on the theoretical model of James Marcia" (p. 164). Building upon Erikson's (1968) theory of psychosocial development, Marcia (1966) formulated and validated a conceptual framework in which he identified four ego-identity statuses. The four statuses are differentiated from one another on the basis of two factors: (1) the experience of a developmental crisis or lack thereof and (2) an identity commitment or lack thereof. Marcia's theory can be applied to specific areas of identity commitment, including the occupational, religious, and political realms. The four statuses and their defining attributes are as follows: (1) *achieved* identity, which is said to exist when a crisis has been experienced and a satisfactory resolution attained, (2) *foreclosed* identity, which occurs when a commitment is made in the absence of a crisis, (3) the *moratorium* status, which exists while an individual is in the midst of a crisis that has not yet been resolved, and (4) *diffused* identity, which exists in individuals who have experienced neither a crisis nor a commitment.

Chickering's Vectors of Development

A theory set forth by Chickering (Chickering & Reisser, 1993) highlighted the relevance of Erikson's (1968) work to student affairs practice, by enumerating seven dimensions of development, termed *vectors*, which are typically of major concern to traditional-aged college students: (1) *developing competence*, (2) *managing emotions*, (3) *moving through autonomy toward interdependence*, (4) *developing mature interpersonal relationships*, (5) *establishing identity*, (6) *developing purpose*, and (7) *developing integrity*. Recognized as the central developmental task of the college years, the establishment of identity is affected by each of the other vectors.

Identity and Human Diversity

As recently noted in the professional literature (Evans, 2016), much of the past decade's research on college student development has centered specifically on *social identity development*, which has been defined as "the process by which people come to understand their social identities (ethnicity, race, gender, sexual orientation, and others) and how these identities affect other aspects of their lives" (Patton et al., 2016, p. 67). Because social identities, as well as the differential access to power and privilege that attend to them, are influenced by the judgments of others, they are also subject to change over time and can likewise differ across geographical locations (Patton et al., 2016).

Among the factors that likely account for the growing interest in social identity development within American higher education today is the increasing diversity of both the U. S. college student population (Eagan et al., 2016) and that of the nation as a whole (Humes, Jones, & Ramirez, 2011). American colleges and universities have become progressively more committed to the cultivation of diverse campus communities as a means of promoting outcomes associated with both learning and democracy (Gurin, Dey, Hurtado, & Gurin, 2002). As student affairs professionals have begun to focus more intently on the preparation of future leaders and citizens for a diverse society, the rapidly expanding body of theory pertaining to social identity development has been a welcome addition to the literature of the field.

Theories of Race and Ethnicity

Perhaps nowhere have issues of diversity in American higher education been more contentious than within the realm of race and ethnicity. The continued underrepresentation of racial and ethnic minorities in higher education, coupled with recurring instances of racial bias on American college and university campuses, has resulted in widespread minority student unrest. This new wave of campus activism has, in some instances, been met with various forms of backlash from racial and ethnic majorities (Latham, 2016). Consistent with both the definition of social identity development presented above and key sources of tension on college and university campuses today, much of the theoretical literature on racial and ethnic identity development, among both minority and majority populations, has focused on awareness of social inequity.

Cross's Theory of Psychological Nigrescence

Cross (1991) formulated a widely cited theory of African-American racial identity development, in which he used the term "nigrescence" to describe the transformation that occurs as an African-American's perspective shifts from one that is Eurocentric to one that is distinctively Black. This theory incorporates five stages through which African-Americans typically proceed in developing a heightened awareness of the significance of race in their lives: (1) *pre-encounter*, (2) *encounter*, (3) *immersion-emersion*, (4) *internalization*, and (5) *internalization-commitment*. In a more recent variation on this conceptual framework, levels of racial consciousness instilled in Black children by their parents are differentiated across three categories of emergent racial identity: (1) *high race salience*, (2) *low race salience*, and (3) *internalized racism*. These differentiated preadolescent statuses, in turn, affect experiences of racial identity development in adolescence and adulthood, such that the stages articulated in the original sequence are now understood to be particular to those who undergo a process of conversion in their racial consciousness. The expanded model also allows for further enhancement of an individual's foundational Black identity through a process known as *nigrescence recycling* (Cross & Fhagen-Smith, 2001). Within the context of college student development, the five stages articulated by Cross (1991) remain a useful framework for understanding common patterns of change as they occur in a campus setting.

Helms's White Identity Development Model

Just as minorities become more aware of the significance of race over time, so too do members of the majority race. Helms (1990) identified two major phases through which White Americans typically proceed in the formation of non-racist Caucasian identities. This model is based on a definition of racism that has three components: (1) *individual racism,* which manifests itself in the discriminatory attitudes and behaviors of individuals, (2) *institutional racism,* which manifests itself in social structures that favor the majority race, and (3) *cultural racism,* which manifests itself in a devaluation of minority culture.

Phase I: Abandonment of Racism

During the initial phase of the process described by Helms, the central task in developing a non-racist White identity is overcoming existing patterns of racism, which might previously have gone unrecognized. Progression through this phase encompasses three successive statuses: (1) *contact,* (2) *disintegration,* and (3) *reintegration.*

Phase II: Defining a Non-Racist White Identity

The second major phase of White identity development is characterized by an abandonment of the assumption of White superiority that marked the previously held view of race. Like the previous phase, this one is also characterized by a sequence of three statuses: (1) *pseudo-independence,* (2) *immersion-emersion,* and (3) *autonomy.*

Phinney's Model of Ethnic Identity Development

Phinney (1996) put forth a model of ethnic identity development that is applicable either to members of racial groups or to more narrowly defined ethnic groups within races. Drawing upon the work of numerous theorists and researchers, Phinney characterized ethnic identity development as a process in which

> adolescents and young adults are assumed to progress over time from an unexamined or received view of their ethnicity – based on attitudes of parents, communities, or society – through a crisis or exploration phase,

in which they immerse themselves in the history and culture of their group, to an achieved, secure sense of their ethnicity.

(p. 145)

Accordingly, she identified three distinct stages of ethnic identity development: (1) *unexamined ethnic identity*, (2) *moratorium or exploration*, and (3) *achieved ethnic identity*.

Theories of Sexuality and Gender

Another area in which the body of literature on social identity development has rapidly expanded is the broad constellation of theoretical constructs pertaining to sexuality and gender. Among the points of differentiation that have been explored in the relevant literature are sex, sexual orientation, gender identity, and gender expression. Consistent with other aspects of social identity, each of these factors can account for variation in power and privilege (Jourian, 2015).

Women's Identity Development

Applying Marcia's (1966) developmental framework, Josselson (1987, 1996) analyzed the characteristics of women who manifested different ego–identity statuses, and drew comparisons among them. From her research, she created more detailed profiles of the women in each category, thereby deepening understanding of the process of identity development as it plays out specifically in the lives of women. To more accurately convey the essence of this process, she articulated—and subsequently amended—her own labeling typology, which also consisted of four categories: (1) *pavers of the way* or *pathmakers* (achievement), (2) *purveyors of the heritage* or *guardians* (foreclosure), (3) *daughters of crisis* or *searchers* (moratorium), and (4) *lost and sometimes found* or *drifters* (diffusion). Among the major issues that women confronted in the process of identity development was *separation-individuation*, meaning the task of separating emotionally from their families of origin. As separation-individuation occurred, they tended to develop a need to replace their families of origin with something else that would serve as the focal point of their lives. Josselson used the term *anchoring* to describe this rechanneling of women's energy. She also found that relationships were often central to women's identities, consistent with previous findings by Chodorow (1978) and Gilligan (1982).

LGBTQ Identity Development

Though sometimes used more strictly to signify "lesbian, gay, bisexual, transgender, and queer" (Stewart & Renn, 2015, p. 1), the acronym LGBTQ is also commonly used as a general term for members of "minoritized sexual orientation or gender identity groups" (p. 2). Although the theoretical literature pertaining to gender identity and expression has expanded in recent years, it has been slower to materialize than that pertaining to sexual orientation. Even so, a number of commonalities have been found in the experiences of non-heterosexual and gender-variant populations, such that prior research on gay, lesbian, and bisexual identity development has informed current understandings of other LGBTQ populations as well (Bilodeau, 2005; Lev, 2004).

Cass's Theory of Gay and Lesbian Identity Development

Cass (1979) formulated a theoretical framework to conceptualize the process through which lesbians and gay men come to identify themselves as homosexual. Cass characterized this process as a struggle to reconcile three separate aspects of one's sexual orientation: (1) one's own view of oneself, (2) one's view of one's own behavior, and (3) one's perception of how one is viewed by others. The theory incorporates six stages of identity formation, progression through which can be interrupted by foreclosure at any stage: (1) *identity confusion*, (2) *identity comparison*, (3) *identity tolerance*, (4) *identity acceptance*, (5) *identity pride*, and (6) *identity synthesis*.

D'Augelli's Model of Lesbian, Gay, and Bisexual Identity Development

D'Augelli (1994) advanced a model of non-heterosexual identity development, in which one's definition of self is shaped by three interacting factors: (1) *personal subjectivities and actions,* (2) *interactive intimacies,* and (3) *sociohistoric connections.* D'Augelli set forth three assumptions upon which his theory was founded: (1) the process of identity development is characterized by changes in views of oneself over the course of the life span, (2) individuals differ among themselves in their processes of development, and (3) individuals are active participants in the construction of their own identities. Consistent with these stipulations, D'Augelli refrained from articulating a fixed sequence of developmental stages, opting instead for an enumeration of six related processes, which can only be fully understood within the social context in which they occur: (1) *exiting heterosexual identity*; (2) *developing a personal lesbian-gay-bisexual identity status*; (3) *developing a lesbian-gay-bisexual social identity*; (4) *becoming a lesbian-gay-bisexual offspring*; (5) *developing a lesbian-gay-bisexual intimacy status*; and (6) *entering a lesbian-gay-bisexual community.*

Theories of Transgender Identity Development

Among the most influential theories of transgender identity development to date is Lev's (2004) model of *transgender emergence*, which charts a process of self-acceptance and disclosure that parallels aspects of the "coming out" experience addressed in much of the literature on gay, lesbian, and bisexual identity development. With an emphasis on implications for supportive psychotherapy, Lev identified a sequence of six common stages of transgender identity development: (1) *awareness*, (2) *seeking information/reaching out*, (3) *disclosure to significant others*, (4) *exploring identity and transition*, (5) *exploring transition and possible body modification*, and (6) *integration and pride*. Based on data from a national sample of individuals representing a broad spectrum of gender-variant identities, Beemyn and Rankin (2011) stopped short of advancing a general sequence of developmental stages, but instead identified major *milestones* that were commonly associated with each of four categories of transgender identity development: (1) *female-to-male transsexual*, (2) *male-to-female transsexual*, (3) *cross-dresser*, and (4) *genderqueer*. Although few authors have examined the development of gender-variant identities specifically within college student populations, case study research by Bilodeau (2005) suggested that D'Augelli's model of gay, lesbian, and bisexual identity development could be successfully adapted and applied to the analysis of six corresponding dimensions of transgender identity development in college.

Theories of Disability

Undoubtedly, a major factor in the growing attention given to the needs of students with disabilities in American higher education is the enactment of relevant federal legislation, coupled with an expanding body of case law that offers guidance on resultant mandates (Grossman, 2014). Increasingly, the legal demands placed on colleges and universities in regard to accommodation of students with disabilities have also come to be seen as opportunities to create more inclusive campus environments, most notably through adoption of universal design principles (Myers, Lindburg, & Nied, 2013).

Evans, Broido, Brown, and Wilke (2017) have called for adoption of a social justice perspective on disability in higher education, which they describe as follows.

> A social justice approach to disability in higher education means beginning with the assumption that people's abilities and rights to contribute to and benefit from higher education are not dependent on their bodies or psyches conforming to dominant norms. It means that we believe the barriers to success in higher education lie in the structural, organizational, physical, and attitudinal aspects of our institutions.
>
> *(p. xiii)*

This stance aligns with widely held perspectives on both social identity development in general (Patton et al., 2016) and issues of identity particular to individuals with disabilities, which have long been recognized as holding both personal and political significance (Linton, 1998; Zola, 1993).

Consistent with the centrality of identity formation to psychosocial development in college, Serebrini, Gordon, and Mann (1994) observed that one of the most obvious developmental issues specific to students with disabilities is the challenge of "integrating a disability into self-identity, which will manifest itself differently depending on when the onset of the disability occurs" (p. 16). In examining the psychology of disability status, Gibson (2006) identified three stages of identity development, each characterized by a different attitude toward the disability: (1) *passive awareness,* (2) *realization,* and (3) *acceptance.* Rejecting the notion of a uniform social identity based on disability, Johnstone (2004) maintained that the identities of individuals with disabilities are personally constructed. Drawing upon the relevant literature, he thus devised a broad classification scheme comprising six general categories of disability identity: (1) *socially ascribed, disempowering,* (2) *overcompensating,* (3) *identities that shift focus away from disabilities,* (4) *empowerment,* (5) *complex,* and (6) *common identity.*

Theories of Religion and Social Class

Both religion and social class, sometimes examined in relation to first-generation college attendance, have been identified in the student development literature as aspects of human diversity that bear upon identity development (Patton et al., 2016). However, both topics have been addressed in the theoretical literature somewhat differently than have other forms of individual variation. While certain theories of faith development have gained a strong foothold within the student affairs literature (Fowler, 2000; Parks, 2011), their focus has generally been on the evolution of one's world view rather than on issues of power and privilege, as would be more typical of social identity theories. Conversely, issues of equity are at the heart of scholarly discourse on social class, yet the theoretical perspectives that have informed contemporary analysis of the topic have often centered on the social conditions that give rise to systemic inequality (Bourdieu & Passeron, 1990; Lareau & Weininger, 2008), as opposed to the significance of such conditions to one's image of self.

Intersectionality and Identity

As illustrated by the multiple dimensions of human diversity addressed in the theoretical literature, the majority or minority status of an individual is not necessarily uniform across all dimensions of social identity. Defined as "the mutually constitutive relations among social identities" (Shields, 2008, p. 301), the concept of *intersectionality* has contributed to more nuanced understandings of the interplay between aspects of personal identity, particularly as they relate to issues of power and privilege. This use of the term was introduced by

Crenshaw (1991), a feminist legal scholar, specifically in relation to the marginalization of women of color, even relative to women and minorities generally. Crenshaw further delineated three distinct forms of intersectionality: (1) *structural intersectionality*, (2) *political intersectionality*, and (3) *representational intersectionality*. Within the literature of higher education, the concept of intersectionality has informed discussion of identity issues pertaining to both students (Jones & Abes, 2013) and faculty (Meyer, 2016), and has been applied to professional practice in the areas of teaching (Ouellett, 2011), student affairs (Wijeyesinghe, 2017), and institutional research (Griffin & Museus, 2011).

Evolving Perspectives on Psychosocial Development in College

As is evident from the review of the theoretical literature presented above, understandings of identity development in college remain in a continuous state of evolution. A similar pattern of ongoing refinement is evident in the broader body of literature on college student development in which psychosocial theories are situated. The expansion of student affairs scholarship over time has yielded both a softening of the boundaries between the cognitive-structural and psychosocial branches of theory and a broadening of their disciplinary moorings.

Constructive Developmentalist Perspectives

Contemporary views of college student development have been increasingly shaped by the works of Kegan (1994), Baxter Magolda (2004), and others who have advanced a perspective that is rooted in both the constructivist and developmentalist traditions. Two key theoretical constructs within the *constructive developmentalist* school of thought are the related processes of *meaning-making* and *self-authorship*, explained by Baxter Magolda and King (2012) as follows.

> Meaning-making capacities reflect how people make sense of (or interpret) their experience, including their assumptions about how to decide what to believe, construct their identities, and engage in relationships with others. The complex meaning-making capacity of self-authorship, characterized by the ability to internally coordinate external influence in the process of defining one's beliefs, identity, and social relations, forms a basis for meeting the complex challenges that college students and other adults face as they navigate life.
>
> *(p. vii)*

Baxter Magolda (2004) used the terms *epistemological, intrapersonal*, and *interpersonal* to distinguish among the dimensions of self-authorship that are concerned with one's beliefs, identity, and social relations, respectively. This view of self-authorship resituates the process of identity development within a holistic framework that incorporates elements of both the psychosocial and cognitive-structural branches of theory and emphasizes growth in both intellectual and emotional autonomy.

Environmental Perspectives

Although developmental theories that emphasize the influence of the college environment on students—traditionally known as *person-environment interaction* theories (Knefelkamp et al., 1978) – are not new, this branch of theory appears to be generating resurgent interest, following a period of relative dormancy. Renn and Arnold (2003) were instrumental in advancing an ecological theory set forth by Bronfenbrenner (1979), through their application of its principles to the psychosocial development of traditional aged college students, with an emphasis on the influence of the student peer culture. In further application of the model to issues of college readiness, Arnold, Lu, and Armstrong (2012) elaborated on influences particular to each of the five subsystems that comprise an individual's environment: (1) *microsystem*, (2) *mesosystem*, (3) *exosystem*, (4) *macrosystem*, and (5) *chronosystem*. While the focus of Bronfenbrenner's work, and subsequent interpretations of it, is on the human environment in which identity development occurs, Strange and Banning (2015) cited four dimensions of campus environments, which together take into account both elements of the built environment and the people and organizations that populate it: (1) *physical*, (2) *aggregate*, (3) *organizational*, and (4) *socially constructed*. A popular model for the creation of campus environments that are supportive of human diversity was initially conceptualized by Hurtado, Milem, Clayton-Pedersen, and Allen (1999), and subsequently, adapted by Chang, Milem, and antonio [sic] (2011). In addition to accounting for the influences of external forces within the *governmental/political* and *sociohistorical* realms, the revised model addresses five dimensions of the institutional context: (1) *compositional diversity*, (2) *historical legacy of inclusion or exclusion*, (3) *psychological climate*, (4) *behavioral climate*, and (5) *organizational/structural diversity*.

Critical and Poststructural Perspectives

In a recent analysis of the evolution of student development theory, Jones and Stewart (2016) used the imagery of waves to represent shifts in the philosophical orientations that have informed emergent theories over time. In their view, the *first wave* is represented by the foundational theories of Erikson (1968), Marcia (1966), Chickering (Chickering & Reisser, 1993), and others, which continue to provide a basic understanding of the changes that occur during the college years, informed by principles of developmental psychology. The *second wave* is reflected in the social identity theories of Cross (1991), Phinney (1996), Cass (1979), and others, which take into account variation in the experiences of diverse student populations. Finally, the *third wave* is encapsulated in theories that also "critique, challenge, and seek to dismantle inequitable power structures" (Jones & Stewart, 2016, p. 21). Jones and Abes (2011) drew similar distinctions between *positivist* and *constructivist* views of knowledge, which correspond to the first and second waves, respectively, and contrasted both with the *critical* and *poststructural* theoretical perspectives that represent the third wave (Jones & Stewart, 2016). In further distinguishing between the critical and poststructural perspectives, Jones and Abes (2011) noted that proponents of the former seek to advance a specific agenda of social reform, while adherents to the latter see potential for multiple forms of resolution and resist imposition of fixed paradigms.

In general, the trend in student development theory has been toward a broader disciplinary grounding, which draws upon the intellectual traditions of both psychology and sociology, and away from a foundation more singularly rooted in psychology (Jones & Abes, 2013; Strayhorn, 2016). As the third wave has ushered in theoretical perspectives that, by their nature, push back against traditional constraints, the disciplinary boundaries that have shaped prevailing views of college student development have grown more porous still. Critical theory, for example, has become a key element of academic curricula in disciplines across the humanities and social sciences, and as such has influenced the study of the disciplines themselves (Malpas & Wake, 2013). The cross-pollination of disciplines will likely continue to manifest itself in the study of college student development in the years ahead, as openness to ascendant theoretical perspectives increases further.

Expanding the Conversation

Based on the theoretical overview presented in this chapter, it appears that Arnett's (2015) work on emerging adulthood holds the potential to both complement and supplement the body of literature that currently informs higher education and student affairs practice. Like the foundational theories of Erikson (1968), Marcia (1966), and Chickering (Chickering & Reisser, 1993), Arnett's (2015) theory situates student development within a broader life stage framework and highlights the centrality of identity formation to psychosocial development in college. The theory also aligns well with overall trends within the literature, which place a growing emphasis on the influence of social context on developmental change in college.

Within the field of developmental psychology, the impact of Arnett's work has already been dramatic. In the years since it was first introduced (Arnett, 2000), the concept of emerging adulthood has become a major focus of research in the field. In 2003, the Society for the Study of Emerging Adulthood (SSEA) was founded as an international association devoted specifically to scholarship on emerging adulthood. Since 2013, SSEA has published *Emerging Adulthood*, a bi-monthly journal devoted exclusively to research on the subject. Through the efforts of a growing community of scholars, much has been learned about aspects of this developmental period, including attitudes toward religion and spirituality (Barry & Abo-Zena, 2014; Smith & Snell, 2009), the influence of family relationships (Fingerman & Yahirun, 2016; McLean, 2016), and physical and mental health issues (Schulenberg & Zarrett, 2006; Swanson, 2016).

Where Arnett's theory, along with the growing body of research that it has inspired, can potentially make its greatest contribution to the student affairs field is in the point of contrast that it raises between developmental issues particular to the life circumstances of college students versus those associated with the broader life stage of emerging adulthood. Although much of the research on emerging adulthood has been conducted on college student populations (Syed, 2016), the generalizability of findings across student versus non-student populations has been and continues to be rigorously interrogated (Arnett, 2016a; Mitchell & Syed, 2015; Schwartz, 2016). A similar debate on generalizability across socioeconomic lines has remained ongoing (Arnett, 2016b; du Bois-Reymond, 2016), spurred on in part by research on experiences of the working class at this same life stage (Hendry & Kloep, 2010; Silva, 2013). Given the growing interest in socioeconomic barriers to enrollment, persistence, and academic success in college (Walpole, 2007), the literature on emerging adulthood holds the potential to enrich understanding of such issues in ways that more narrowly focused research on college students simply cannot.

References

Arnett, J. J. (2000). Emerging adulthood: A theory of development from the late teens through the twenties. *American Psychologist, 55,* 469–480.

Arnett, J. J. (2015). *Emerging adulthood: The winding road from the late teens through the twenties* (2nd ed.). New York, NY: Oxford.

Arnett, J. J. (2016a). College students as emerging adults: The developmental implications of the college context. *Emerging Adulthood, 4,* 219–222.

Arnett, J. J. (2016b). Does emerging adulthood theory apply across social classes? National data on a persistent question. *Emerging Adulthood, 4,* 227–235.

Arnold, K. D., Lu, E. C., & Armstrong, K. J. (2012). *The ecology of college readiness.* ASHE Higher Education Report, 38(5). San Francisco, CA: Jossey-Bass.

Barry, C. M., & Abo-Zena, M. M. (Eds.). (2014). *Emerging adults' religiousness and spirituality: Meaning-making in an age of transition.* New York, NY: Oxford.

Baxter Magolda, M. B. (2004). Self-authorship as the common goal of 21st-century education. In M. Baxter Magolda & P. M. King (Eds.), *Learning partnerships: Theory and models of practice to educate for self-authorship* (pp. 1–35). Sterling, VA: Stylus.

Baxter Magolda, M. B., & King, P. M. (2012). *Assessing meaning-making and self-authorship: Theory, research, and application.* ASHE Higher Education Report, 38(3). San Francisco, CA: Jossey-Bass.

Beemyn, G., & Rankin, S. (2011). *The lives of transgender people.* New York, NY: Columbia University Press.

Bilodeau, B. (2005). Beyond the gender binary: A case study of two transgender students at a Midwestern research university. *Journal of Gay & Lesbian Issues in Education, 3*(1), 29–44.

du Bois-Reymond, M. (2016). Emerging adulthood theory and social class. In J. J. Arnett (Ed.), *The Oxford handbook of emerging adulthood* (pp. 47–61). New York, NY: Oxford.

Bourdieu, P., & Passeron, J -C. (1990). *Reproduction in education, society and culture* (2nd ed.). Newbury Park, CA: Sage.

Bronfenbrenner, U. (1979). *The ecology of human development: Experiments by nature and design.* Cambridge, MA: Harvard University Press.

Carpenter, S. L., Dean, S., & Haber-Curran, P. (2016). The philosophical heritage of student affairs. In N. Zhang (Ed.), *Rentz's student affairs practice in higher education* (5th ed., pp. 3–27). Springfield, IL: Thomas.

Cass, V. C. (1979). Homosexual identity formation: A theoretical model. *Journal of Homosexuality, 4*(3), 219–235.

Chang, M. J., Milem, J. F., & antonio, a. l. [sic]. (2011). Campus climate and diversity. In J. H. Schuh, S. R. Jones, & S. R. Harper (Eds.), *Student services: A handbook for the profession* (5th ed., pp. 43–58). San Francisco, CA: Jossey-Bass.

Chickering, A. W., & Reisser, L. (1993). *Education and identity* (2nd ed.). San Francisco: Jossey-Bass.

Chodorow, N. (1978). *The reproduction of mothering: Psychoanalysis and the sociology of gender.* Berkeley, CA: University of California Press.

Crenshaw, K. (1991). Mapping the margins: Intersectionality, identity politics, and violence against women of color. *Stanford Law Review, 43*, 1241–1299.

Cross, W. E., Jr. (1991). *Shades of black: Diversity in African-American identity.* Philadelphia, PA: Temple University Press.

Cross, W. E., Jr., & Fhagen-Smith, P. (2001). Patterns of African American identity development: A life span perspective. In C. L. Wijeyesinghe & B. W. Jackson III (Eds.), *New perspectives on racial identity development: A theoretical and practical anthology* (pp. 243–270). New York, NY: New York University Press.

D'Augelli, A. R. (1994). Identity development and sexual orientation: Toward a model of lesbian, gay, and bisexual development. In E. J. Trickett, R. J. Watts, & D. Birman (Eds.), *Human diversity: Perspectives on people in context* (pp. 312–333). San Francisco, CA: Jossey-Bass.

Eagan, M. K., Stolzenberg, E. B., Ramirez, J. J., Aragon, M. C., Suchard, M. R., & Rios-Aguilar, C. (2016). *The American freshman: Fifty-year trends, 1966–2015.* Los Angeles, CA: Higher Education Research Institute, UCLA.

Erikson, E. K. (1968). Life cycle. In D. L. Sills (Ed.), *International encyclopedia of the social sciences* (Vol. 9., pp. 286–292). New York, NY: Macmillan.

Evans, N. J. (2016). Preface. In L. D. Patton, K. A. Renn, F. M. Guido, & S. J. Quaye (Eds.), *Student development in college: Theory, research, and practice* (3rd ed., pp. xix–xxiv). San Francisco, CA: Jossey-Bass.

Evans, N. J., Broido, E. M., Brown, K. R., & Wilke, A. K. (2017). *Disability in higher education: A social justice approach.* San Francisco, CA: Jossey-Bass.

Fingerman, K. L., & Yahirun, J. (2016). Emerging adulthood in the context of family. In J. J. Arnett (Ed.), *The Oxford handbook of emerging adulthood* (pp. 163–176). New York, NY: Oxford.

Fowler, J. W. (2000). *Becoming adult, becoming Christian: Adult development and Christian faith.* San Francisco, CA: Jossey-Bass.

Gibson, J. (2006). Disability and clinical competency: An introduction. *The California Psychologist, 39*, 6–10.

Gilligan, C. (1982). *In a different voice: Psychological theory and women's development.* Cambridge, MA: Harvard University Press.

Griffin, K. A., & Museus, S. D. (Eds.). (2011). *Using mixed-methods approaches to study intersectionality in higher education.* New Directions for Institutional Research, n. 151. San Francisco, CA: Jossey-Bass.

Grossman, P. D. (2014). The greatest change in disability law in 20 years. In M. L. Vance, N. E. Lipsitz, & K. Parks (Eds.), *Beyond the Americans with Disabilities Act: Inclusive policy and practice for higher education* (pp. 3–19). Washington, DC: NASPA.

Gurin, P., Dey, E. L., Hurtado, S., & Gurin, G. (2002). Diversity and higher education: Theory and impact on educational outcomes. *Harvard Educational Review, 72*(3), 330–366.

Helms, J. E. (1990). Toward a model of white racial identity development. In J. E. Helms (Ed.), *Black and white racial identity: Theory, research, and practice* (pp. 49–66). Westport, CT: Greenwood.

Hendry, L. B., & Kloep, M. (2010). How universal is emerging adulthood? An empirical example. *Journal of Youth Studies, 13*(2), 169–179.

Humes, K. R., Jones, N. A., & Ramirez, R. R. (2011). *Overview of race and Hispanic origin: 2010.* Report no. C2010BR-02. Washington, DC: U.S. Census Bureau.

Hurtado, S., Milem, J., Clayton-Pedersen, A., & Allen, W. (1999). *Enacting diverse learning environments: Improving the climate for racial/ethnic diversity in higher education.* ASHE-ERIC Higher Education Report, 26(8). Washington, DC: The George Washington University, Graduate School of Education and Human Development.

Johnstone, C. J. (2004). Disability and identity: Personal constructions and formalized supports. *Disability Studies Quarterly, 24*(4). Retrieved May 25, 2017 from http://dsq-sds.org/article/view/880/1055

Jones, S. R., & Abes, E. S. (2011). The nature and uses of theory. In J. H. Schuh, S. R. Jones, & S. R. Harper (Eds.), *Student services: A handbook for the profession* (5th ed., pp. 149–167). San Francisco, CA: Jossey-Bass.

Jones, S. R., & Abes, E. S. (2013). *Identity development of college students: Advancing frameworks for multiple dimensions of identity.* San Francisco, CA: Jossey-Bass.

Jones, S. R., & Stewart, D -L. (2016). Evolution of student development theory. In E. S. Abes (Ed.), *Critical perspectives on student development theory* (pp. 17–28). New Directions for Student Services, n. 154. San Francisco, CA: Jossey-Bass.

Josselson, R. (1987). *Finding herself: Pathways to identity development in women.* San Francisco, CA: Jossey-Bass.

Josselson, R. (1996). *Revising herself: The story of women's identity from college to midlife.* New York, NY: Oxford.

Jourian, T. J. (2015). Evolving nature of sexual orientation and gender identity. In D-L. Stewart, K. A. Renn, & G. B. Brazelton (Eds.), *Gender and sexual diversity in U.S. higher education: Contexts and opportunities for LGBTQ college students* (pp. 18–30). New Directions for Student Services, n. 152. San Francisco, CA: Jossey-Bass.

Kegan, R. (1994). *In over our heads: The mental demands of modern life.* Cambridge, MA: Harvard University Press.

Knefelkamp, L., Widick, C., & Parker, C. A. (1978). Editors' notes: Why bother with theory? In L. Knefelkamp, C. Widick, & C. A. Parker (Eds.), *Applying new developmental findings* (pp. vii–xvi). New Directions for Student Services, n. 4. San Francisco, CA: Jossey-Bass.

Lareau, A., & Weininger, E. B. (2008). Class and the transition to adulthood. In A. Lareau & D. Conley (Eds.), *Social class: How does it work?* (pp. 118–151). New York, NY: Russell Sage Foundation.

Latham, W. H. (2016). Embracing campus diversity and addressing racial unrest: How higher ed can take the lead in confronting this modern civil rights issue. *University Business, 19*(11), 52.

Lev, A. I. (2004). *Transgender emergence: Therapeutic guidelines for working with gender-variant people and their families.* Binghamton, NY: Haworth.

Linton, S. (1998). *Claiming disability: Knowledge and identity.* New York, NY: New York University Press.

Malpas, S., & Wake, P. (2013). Editors' introduction to the first edition. In S. Malpas & P. Wake (Eds.), *The Routledge companion to critical and cultural theory* (2nd ed., pp. viii–x). New York, NY: Routledge.

Marcia, J. E. (1966). Development and validation of ego–identity status. *Journal of Personality and Social Psychology, 3*, 551–558.

Marcia, J. E. (1993). The status of the statuses: Research review. In J. E. Marcia, A. S. Waterman, D. R. Matteson, S. L. Archer, & J. L. Orlofsky (Eds.), *Ego identity: A handbook for psychosocial research* (pp. 22–41). New York, NY: Springer-Verlag.

Mayhew, M. J., Rockenbach, A. N., Bowman, N. A., Seifert, T. A., Wolniak, G. C., Pascarella, E. T., & Terenzini, P. T. (2016). *How college affects students, volume 3: 21st century evidence that higher education works.* San Francisco, CA: Jossey-Bass.

McLean, K. C. (2016). *The co-authored self: Family stories and the construction of personal identity.* New York, NY: Oxford.

Meyer, L. D. (2016). Triple threat: Multiple identities in the academy. In B. L. H. Marina & S. Ross (Eds.), *Beyond retention: Cultivating spaces of equity, justice, and fairness for women of color in U.S. higher education* (pp. 165–179). Charlotte, NC: Information Age.

Mitchell, L. L., & Syed, M. (2015). Does college matter for emerging adulthood? Comparing developmental trajectories of educational groups. *Journal of Youth and Adolescence, 44*, 2012–2027.

Myers, K. A., Lindburg, J. J., & Nied, D. M. (2013). *Allies for inclusion: Disability and equity in higher education.* ASHE Higher Education Report, 39(5). San Francisco, CA: Jossey-Bass.

Ouellett, M. L. (Ed.). (2011). *An integrative analysis approach to diversity in the college classroom.* New Directions for Teaching and Learning, n. 125. San Francisco, CA: Jossey-Bass.

Parks, S. D. (2011). *Big questions, worthy dreams: Mentoring emerging adults in their search for meaning, purpose, and faith* (2nd ed.). San Francisco, CA: Jossey-Bass.

Pascarella, E. T., & Terenzini, P. T. (1991). *How college affects students: Findings and insights from twenty years of research.* San Francisco, CA: Jossey-Bass.

Pascarella, E. T., & Terenzini, P. T. (2005). *How college affects students, volume 2: A third decade of research.* San Francisco, CA: Jossey-Bass.

Patton, L. D., Renn, K. A., Guido, F. M., & Quaye, S. J. (2016). *Student development in college: Theory, research, and practice* (3rd ed.). San Francisco, CA: Jossey-Bass.

Phinney, J. S. (1996). Understanding ethnic diversity: The role of ethnic identity. *American Behavioral Scientist, 40*(2), 143–152.

Renn, K. A., & Arnold, K. D. (2003). Reconceptualizing research on college peer culture. *Journal of Higher Education, 74*(3), 261–291.

Renn, K. A., & Reason, R. D. (2013). *College students in the United States: Characteristics, experiences, and outcomes.* San Francisco, CA: Jossey-Bass.

Rentz, A. L. (1994). The emergence of student development. In A. L. Rentz (Ed.), *Student affairs: A profession's heritage* (2nd ed., pp. 257–261). Lanham, MD: University Press of America.

Schulenberg, J. E., & Zarrett, N. R. (2006). Mental health during emerging adulthood: Continuity and discontinuity in courses, causes, and functions. In J. J. Arnett & J. L. Tanner (Eds.), *Emerging adults in America: Coming of age in the 21st century* (pp. 135–172). Washington, DC: American Psychological Association.

Schwartz, S. J. (2016). Turning point for a turning point: Advancing emerging adulthood theory and research. *Emerging Adulthood, 4*, 307–317.

Smith, C., & Snell, P. (2009). *Souls in transition: The religious and spiritual lives of emerging adults.* New York, NY: Oxford.

Serebrini, R. R., Gordon, S. E., & Mann, B. A. (1994). Student development theories as related to students with disabilities. In D. Ryan & M. McCarthy (Eds.), *A student affairs guide to the ADA & disability issues* (pp. 15–32). Washington, DC: NASPA.

Sherman, G. L. (2014). *Refocusing the self in higher education: A phenomenological perspective.* New York: Routledge.

Shields, S. A. (2008). Gender: An intersectionality perspective. *Sex Roles, 59*, 301–311.

Silva, J. M. (2013). *Coming up short: Working-class adulthood in an age of uncertainty.* New York, NY: Oxford.

Stewart, D-L., & Renn, K. A. (2015). Editors' notes. In D-L. Stewart, K. A. Renn, & G. B. Brazelton (Eds.), *Gender and sexual diversity in U.S. higher education: Contexts and opportunities for LGBTQ college students* (pp. 1–8). New Directions for Student Services, n. 152. San Francisco, CA: Jossey-Bass.

Strange, C. C., & Banning, J. H. (2015). *Designing for learning: Creating campus environments for student success* (2nd ed.). San Francisco, CA: Jossey-Bass.

Strayhorn, T. L. (2016). *Student development theory in higher education: A social psychological approach.* New York, NY: Routledge.

Swanson, J. A. (2016). Trends in literature about emerging adulthood: Review of empirical studies. *Emerging Adulthood, 4*, 391–402.

Syed, M. (2016). Continuity and change in *Emerging Adulthood. Emerging Adulthood, 4*, 375–377.

Walpole, M. (2007). *Economically and educationally challenged students in higher education: Access to outcomes.* ASHE Higher Education Report, 33(3). San Francisco, CA: Jossey-Bass.

Wijeyesinghe, C. L. (Ed.). (2017). *Enacting intersectionality in student affairs.* New Directions for Student Services, n. 157. San Francisco, CA: Jossey-Bass.

Zola, I. K. (1993). Self, identity and the naming question: Reflections on the language of disability. *Social Science and Medicine, 36*(2), 167–173.

4

EMERGING ADULTHOOD THROUGH THE LENS OF SOCIAL IDENTITY

Rosemary J. Perez and Lisa Landreman

In this chapter, we consider the ways socially constructed identities influence how emerging adulthood is conceptualized and understood. The chapter begins with our shared assumptions about student development and a review of key terms. Next, we review the existing emerging adulthood literature and the extent to which it considers varied lived experiences and developmental trajectories based on individuals' socially constructed identities. The chapter continues by exploring how understandings of emerging adulthood evolve when socially constructed identities in the context of power, privilege, and oppression are considered. We conclude with implications for research and student affairs practice.

Assumptions and Key Terms

Our examination of emerging adulthood is reflective of our shared assumptions, beliefs, and values. First, our work is shaped by the social constructivist paradigm (Lincoln & Guba, 2000). This paradigm asserts that people construct their realities by making meaning of their experiences, which are shaped by the social worlds and cultures they are embedded within. Similarly, we view adulthood as a social construction that is defined and redefined by individuals and groups in ways that are culturally and historically relevant (Arnett, 2000, 2015).

Second, we view socially constructed identities as essential components when conceptualizing human development. Although theories of development may not foreground social identity, we believe it is difficult to examine movement into adulthood without considering individuals' socially constructed identities since they affect how people navigate their worlds and how they interact with others. Thus, socially constructed identities influence but do not determine how individuals experience and construct their understandings of reality and of adulthood (Patton, Renn, Guido, & Quaye, 2016).

Third, we believe that power, privilege, and oppression are embedded throughout society to advantage some groups and to actively subordinate others (Young, 2013). Oppression is sustained through unquestioned norms, beliefs, and cultural practices and through the creation of political, economic, and social structures that are designed to perpetuate unearned advantages for privileged groups and limit opportunities for subordinated groups. With this in mind, our chapter reflects our shared understanding that power, privilege, and oppression shape people's: (1) lived experiences and their interpretations of them, (2) access to resources and opportunities, and (3) constructions of knowledge. Although we have some shared assumptions, beliefs, and values, our understandings of them and of emerging adulthood have been shaped by our socially constructed identities and lived experiences.

Emerging Adulthood and Socially Constructed Identities

As conceptualized by Arnett (2000, 2015), the notion of emerging adulthood is consistent with the social constructivist paradigm in that individuals' understandings of the transition to adulthood are defined within historical and cultural contexts. In advancing the notion of emerging adulthood, Arnett (2000, 2015) asserted that the transition to adulthood within industrialized nations such as the U.S. has been elongated, given cultural shifts that have occurred due to the technology revolution, the sexual revolution, the women's movement, and the youth movement. This extended journey toward the traditional markers of adulthood (e.g., marriage or long-term partnership, parenthood, long-term job/career) is characterized by five pillars: (1) engaging in identity exploration, (2) experiencing instability, (3) becoming more self-focused as individuals re-center themselves, (4) feeling in-between, and (5) perceiving possibilities (Arnett, 2000, 2015).

Although emerging adulthood is situated historically and culturally, scholars have questioned the extent to which this phase of life and its associated developmental tasks are reflective of all individuals' lived experiences (Furstenberg, 2016; Syed & Mitchell, 2013). Specifically, these critics have asserted that emerging adulthood centralizes the experience of White, middle class individuals such that we are left to ask if those with minoritized identities "get to be emerging adults" (Syed & Mitchell, 2013, p. 91) or if this experience is reserved for those with privileged identities. A growing body of research has explored the ways individuals' socially constructed identities affect their pathways to and through emerging adulthood (e.g., Cohler & Michaels, 2013; Norona, Preddy, & Welsh, 2016; Silva, 2016; Syed & Mitchell, 2016).

While studies of emerging adulthood acknowledge cultural context and are increasingly identity conscious, they may not adequately attend to the ways that power, privilege, and oppression influence how emerging adulthood is conceptualized and experienced. The notion of adulthood is a tool of social reproduction that maintains the "social and economic status quo with little attention to issues of inequality" (Hammack & Toolis, 2014, p. 50). Dominant adulthood narratives are reinforced through family, personal relationships, and social institutions (McLean, 2016) since these agents of socialization emphasize and normalize marriage, parenthood, and long-term employment as essential to the transition to adulthood. We must expand our understandings of emerging adulthood to be conscious of power and cognizant of the ways that privilege and oppression influence how we understand adulthood and individuals' journeys toward it.

Race and Ethnicity

Although the research that gave rise to the concept of emerging adulthood was conducted on a structurally diverse sample, scholars have questioned if developmental processes associated with this period differ across racial and ethnic groups (Syed & Mitchell, 2013, 2016). Notably, Arnett's (2000, 2015) conception of adulthood in industrialized nations prioritizes independence and autonomy as goals. This view of adulthood is reflective of dominant, White Western values (Hammack & Toolis, 2014; Syed & Mitchell, 2013) and may not resonate with those who come from collectivist cultures that emphasize interdependence and duty to family over individualism (Syed & Mitchell, 2013). Furthermore, some have argued that Arnett's work does not adequately account for how oppression shapes the five pillars of emerging adulthood for racially minoritized individuals (Syed & Mitchell, 2013, 2016).

Given these critiques, a growing body of research has examined potential differences in pathways through the five pillars of emerging adulthood across racial and ethnic groups. For example, Syed and Mitchell (2013) indicated that it is unclear whether the age of instability is experienced similarly across racial and ethnic groups. While their analysis of 2012 U.S. Census data suggested that jobs were unstable for all racial and ethnic groups, they found that residential instability for Black and Latinx individuals continued through emerging adulthood and into their 30s (Syed & Mitchell, 2013). Although not explicit, these findings reflect how racism is embedded into financial institutions and housing policies (Young, 2013) leading to limited opportunities for racially minoritized individuals to find or own long-term housing. The age of instability for racially and ethnically minoritized individuals may not be a choice, but rather a product of institutionalized oppression that may be minimized when simply framed as an elongated transition into adulthood.

Researchers have also examined relationship instability with particular attention to family conflict. Specifically, scholars have studied intergenerational conflicts that occur as immigrant adolescents and emerging adults negotiate acculturation and assimilation in the U.S. (Syed & Mitchell, 2013, 2016). Inter-generational conflicts are associated with increased stress and lower academic performance; moreover, the effects are more pronounced for Asian Americans than they are for White and Latinx individuals (Syed & Mitchell, 2013, 2016). Since many Asian American cultures are rooted in collectivism and filial piety, acculturation may alleviate pressures outside the home while creating new tensions with family members. This pattern suggests that, for some, the age of instability is reflective of White privilege since White individuals are from the dominant culture and are not pressured to acculturate. In contrast, instability in familial relationships for some racially and ethnically minoritized individuals is intertwined with living a bicultural experience and negotiating pressures to conform to cultural norms rooted in Whiteness. Similarly, the notion of emerging adulthood as a time of self-focus has varying degrees of cultural relevance for individuals. Arnett (2015) found that Black and Latinx emerging adults perceived their parents to be more involved in their lives than they preferred when compared to their White peers. The age of instability for racially and ethnically minoritized emerging adults is linked to navigating cultural constraints. Tight familial ties can be a source of strength for racially minoritized emerging adults (Yosso, 2005) and they can concurrently feel like a barrier to independence.

More closely examining the age of possibilities in the context of oppression leads one to wonder to whom opportunities are afforded given the realities of racism in the U.S. and in other industrialized nations. Racism embedded within schools and schooling has cumulative impact that affects racially minoritized students' success and pursuit of postsecondary education (Syed & Mitchell, 2013, 2016). While access to higher education has increased across racial and ethnic groups, Black, Latinx, and American Indian individuals continue to persist and graduate at lower rates than their White peers (National Center for Educational Statistics, 2016). Furthermore, the effects of racism on minoritized individuals is linked to increased stress and anxiety, decreased self-esteem, feelings of isolation, and negative physical health (Syed & Mitchell, 2013, 2016). With these disparities in mind, Syed and Mitchell (2013) questioned if racially minoritized emerging adults had the privilege to be optimistic about their futures. Moreover, it is unclear if racially minoritized individuals are afforded opportunities to experience the age of feeling in-between given the ways stereotypes and racism affect their lived experiences.

While racism remains pervasive in our society, research suggests that racially minoritized emerging adults remain optimistic about their futures and have high aspirations (Syed & Mitchell, 2013, 2016). Rather than ascribing to deficit perspectives, racially minoritized emerging adults may leverage their strengths and forms of cultural wealth in response to systems of oppression. In doing so, they are able to use cultural, social, linguistic, navigational, aspirational, and resistant forms of capital (Yosso, 2005) to empower themselves and their communities as they traverse the journey toward adulthood.

Despite identity exploration being a key component of emerging adulthood, the notion of identity exploration as described by Erikson (1968), and subsequently, by Arnett (2000, 2015) does not adequately account for the process of racial and ethnic identity exploration. Rather, identity is broadly defined as race neutral and occurring through one's relationships, work, and worldviews. Because the theory omits race, the notion of identity exploration in emerging adulthood centralizes Whiteness. As such, emerging adulthood ignores the fundamentally different tasks of developing a sense of self that occurs for those who hold dominant and subordinated racial and ethnic identities. Theories of minoritized racial and ethnic identity (Patton et al., 2016) development illustrate increasingly complex understandings of oneself as a racialized being that holds membership in a subordinated group. To varying degrees, these theories also describe minoritized racial and ethnic identity development as a process of grappling with internalized oppression and developing a positive view of one's self and of one's racial and ethnic groups. As emerging adults explore their identities, racially minoritized individuals do not have the privilege to ignore race and the effects of racism while their White peers can. Thus, it is essential to use a race-conscious lens to conceptualize identity exploration during emerging adulthood.

Social Class

Social class "is an experience of shared economic circumstances and shared social and cultural practices in relation to positions of power" (Zandy, 1996, p. 8). It refers to one's sociocultural background that influences self-perceptions, attitudes, and behaviors. Examining social class identities and experiences is relatively new, and currently, no specific theories regarding social class identity development exist. The focus on identity exploration and self-fulfillment of the late teens and early 20s college attenders is often contrasted to the struggles to make a living wage for those from lower social classes (Arnett, 2016).

One's experience with social class is shaped by other aspects of social identity such as race, gender, sexual orientation, or ability, and cannot be adequately discussed without acknowledging these intersections. However, few studies related to social class address this intersectionality and most, as it is related to college students (e.g., emerging adults), are focused on White students (Patton et al., 2016). Different from other social identity groups who may draw from a group identity grounded in shared experiences, social class operates as an unconscious collective (Bottero, 2004), further complicating our ability to understand the dynamics of social class on development.

The uneven distribution of social capital has increased and has contributed to an "opportunity gap" based on social class (Putnam, 2015, p. 207). This differential access to social capital affects who attends and who is successful in college. Much of the scholarship regarding poor and working class students who attend college discusses the challenges they face and how they strategically maneuver an alienating college environment where they don't often know the "rules" of these spaces (Borrego, 2004). This body of research illustrates that many poor and working class students must negotiate their home environment and their college campus, which often hold significantly different values. Although poor and working class students may have strong relational ties to family and community, these connections often have less access to networks that help with job acquisition, college placement, or addressing health issues. Grounded in theories on understanding cultural capital, Lehmann (2014) found that working-class students were successful once they were integrated into the college environment, which may distance them from the values of their families and home communities.

A major criticism of the cultural capital scholarship applied to poor and working class college students is the underlying assumption that these students are "disadvantaged" or "lacking" in some area needed for college success. The dominant narrative that poor and working class students lack the necessary cultural capital to be successful in the college environment fails to interrogate how social capital is obtained or used to maintain exclusion (Warr, 2006). As noted above, the concept of "community cultural wealth" as introduced by Yosso (2005) introduced six forms of assets or resources that minoritized communities often bring to higher education. These forms of capital challenge the notion that people of color lack the social and cultural capital required for social mobility and include: aspirational, linguistic, familial, social, navigational, and resistant capital. This framework not only challenges the dominant discourses that shape social class but it also acknowledges class-based notions of inequality and the intersections of class and race (Patton et al., 2016). However, students of color and poor and working-class students can internalize dominant cultural beliefs about what it takes to succeed, which can shape their experiences, and subsequently, their transition to adulthood.

Arnett (2015) contends that, from its origins, the research on emerging adulthood has been inclusive of participants from a wide range of social class backgrounds. He reviewed a national survey that examined 18–25 year-olds' responses on a range of topics related to adulthood, comparing their social class backgrounds. Furthermore, he found no significant differences among the five pillars of emerging adulthood (i.e., identity exploration, instability, self-focus, feeling in between, and possibilities/optimism) with respect to social class (Arnett, 2015). Arnett found more similarities than differences reported regarding the participants' expectations for adulthood, their emotional lives, and their attitudes toward school, work, love, sex, and marriage. Across social class membership, people in this age range indicate that they are exploring the implications of their identity in love and work and are moving toward commitments. In contrast to the belief that emerging adults from lower social classes are pessimistic about their future, the Clark University Poll of Emerging Adults survey found that despite their family's financial resources and social capital, they were more likely than their middle and upper class peers to believe that they would have better lives than their parents (Arnett, 2015). As could be predicted, however, poor and working class emerging adults from the survey also were more likely to report that they could not get the kind of education they needed because of the lack of financial resources.

As the median age for entering stable work, marriage, and parenthood has been steadily delayed over the last half-century, there is benefit to reimagining a new life stage to understanding adult development. However, there remains much to be understood about how people from poor and working class groups experience the stage of emerging adulthood as compared to their middle and upper-class peers. Questions of identity, stability, and possibilities will likely look different for members of various class groups, despite their agreement that they experience these stages. As Arnett (2016) emphasizes, "one stage, many paths" (p. 234).

However, when that path includes continued education, this statement becomes more complicated. Despite their reported optimism, postsecondary education can have a significant influence on a person's "path" through any one of the emerging adulthood pillars. The lack of financial resources for poor and working class students has a significant impact on their ability to obtain the appropriate education for their needs. The variations related to how emerging adulthood is experienced among the poor and working class as compared to their counterparts from other social classes are differences that most often reflect inequality and oppression. As many critics contend, the conclusion that class differences in psychological development do not substantially differ is premature (Furstenberg, 2016). In order to change the discourse on the impact of social class on emerging adulthood, the effects of oppression on social class identities that are most often unconsciously experienced collectively need to be better understood. Despite the lack of class-consciousness in many theories of development, social class and income inequalities are core to identity development (Gupton & Miksch, 2016).

Gender

Arnett (2000, 2015) was cognizant of how gender roles influence the transition from adolescence into adulthood. In part, this sensitivity is linked to the ways the women's movement challenged the notion that women's primary goals were to marry and raise children. As women increased their participation in higher education, delayed or decided not to marry or have children, and worked outside of the home, traditional gender roles were contested and contributed to the development of emerging adulthood as a new life stage within the U.S. and other industrialized nations.

Since the rise of emerging adulthood has been linked to shifts in how individuals navigate gender roles, scholars have consistently examined gender differences in how men and women experience the five pillars of this phase of life (e.g., Arnett, 2015; Norona et al., 2016). For example, studies have suggested that there are gendered differences in how individuals explore and express their identities through narratives. Specifically, girls are encouraged to be more emotional and relational in how they narrate the stories of their lives while boys are socialized to convey fewer feelings and to be more direct (Norona et al., 2016). However, Norona et al. (2016) indicated that the differences between men's and women's autobiographies decrease over time and across gender as individuals explore compassion for others, relationships, and life goals rather than their gender roles. Missing from this research (and research on gender differences in emerging adulthood theory) is an acknowledgement or exploration of nondominant conceptions and experiences with gender identity. Examples of this include individuals who identify as transgender (those whose gender identity is different from their sex assignment at birth), agender (those who do not identify with gender), or genderqueer (those whose gender is not exclusively feminine or masculine). While the findings suggest that gender may influence how emerging adults express or narrate their experiences, they also indicate that gender roles do not determine what individuals grapple with as they explore their identities. And yet, the constraints of gender roles, sexism, and genderism (Bilodeau, 2013) remain such that pathways to identity may be experienced differently as individuals explore and make commitments (Josselson, 1996).

Considerable research has also attended to the ways gender roles and expectations affect emerging adults' familial, peer, and romantic relationships. While women and men tend to have more positive relationships with parents after moving out of the home, men tend to have less contact with their families than women (Norona et al., 2016). This pattern may reflect gendered expectations in that women may have more familial obligations and may be viewed as less independent and in need of protection than peers who are men. Men and women appear to have similar experiences in friendships, though women tend to interact through sharing stories while men tend to interact via activities (Norona et al., 2016). These gendered ways of engaging with peers are consistent with socialization patterns that prescribe masculine and feminine interactions (Davis, 2002). Similarly, women and men have similar interests in and patterns of moving toward long-term romantic relationships. Yet, gendered expectations about sexuality influence how emerging adults engage in this process since women tend to report having less casual sex and more actively exploring their sexual identity than their peers who are men (Arnett, 2015; Norona et al., 2016). While the women's movement in part gave rise to emerging adulthood, gender roles and sexism continue to influence how individuals navigate this phase of life.

Although discussions of gender in the emerging adulthood literature have tended to focus on gender roles and gender socialization, some scholars have also examined how biological differences may affect individuals' identity exploration and relationships (Norona et al., 2016). These scholars acknowledge that gender and sex are distinct concepts; however, tightly linking them in the literature reifies the gender binary (Lev, 2004) by focusing on how gender is embodied. Moreover, attending to how biological differences based on sex (e.g., hormones, body composition) influence gender-related experiences is a form of essentialism that suggests biological traits affect and possibly determine how individuals experience social constructions such as adulthood. In this regard, coupling discussions of biological sex with explorations of gender can affirm rather than contest the limitations of the gender binary and dichotomous gender roles.

As mentioned, the emerging adulthood literature acknowledges dominant narratives related to gender but does so from a binary perspective (Lev, 2004). In so doing, emerging adulthood as currently conceptualized may perpetuate cissexism in that it normalizes the experiences of cisgender people and marginalizes the experiences of trans★ and genderqueer individuals. There is limited research that attends to how trans★ individuals navigate the five pillars of emerging adulthood, but findings from the National Center for Transgender Equality's 2015 survey highlighted that members of the trans★ community experience greater violence, economic and housing instability, workplace and healthcare discrimination, and psychological distress than cisgender peers (James et al., 2016). Given the effects of cissexism and transphobia on trans★ and genderqueer emerging adults, there is a need to reframe how we conceptualize this period of life to contest rather than to reaffirm the gender binary.

Sexual Orientation

Arnett (2000, 2015) argued that the rise of emerging adulthood was due in part to the sexual revolution during which standards of sexual morality shifted such that "young people no longer had to enter marriage in order to have a regular sexual relationship" (Arnett, 2015, p. 5). While attitudes toward sex and marriage evolved, it is critical to ask for whom have these standards changed given that constructions of adulthood are defined in terms of "compulsory heterosexuality and reproduction" (Hammack & Toolis, 2014, p. 50). Morgan (2016) argued that the transition to adulthood in the U.S. and other industrialized nations is "equated to heteronormative milestones such as marriage and parenthood, for which there are many structural barriers" (p. 263) for sexually minoritized individuals. In essence, how we conceptualize adulthood fails to acknowledge the ways in which oppression affects lesbian, gay, and bisexual (LGB) individuals' abilities to achieve the "traditional" markers of adulthood.

Ample research exists comparing LGB and heterosexual relationships within the emerging adulthood literature. Notably, there are few differences in the duration of and satisfaction within LGB and heterosexual romantic relationships, despite the stigma and discrimination that sexually minoritized partners face (Cohler & Michaels, 2013). Regardless of sexual orientation, many emerging adults express a desire to be in a long-term, monogamous relationship and to become parents. However, same-sex couples frequently face legal barriers to adopting children or may encounter financial barriers if they choose to expand their families via surrogacy or the use of reproductive technologies (Cohler & Michaels, 2013). These barriers have been compounded by the recency of same-sex couples' ability to marry and access partner benefits, as well as ongoing prejudices that characterize LGB individuals as deviants or as immoral. In effect, LGB individuals are continually affected by heterosexism and homophobia as they navigate the five pillars of emerging adulthood.

There are notable differences in how scholars characterize the process of identity exploration for LGB and heterosexual individuals. Some theorists have suggested that the process of identity exploration for LGB individuals involves recognizing that one is not heterosexual, internalizing and making meaning of having a minoritized identity based on sexual orientation, disclosing one's sexual identity to others, and developing pride in one's LGB identity (e.g., D'Augelli, 1994). These theories describe developmental milestones and pathways that are reflective of being embedded within heteronormative cultures. They acknowledge that heterosexuality is consistently viewed as a normative sexual identity, and as a result, individuals who are LGB engage in a process of exploring, coming to accept, and disclosing their sexual identity to others. Collectively, theories of sexual identity development highlight the ways in which oppression leads to different processes of identity exploration for LGB and heterosexual individuals. And yet, they do not reflect the penalties (e.g., marginalization, violence, discrimination) that LGB emerging adults may experience if they openly express their sexual identities.

Oppression also shapes how LGB individuals experience the age of instability. For instance, Arnett (2006) noted that sexually minoritized individuals who come out to unsupportive family members may struggle more to get assistance and support from them during the period of emerging adulthood than their heterosexual peers. As such, LGB individuals without familial support may experience instability and move toward independence more quickly than those who have more accepting families. In lieu of familial support, sexually minoritized people may work more actively to find and create affirming friendships and kinship networks (Arnett, 2006). Notably, engagement with other LGB individuals is a milestone described by theories of minoritized sexual identity development (D'Augelli, 1994) and is a part of cultivating a positive view of one's LGB identity.

Furthermore, LGB individuals may experience instability at work based on their sexual orientation. Cohler and Michaels' (2013) synthesis of literature suggests that while LGB emerging adults are increasingly comfortable being "out" at work, this opportunity is not always afforded to them. In particular, those LGB individuals employed by corporations were more hesitant to disclose their sexual identity than those working in other sectors. This is consistent with a pattern of LGB people historically choosing careers where "work did not lead to situations in which it became important to disclose your gay or lesbian identity or to find those few 'gay friendly' careers that supported diverse sexualities" (Cohler & Michaels, 2013, p. 110). While attitudes toward sexually minoritized individuals are more positive than they have been historically and career options are expanding, heterosexism and homophobia affect how LGB individuals may perceive the age of possibilities and how they may experience the age of instability (Cohler & Michaels, 2013).

Ability

Much scholarship on the transition to adulthood for people with disabilities is aimed at exploring the challenges faced by youth with disabilities as they navigate the environmental barriers they must contend with in a world that was not designed for them (Stewart et al., 2010). The range of people who may have experienced discrimination or other negative consequences based on their disability may be far greater than those who identify with the term *disability*, and includes those with developmental, medical, neurological, physical, and psychological disabilities. What connects the experiences of emerging adults with diverse disabilities is "having to contend with a culture that sees disability through fear, pity, or shame and teaches [them] to regard disability as a tragedy" (Adams, Bell, & Griffin, 2007, p. 336). With this in mind, it is important to distinguish research that explores health issues and emerging adulthood from a medical model of disability. The medical model looks at disability as a defect or loss of function that resides in the individual. A social constructionist view of disability defines disabilities as problems that reside in the environment that fail to accommodate the needs of individuals with disabilities (Gibson, 2006).

Addressing ableism (i.e., oppression based on ability) and theorizing how disabilities may affect emerging adulthood theory is complicated. Many people who have conditions that qualify under the American with Disabilities Act (1990) as a disability do not actually identify as a person with a disability. For some, the decision to identify or not to identify with the term is a political issue. For others, it may be due to a lack of awareness or self-awareness (i.e., their condition may not be a salient component of their identity or they may not be aware that their condition falls under the ADA as a disability). Disability saliency for some may be related to the intersectionality of their other identities as these other identities may mitigate their experiences with discrimination based on their ability. One does not have to identify as a person with a disability to experience oppression based on their disability or to have their transition to adulthood impacted by their disability. The wide range of disabilities leads to varying experiences navigating environments and oppression.

These differences make it difficult to address oppression based on ability and to theorize how one's disability affects their transition to adulthood. An important component of counseling youth with disabilities is acceptance of their disability and integrating it into a positive self-concept (Meyer, Hinton, & Derzis, 2015). Understanding "disability identity development" includes both this acceptance and what Atkinson, Morten, and Sue (1993) framed as minority identity development. This framework positions the disability identity in a context that acknowledges people with disabilities experience oppression as they navigate their environments. Emerging adults' acceptance of their disability and their understanding of its saliency to how they construct their identity can have a great impact on their transition to adulthood.

Stewart et al. (2010) conducted a literature review of the vast and growing body of published, 'evidence-based' literature about the transition to adulthood for youth with disabilities. In most cases, the transition to adulthood was identified as the successful achievement of a variety of outcomes associated with "adult life" such as participation in educational and career planning, community participation, self-determination, inclusion, independent living, and quality of life (as cited in Stewart et al., 2010). The success of the transition to adulthood was based on the ease with which emerging adults with disabilities could access supports that enabled them to fully participate in what is thought of as adult living (as cited in Stewart et al., 2010). The transition to adulthood is complicated by the challenges and vulnerabilities that many emerging adults with disabilities face in their transition to their physical, social, and learning environments. Leiter and Waugh (2009) found that by age 30, adults with disabilities are twice as likely to be living with their parents. They identified four factors that influence this living situation for emerging adults with disabilities: (1) educational and economic opportunities; (2) associated changes in norms regarding co-residence with parents; (3) family resources and supports in the transition to adulthood; and (4) requirements for care assistance. Although uncertainty is considered developmentally appropriate (Arnett, 2015), understanding the complex circumstances that emerging adults with disabilities face as compared to their peers without disabilities can better inform theory on emerging adulthood for people with disabilities.

Despite increased awareness of the Americans with Disabilities Act (1990) and the work of activists in the disabilities rights movement, it is only recently that literature has begun to acknowledge that the "transition to adulthood is more than just a service approach, as it involves a process of taking on new roles and adapting or changing existing roles for youth and their families" (as cited in Stewart et al., 2010, p. 2). Notably, evidence suggests that emerging adults "have the same aspirations and want the same outcomes, [but] most research on transition to adulthood is separate for youth with and without disabilities" (Stewart et al., 2010, p. 12). The challenges emerging adults face in transitioning to adulthood are compounded for those with disabilities because they experience disability-related challenges that are not accounted for within their developmental stage experience (Mannino, 2015).

Future Considerations

This chapter provided a brief overview and rationale for understanding the influence of cultural experiences and social identity development processes on the transition to adulthood for minoritized individuals. As introduced by Furstenberg (2016), it may be more helpful to think of Arnett's (2000, 2015) emerging adulthood theory as a conceptual framework rather than a theory when working with college students. Key to this framework is an understanding that "… the locus of developmental processes that may have once occurred during adolescence may be happening later" (Furstenberg, 2016, p. 237). It is likely that many emerging adults share similar feelings and experiences, regardless of their intersecting socially constructed identities. What they also share is that their intersecting identities and experiences with power, privilege, and oppression can have a significant effect on their movement through the five pillars of emerging adulthood.

It is important to use caution in generalizing agreement to questions on a survey related to the five pillars of the emerging adulthood stages to the participants' real lives (du Bois-Reymond, 2016). The initial item agreements along class, gender, sexual orientation, or other socially constructed identities must be further interrogated to ascertain the meaning made by members of various groups in their sociohistorical context and how their identities relate to their positions in society (du Bois-Reymond, 2016). Emerging adulthood's basis in demographic data easily tracks trends in modern life that Arnett (2000, 2015) recommends be considered within different cultural contexts. Although Arnett (2015) cautions against a universal application to his theory, without further research, an awareness of the historical and cultural context that shaped the theory, and attention to the diverse experiences and identities of emerging adults, there is potential to use the theory in ways that perpetuate dominant narratives of what constitutes a "normal" transition into adulthood.

In reviewing the complications social identity development and experiences with oppression may bring to emerging adulthood theory, we recommend continued analysis and cognizance of the nuanced, complex, and intersecting experiences of women, people of color, people with disabilities, LBGTQ individuals, and those from other marginalized social identity groups (e.g., poor and working class, religious minorities, immigrants). Increased understandings of minoritized individuals' experiences may call for new components to an emerging adulthood framework. The developmental demands minoritized emerging adults experience are different from those of their peers who are navigating systemic oppression from positions of privilege. These experiences need to be incorporated into our understandings of theories of human development including emerging adulthood. Furthermore, how we conceptualize emerging adulthood will evolve as social movements challenge social inequalities. For example, views of adulthood may change in light of the Black Lives Matter movement and the struggle for transgender equality. As such, research that examines the pathways to and through adulthood must shift to reflect the changes in our social and historical context.

Student affairs professionals are well aware that experiences students have in early adulthood—and in college—can cause them to engage in reflection and to develop more complex thinking, and can have a long-lasting impact on their identity development (Patton et al., 2016). The cultural context of becoming an adult has changed, which calls our former understandings of the developmental processes of traditional aged college students into question. Postsecondary educators, including student affairs practitioners, must keep current with social, economic, and cultural trends that affect students. Despite the challenges faced by researchers who are on a quest for measuring developmental processes with empirical data, Arnett's (2000, 2015) theory of emerging adulthood can be a useful tool for practitioners. It reminds us that despite laws in the U.S. that define students as adults at 18, enabling a number of privileges (e.g., voting), they are encountering important life transitions. We have an opportunity to facilitate these transitions by better understanding these pathways, and in doing so, we have the potential to be better guides and companions on and through their journeys to adulthood.

References

Adams, M., Bell, L. A., & Griffin, P. (2007). *Teaching for diversity and social justice* (2nd ed.). New York, NY: Routledge.

Americans with Disabilities Act of 1990, Pub. L. No. 101–336, 104 Stat. 328 (1990).

Arnett, J. J. (2000). Emerging adulthood: A theory of development from the late teens through the twenties. *American Psychologist, 55*, 469–480.

Arnett, J. J. (2006). The psychology of emerging adulthood: What is known, and what remains to be known? In J. J. Arnett & J. L. Tanner (Eds.), *Emerging adults in America: Coming of age in the 21st century* (pp. 303–330). Washington, DC: American Psychological Association.

Arnett, J. J. (2015). *Emerging adulthood: The winding road from the late teens through the twenties* (2nd ed.). New York, NY: Oxford.

Arnett, J. J. (2016). Does emerging adulthood theory apply across social classes? National data on a persistent question. *Emerging Adulthood, 4*, 227–235.

Atkinson, D. R., Morten, G., & Sue, D. W. (Eds.). (1993). *Counseling American minorities: A cross-cultural perspective* (4th ed.). Madison, WI: W.C. Brown & Benchmark.

Bilodeau, B. (2013). Developing gender-inclusive facilitation: Understanding genderism. In L. Landreman (Ed.), *The art of effective facilitation: Reflections from social justice educators* (pp. 67–80). Sterling, VA: Stylus.

du Bois-Reymond, M. (2016). Emerging adulthood theory under scrutiny. *Emerging Adulthood, 4*, 242–243.

Borrego, S. (2004). *Class matters: Beyond access to inclusion*. Washington, DC: National Association of Student Affairs Administrators in Higher Education.

Bottero, W. (2004). Class identities and the identity of class. *Sociology, 38*, 985–1003.

Cohler, B. J., & Michaels, S. (2013). Emergent [sic] adulthood in lesbian and gay lives: Individual development, life course, and social change. In C. J. Patterson & A. R. D'Augelli (Eds.), *Handbook of psychology and sexual orientation* (pp. 102–117). New York, NY: Oxford.

D'Augelli, A. R. (1994). Identity development and sexual orientation: Toward a model of lesbian, gay, and bisexual development. In E. J. Trickett, R. J. Watts, & D. Birman (Eds.), *Human diversity: Perspectives on people in context* (pp. 312–333). San Francisco, CA: Jossey-Bass.

Davis, T. L. (2002). Voices of gender role conflict: The social construction of college men's identity. *Journal of College Student Development, 43*, 508–521.

Erikson, E. H. (1968). *Identity: Youth and crisis*. New York, NY: Norton.

Furstenberg, F. (2016). Social class and development in early adulthood: Some unsettled issues. *Emerging Adulthood, 4*, 236–238.

Gibson, J. (2006). Disability and clinical competency: An introduction. *The California Psychologist, 39*, 6–10.

Gupton, J. T., & Miksch, K. (2016). A theory of equity: A social and legal analysis of college access for low-income students. In P. A Pasque, N. Ortega, J. C. Bukhardt, & M. P. Ting (Eds.), *Transforming understandings of diversity in higher education* (pp. 44–53). Sterling, VA: Stylus.

Hammack, P. L., & Toolis, E. (2014). Narrative and the social construction of adulthood. In. B. Schiff (Ed.), *Rereading personal narrative and life course* (pp. 43–56). New Directions for Child and Adolescent Development, n. 145. San Francisco, CA: Jossey-Bass.

Lehmann, W. (2014). Habitus transformation and hidden inquiries: Successful working-class university students. *Sociology of Education, 87*, 1–13.

Leiter, V., & Waugh, A. (2009). Moving out: Residential independence among young adults with disabilities and the role of families. *Marriage & Family Review, 45*(5), 519–537.

Lev, A. I. (2004). *Transgender emergence: Therapeutic guidelines for working with gender-variant people and their families*. Binghamton, NY: Haworth.

Lincoln, Y. S., & Guba, E. G. (2000). Paradigmatic controversies, contradictions, and emerging consequences. In N. K. Denzin & Y. S. Lincoln (Eds.), *Handbook of qualitative research* (2nd ed., pp. 163–188). Thousand Oaks, CA: SAGE.

James, S. E., Herman, J. L., Rankin, S., Keisling, M., Mottet, L., & Anafi, M. (2016). The Report of the 2015 U.S. Transgender Survey. Washington, DC: National Center for Transgender Equality.

Josselson, R. (1996). *Revising herself: The story of women's identity from college to midlife*. New York, NY: Oxford.

Mannino, J. E. (2015). Resilience and tranistioin to adulthood among emerging adults with disabilities. *Journal of Pediatric Nursing, 30*(5), 131–145.

McLean, K. C. (2016). *The co-authored self: Family stories and the construction of personal identity*. New York, NY: Oxford.

Meyer, J. M., Hinton, V. M., & Derzis, N. (2015). Emerging adults with disabilities: Theory, trends, and implications. *Journal of Applied Rehabilitation Counseling, 46*(4), 3–10.

Morgan, E. M. (2016). Contemporary issues in sexual orientation and identity development in emerging adulthood. In J. J. Arnett (Ed.), *The Oxford handbook of emerging adulthood* (pp. 262–279). New York, NY: Oxford.

Norona, J. C., Preddy, T. M., & Welsh, D. P. (2016). How gender shapes emerging adulthood. In J. J. Arnett (Ed.), *The Oxford handbook of emerging adulthood* (pp. 62–86). New York, NY: Oxford.

Patton, L. D., Renn, K. A., Guido, F. M., & Quaye, S. J. (2016). *Student development in college: Theory, research, and practice* (3rd ed.). San Francisco, CA: Jossey-Bass.

Putnam, R. D. (2015). *Our kids: The American dream in crisis.* New York, NY: Simon & Schuster.

Silva, J. M. (2016). High hopes and hidden inequalities: How social class shapes pathways to adulthood. *Emerging Adulthood, 4*, 239–241.

Stewart, D., Freeman, M., Law, M., Healy, H., Burke-Gaffney, J., Forhan, M., … Guenther, S. (2010). Transition to adulthood for youth with disabilities: Evidence from the literature. In J. H. Stone & M. Blouin (Eds.). *International encyclopedia of rehabilitation.* Retrieved from http://cirrie.buffalo.edu/encyclopedia/en/article/110/

Syed, M., & Mitchell, L. L. (2013). Race, ethnicity, and emerging adulthood: Retrospect and prospects. *Emerging Adulthood, 1*(2), 83–95.

Syed, M., & Mitchell, L. L. (2016). How race and ethnicity shape emerging adulthood. In J. J. Arnett (Ed.), *The Oxford handbook of emerging adulthood* (pp. 87–101). New York, NY: Oxford.

U.S. Department of Education, National Center for Education Statistics. (2016). *The condition of education 2016* (NCES 2016–144), Educational Attainment of Young Adults.

Warr, D. J. (2006). Gender, class, and the art and craft of social capital. *The Sociological Quarterly, 47*, 497–520.

Yosso, T. J. (2005). Whose culture has capital? *Race, Ethnicity and Education, 8*(1), pp. 69–91.

Young, I. M. (2013). Five faces of oppression. In M. Adams, W. J. Blumenfeld, R. Castañeda, H. W. Hackmann, M. L. Peters, & X. Zúñiga (Eds.), *Readings for diversity and social justice* (3rd ed., pp. 35–45). New York, NY: Routledge.

Zandy, J. (1996). Decloaking class: Why class identity and consciousness count. *Race, Gender, Class, 4*(1), 7–23.

5

GENERATIONAL THEORY AND EMERGING ADULTHOOD

Joseph L. Murray

Within the student affairs field, it is widely recognized that familiarity with the characteristics of American college students constitutes requisite knowledge for entry into professional practice (Wells, 2015). While theories of psychosocial development offer insight on traits associated with a wide spectrum of life stages (Erikson, 1968; Havighurst, 1972), including the period that has traditionally encompassed the college years (Chickering & Reisser, 1993; Marcia, 1966), the influence of social and cultural factors on the developmental process suggests that at least some measure of instability in these patterns is inevitable over time. A growing body of literature on the dynamics of generational change creates a context for interpretation of psychosocial theory in a world that is continuously in flux. This chapter provides an analysis of generational differences among student cohorts, with attention to the unique characteristics of today's traditional aged undergraduates.

Understanding Generational Cohorts

Numerous authors have studied differences that have emerged over time in the characteristics and outlooks of successive generations of Americans. Strauss and Howe (1991) have defined a generation as "a cohort-group whose length approximates the span of a phase of life and whose boundaries are fixed by peer personality" (p. 60). A phase of life covers approximately 22 years, and the peer personality of a generation is a profile of its typical member, based on those attributes that are most representative of the generation as a whole. The peer personality reflects the unique perspective that is shared by the members of a generation, as a product of their having experienced a common cultural history, informed by a relatively uniform level of maturity at each step of the way.

The axiom that history repeats itself is pertinent to the study of generational differences insofar as changes in the mood of the nation have been found to follow cyclical patterns, which manifest themselves in the peer personalities of the generations that occupy various points in time. In studying one aspect of national mood, Levine (1980) drew a distinction between periods of *individual ascendancy*, in which members of a society direct their attention and energy primarily toward protecting their personal interests, versus periods of *community ascendancy*, in which their attention and energy become more outwardly focused on strengthening ties to others and advancing the common good. In examining the historical record, Levine found that fluctuations in the national mood have repeatedly followed a cycle in which a gradual shift toward community ascendancy continues until a war or other national crisis prompts an abrupt swing toward individual ascendancy. Although subsequent research by Levine and Cureton (1998) suggests that global conditions can occasionally disrupt this cycle, the relationship between the spirit of the times and the temperament of the generation that comes of age in a given era remains a symbiotic one in which history shapes people and people shape history.

Strauss and Howe (1991) observed a similar pattern of cultural change, involving repeated passage between two alternating types of *social moments*. The authors defined a social moment as "an era, typically lasting about a decade, when people perceive that historic events are radically altering their social environment" (p. 71). The two types of social moments are *secular crises* and *spiritual awakenings*. During a secular crisis, the members of a society focus their attention primarily on functional aspects of public life, whereas during a spiritual awakening, their attention shifts toward more private questions of meaning and value. Social moments are punctuated by periods of relative stability, and generally coincide with every second generation's passage from youth toward adulthood.

The prevailing dispositions of successive generations tend to alternate between two complementary styles, labeled *dominant* and *recessive*. Dominant generations are those that transition from their youth in the midst of social moments and are prone to advance change, while recessive generations are those whose birth coincides with social moments and who tend to temper change (Strauss & Howe, 1991). Edmunds and Turner (2002) drew a similar distinction between *active* and *passive* generations, the former characterized by a tendency toward transformation of their nations' intellectual and cultural life, and the latter by a general acceptance of the status quo. The authors focused specifically on the influence of traumatic global events on certain generations' collective inclination toward forward thinking. Examining political change, in particular, Bessant (2014) saw potential for digital media to amplify the impact of social activism on the part of rising generations.

Currently, there are seven living generations of Americans, categorized by their years of birth: (1) *World War II Generation*, born before 1933; (2) *Swing Generation*, born from 1933 to 1945; (3) *Baby-Boom Generation*, born from 1946 to 1964;

(4) *Generation X*, born from 1965 to 1976; (5) *Millennial Generation*, born from 1977 to 1994; (6) *iGeneration*, born from 1995 to 2009; and (7) *Recession Generation*, born after 2009 (New Strategist Press, 2013). Whereas generational labels are largely a product of popular parlance, it is perhaps to be expected that authors vary in their chosen terminology. For example, Strauss and Howe (1991) have referred to the World War II Generation, Swing Generation, and Generation X as the *G.I. Generation*, *Silent Generation*, and *Thirteenth Generation,* respectively, while other authors have referred to iGeneration as *iGen* (Twenge, 2017), *Generation Z* (Seemiller & Grace, 2016), and *Gen Z* (Beltramini & Buckley, 2014; Koulopoulos & Keldsen, 2014).

It should be noted, as well, that demographers have not established completely uniform thresholds between generations. For example, the Baby-Boom Generation has sometimes been defined as including those born from 1943 to 1960 (Strauss & Howe, 1991), or more generally, "between the mid 1940s and early 1960s" (Steinhorn, 2006, p. xii). Gillon (2004) drew a further distinction between *Boomers*, who were born between 1945 and 1957, and *Shadow Boomers*, who were born between 1958 and 1964. Lancaster and Stillman (2002) introduced the term, *cusper*, in reference to those who are born at either end of a generation, and consequently, may identify to some extent with the generation before or after it. The authors observed that such individuals can often play an important role in mediating dialogue between members of different generations.

Characteristics and Values of Traditional Aged Undergraduates

Beyond the general literature on successive age cohorts, ongoing studies of America's student population have more specifically tracked changes in the characteristics of those making the transition from high school to college over time. The findings of such research clearly hold implications for the work of faculty, administrators, and student affairs professionals in higher education. To be clear, the reference here is to research on differences among successive generations of traditional aged students, as opposed to another extensive body of literature pertaining to differences in characteristics of traditional versus non-traditional aged students (Cross, 1992; Knowles, Holton, & Swanson, 2015; Merriam, Caffarella, & Baumgartner, 2007). While the latter addresses developmental change within the individual, the former is concerned instead with collective change that occurs from one generation to the next.

An influential trilogy of national studies, focused specifically on college students, has offered direct points of comparison across cohorts enrolled in higher education over the past half-century. In the first of these investigations, Levine (1980) found that the students of the late 1970s were much more materialistic than their predecessors of the 1960s and less focused on contributing to the common good or enacting social change. In replicating the study almost 20 years later, Levine and Cureton (1998) found an enduring concern for financial security and material comfort among the students of the 1990s, which gave rise to a pragmatic approach to higher education. However, this younger student cohort simultaneously desired to make a difference in the world. In the words of the authors, these students demonstrated a commitment to both "doing well" and "doing good" (p. 157). In the most recent iteration of this line of research, Levine and Dean (2012) found growing influences of social, technological, and economic change on today's students, who will face an array of unprecedented challenges for which many have appeared to be unprepared.

This trend aligns with findings from the *Cooperative Institutional Research Program (CIRP),* which indicate similar patterns in regard to the values and priorities of the current generation of college students. Among those entering college in 2010, 71.2% indicated that increased earning power was a "very important" motive for attending college (Pryor, Hurtado, DeAngelo, Blake, & Tran, 2010, p. 31), compared with only 49.9% of those entering college in 1976 (Pryor, Hurtado, Saenz, Santos, & Korn, 2007). Additionally, 77.4% indicated that "being well off financially" (Pryor et al., 2010, p. 38) was among their highest personal priorities. However, 69.1% similarly endorsed the importance of "helping others in difficulty" (p. 38), and the percentage of students that anticipated participating in community service or voluntarism in college increased from 16.9% in 1990 to 32.1% in 2010 (Pryor et al., 2007, 2010). In a similar survey of young adults, sponsored by the Pew Research Center, service appeared to be assigned even higher priority than wealth, with 21% of respondents indicating that "helping others in need" was among their most important aspirations, compared with only 15% for "having a high-paying career" (Taylor & Keeter, 2010, p. 2). The study also revealed that 57% of participants had engaged in voluntarism within the previous year.

Demographically and attitudinally, the overall trend has been toward advancement of more inclusive campus communities over time. Undergraduate students have become more ethnically diverse than previous generations were (Howe & Strauss, 2007). They are also more comfortable with diversity and more open in their attitudes toward race, sexual orientation, and gender roles (Alsop, 2008; Levine & Dean, 2012). Even so, political views appear to have become more polarized over time, and traditional notions of liberalism and conservatism have been challenged by a more complex realignment of political sentiment across a host of controversial issues (Broido, 2004).

The Millennial Shift

The turn of a millennium, by its nature, invites both retrospection and prognostication, and by virtue of its rarity in the course of history, inescapably comes to be seen as a significant point of transition within a culture. Indeed, the challenge of *periodization,* meaning the division of history into designated eras, has long been plagued by "the attempt to make periods and centuries coincide" (Le Goff, 2015, p. 3), even among trained historians. This tendency, coupled with the demographic strength of the Millenial cohort, helps explain the attention focused on both the generation itself and the social conditions that might account for its collective traits.

According to Howe and Strauss (2000), Millennial children were carefully protected by their parents and raised to believe that they were precious and loved. As a consequence of their upbringing, members of this generation have typically grown up to be optimistic and self-assured. Trends in education have also led them to become more collaborative and driven to excel than previous generations have been, reflecting an internalization of the pressure to succeed that has been imposed upon them for much of their lives. Millennials have also been described as trusting and supportive of the social institutions and values of their elders.

Dealing more broadly with the characteristics of those born from the 1970s through the 1990s, Twenge (2006) offered a synthesis of major findings from numerous psychological studies of post-Baby-Boom Americans. Her analysis painted an unflattering portrait of a nation of young people consumed by narcissism, which inspired her to label them *Generation Me*. In examining the root of the problem, Twenge laid blame at the foot of the self-esteem movement that came to dominate educational and parenting practices at the time of their childhood. Beyond the overarching issue of self-absorption, she also found evidence of more prevalent anxiety, depression, and loneliness among young people than in generations past, despite their widespread tolerance, self-confidence, and ambition. Twenge's (2013) contention that narcissism had risen among recent generations of young people was subsequently challenged by Arnett (2013), based on questions concerning validity of instrumentation, overgeneralization of findings, and inconsistency with other research.

Like Twenge, Putnam (2000), a political scientist, also observed an enduring generational shift in attitudes and behaviors, in advance of the new millennium. However, in this case, the change originated with the Baby-Boom Generation itself. Citing a wealth of quantitative indicators, Putnam argued that the nation, as a whole, had become less socially engaged during the final third of the 20th century. Further examination of the data revealed differences across generations in the depth of their engagement, even during corresponding life stages, with more recent generations showing greater social isolation at each stage.

In addition to generational change, Putnam (2000) attributed the modern erosion of community life to changes in the cultural and geographic landscape of the nation. He cited greater demands on time and resources, due in part to the increased prevalence of dual-career households, together with mass migration to the suburbs and the advent of television and other forms of electronic entertainment, as factors contributing to this trend. In a similar vein, Oldenburg (1989), a sociologist, lamented the concurrent disappearance of *third places*, familiar gathering spaces—neither home nor workplace—where community life had been widely fostered in earlier times.

The Role of Parents

In examining the lasting impact of the Millennial Generation on college campuses, a number of authors have focused primarily on the characteristics of their parents. The term, *helicopter parent*, has been widely used to capture the degree to which many parents have remained actively involved in their sons' and daughters' daily lives, even after sending them off to college (Alsop, 2008; Carney-Hall, 2008; Howe & Strauss, 2007; Levine & Dean, 2012; Tapscott, 2009; Taub, 2008; Wartman & Savage, 2008). In addition to maintaining frequent contact with their sons and daughters, many parents do not hesitate to intervene in situations where they feel the interests of their offspring are at stake (Lowery, 2004). Such advocacy has been a likely factor in some students' difficulty in taking initiative on their own behalf, especially in dealing with faculty members (Wilson, 2004). Nevertheless, the potential for parents to play a supportive role in promoting student development has generally been acknowledged (Carney-Hall, 2008; Taub, 2008).

Accordingly, various authors have recommended that college administrators devise mechanisms for parental involvement in higher education, which maintain appropriate boundaries and do not compromise the traditional role of the undergraduate institution in promoting students' independence (Daniel, Evans, & Scott, 2001; Lowery, 2004). Practitioners in the field have begun to heed this call, as reflected in the establishment of the Association of Higher Education Parent/Family Programs Professionals (AHEPPP) in 2008 (AHEPPP, n.d.) and the initial publication of a related set of professional standards by the Council for the Advancement of Standards in Higher Education (CAS) four years later (Mitstifer, 2012).

As the sons and daughters of Gen Xers began heading off to college in greater numbers, Howe and Strauss (2007) noted that the helicopter parent had begun to give way to the *stealth fighter parent*, who approaches the education of his or her offspring with the same self-protective and pragmatic consumer orientation that has long characterized the generation that came of age in the closing decades of the 20th century. As reported by Levine and Dean (2012), it is often student affairs professionals who bear the brunt of such parents' discontent, when their sons' and daughters' experiences of college fall short of expectations. Whereas Boomer parents have generally been interested in the societal function of higher education, Gen X parents have tended to be more concerned about the personal benefits that it can provide for their sons and daughters. Millennials' tendency to make decisions in collaboration with their parents and to share their parents' preference for brand name consumption has had a lasting impact on the practice of admissions and enrollment management by elevating the significance of institutional reputation as a factor in the successful recruitment of prospective students (Howe & Strauss, 2007).

The Significance of Technology

The arrival of Millennials on campus coincided with unprecedented advances in technology (Howe & Strauss, 2007). Research on incoming college students, over the past 20 years, has indicated a dramatic increase in both their overall use of electronic devices and their reliance on the Internet as a resource for carrying out their academic work (Pryor et al., 2007). Having lived their entire lives in a world where digital communication has been a part of daily life (Levine & Dean, 2012; Twenge, 2017), today's undergraduates are distinguished from prior generations of students in their ability to adapt to technological change, and have thus, earned the moniker of the *Net Generation* (Junco & Mastrodicasa, 2007; Tapscott, 1998, 2009).

Perhaps nowhere is the influence of technology on the lives of today's college students more evident than in the realm of social networking. The percentage of American college students using Facebook alone has been reported at anywhere from 79% to 99% (Junco, 2014), and most students' experiences with social networking predate their arrival on campus. Data from the fall 2010 *CIRP* questionnaire revealed that 77.7% of incoming first-year students had devoted an average of one hour or more per week to use of social networking sites during their senior year of high school (Pryor et al., 2010).

Turkle (1984), a sociologist and psychologist, has long been interested in the developmental impact of successive generations' interaction with machines that exhibit progressively more realistic human properties. In studying children's and adolescents' experiences with electronic toys and rudimentary computer programming, she drew links to Erikson's concepts of initiative, industry, and identity. Insofar as identity formation undergirds multiple aspects of psychosocial development in college (Chickering & Reisser, 1993), one aspect of life in the digital age that is of particular relevance to student affairs is the malleability of self-presentation that is made possible through the Internet, a phenomenon that Turkle (1995) subsequently explored in a study of multi-user online games.

In the final installment of a trilogy that spanned almost three decades, Turkle (2012) analyzed the sociological significance of the growing array of online networking sites and portable communication devices that keep us connected to masses of personal acquaintances, while simultaneously ensuring that our communication with these "friends" remains comfortably superficial. Her conclusion is that the resultant terms of social interaction have too often left us with a paradoxical deficiency in both intimacy and solitude. This realization has since prompted her to issue an urgent plea for the restoration of face-to-face conversation as a fundamental element of our culture, citing its positive impact on our capacity for empathy, connection, creativity, and fulfillment (Turkle, 2015). Given the depth of current students' immersion in the cyber world, Turkle's work suggests that their ability to build satisfying relationships and to find a sense of meaning and purpose in life will remain a pressing concern for the immediate future.

As a more practical matter, today's students are extremely comfortable in using technology, and the ease with which they have incorporated it into their lives has in turn led them to value efficiency. Increased accessibility of information has also enabled them to develop a relatively broad global perspective (Lancaster & Stillman, 2002), perhaps reinforcing their openness to new ideas and diverse points of view. Citing numerous ways in which the values and expectations of today's young people have been shaped by technology, Tapscott (2009) identified eight generational "norms" that they have consistently pursued across multiple facets of their lives: (1) *freedom*, (2) *customization*, (3) *scrutiny*, (4) *integrity*, (5) *collaboration*, (6) *entertainment*, (7) *speed*, and (8) *innovation*. In light of both the practical advantages of technology and the enthusiasm with which it has been received by this generation of students, Lowery (2004) has urged educators to continue to explore new ways of incorporating its use into the delivery of services on their campuses, just as Junco (2014) has called more specifically for the use of social networking as a means of connecting with today's undergraduates.

Teaching Today's Students

Given Millennials' pragmatic orientation toward education, it should perhaps come as no surprise that they would often prefer educational activities that are of practical value and that can be expected to yield tangible benefits to them. Consistent with popular perceptions of job prospects for graduates in various disciplines, they have tended to be drawn more to science and mathematics than to the humanities (Howe & Strauss, 2007). Over the past decade, it appears that little has changed in regard to students' instrumentalist view of higher education. As recently explained by Twenge (2017), "they go to college to get a better job and make more money, not necessarily to improve their minds" (p. 309).

Conventional by nature, and having experienced a protective upbringing, contemporary students often desire a psychologically safe and well-ordered campus environment. Today's undergraduates tend to be respectful of authority and eager to please. In particular, many of today's students strive to make a favorable impression on their professors and are heavily focused on earning good grades as a measure of their academic achievement (Howe & Strauss, 2007; Twenge, 2017). While undergraduate students have been widely portrayed as having high educational aspirations (DeBard, 2004), but unrealistically low expectations of the amount of effort required to achieve their goals (Wilson, 2004), this pattern appears to be changing. Those students who have come of age amidst the Great Recession and its aftermath have held relatively pessimistic views of their prospects for success and have generally been willing to work hard for good grades. Even so, their reliance on information technology has often resulted in shorter attention spans, less use of print media, and relatively indiscriminate consumption of information (Twenge, 2017).

The limits of students' immersion in academics came to the fore in a highly publicized study by Arum and Roksa (2011), which served as the basis for their book, *Academically Adrift: Limited Learning on College Campuses*. Upon its release, the book raised widespread concern about the lack of significant gains in undergraduate students' advanced cognitive skills over the course of four years in college. In examining their data, the authors found that students often were not sufficiently challenged by their course instructors. However, peer culture also appeared to be a major factor in the underperformance of American colleges and universities in promoting academic learning. Students often viewed college as primarily a social experience and devoted an inordinate amount of time and energy to peer interaction, while placing relatively little focused attention on academics.

In a follow-up study, with more direct links to the prior literature on emerging adulthood, Arum and Roksa (2014) found that recent graduates were also more likely to retrospectively cite social learning as the principal benefit of their undergraduate education. In this more recent work, the authors also directly addressed the role of the student affairs profession in elevating personal development to the status of a major educational goal, arguing that this realignment of priorities had diminished the primacy of academics within the mission of American higher education.

Regardless of its source, the gregarious nature of the Millennial Generation seems to have had a lasting influence on views of college teaching. Although there is a need for further research on the impact of group study on academic learning (Arum & Roksa, 2011), students' preference for collaboration has generally been seen as lending support to the use of interactive pedagogies (Wilson, 2004). In this regard, Twenge (2017) has suggested that student attitudes might be changing somewhat. She notes that current undergraduates sometimes enjoy class discussion, but tend to place their highest priority on mastery of content for which they will be held accountable. Thus, they have no objection to lecture, provided that it enhances their performance on tests. Findings from a recent survey of college faculty suggest, further, that students have become more passive in class discussion than their predecessors of just five years ago (Twenge, 2017).

Supervising Today's Student Workers

Multiple studies have shown that a majority of undergraduate students now work during their enrollment in college (Perna, 2010), owing in part to the centrality of student employment to the financial aid system (Baum, 2010). Within student affairs, undergraduate resident assistants and other peer helpers have long played a vital role in the delivery of programs and services (Blimling, 2010; Newton & Ender, 2010). Over time, student affairs professionals have also come to recognize the educational benefits of on-campus employment for student workers themselves (Perozzi, 2009). Thus, supervision of student staff can now be viewed as a widely available means by which to promote learning and development in college.

The management literature offers unique insight on the supervision of the current generation of emerging adults in organizational settings. According to Lancaster and Stillman (2002), the collaborative orientation of today's young people often leads them to expect opportunities to provide input on decisions affecting the organizations in which they work. They have also tended to prefer frequent and immediate feedback on their performance (Alsop, 2008; Lancaster & Stillman, 2002), a pattern that has been similarly observed in classroom settings (Wilson, 2004). They are generally motivated by work that they find meaningful. Further, they tend to be comfortable with multitasking and prefer to develop skills across a broad array of activities rather than focusing on a narrow area of specialization. Likewise, they often place a high priority on balancing work with other aspects of their lives and tend to appreciate flexible working conditions that enable them to achieve this balance (Alsop, 2008; Lancaster & Stillman, 2002).

While emerging adults' preferred working conditions have shown little change over the past 20 years, the intervening economic downturn appears to have tempered their expectations. Recent research suggests that the newest entrants into the workforce are less confident and less entitled than those who came before them. They also tend to be more realistic in their expectations for advancement and manifest a stronger work ethic. Due to the rising cost of higher education and the accumulation of debt that it brings, college students and recent graduates appear to have grown more willing to trade intrinsic enjoyment of their work for more generous compensation (Twenge, 2017).

Today's youngest workers value job security, but do not take it for granted. Thus, in supervising student workers, professional staff would do well to offer reassurance that their subordinates are meeting expectations in those areas where they are performing well, in addition to offering any corrective advice that might be needed. Insofar as the casual nature of electronic communication, coupled with its heavy reliance on visual imagery, appears to have diminished the newest generation of job seekers' ability to present their qualifications to prospective employers effectively (Twenge, 2017), the role of on-campus supervisors in providing career mentoring to their protégées should also be given its proper attention.

Transitioning to Generation Z

As the last of the Millennials have made their way through America's colleges and universities, prognosticators within higher education and elsewhere have begun to shift their attention to the next generation of undergraduate students, variously labeled iGeneration (New Strategist Press, 2013), iGen (Twenge,

2017), Generation Z (Seemiller & Grace, 2016), or Gen Z (Beltramini & Buckley, 2014; Koulopoulos & Keldsen, 2014). In an earlier bid for naming rights, Howe and Strauss (2007) dubbed this cohort the *Homeland Generation*, but had little more to say about them other than to note that they would be largely shaped by the parenting styles of Gen X, though half would be born to Millennials. Shying away from even setting rigid temporal bounds on this new generation, the authors placed its years of birth from the 2000s through the mid-2020s. Others have since placed the front end of this range at 1995 to 2000 (Beltramini & Buckley, 2014; New Strategist Press, 2013). Striving for inclusivity, Koulopoulos and Keldsen (2014) placed its beginning within "a band of ten years on either side of the year 2005" (p. 2).

Despite having been shaped by the times into which they were born, members of Gen Z have varied widely in the specific experiences of their youth, and have sometimes manifested surprising traits. As students, more of them have been homeschooled than have members of any other generation in recent history. Among those enrolled in traditional public schools, standardized testing and school violence have increasingly come to be seen as basic facts of life. However, even for these students, opportunities for learning are no longer seen as confined to formal academic settings, owing largely to advances in information technology (Beltramini & Buckley, 2014). Having grown up in the digital era, members of Generation Z are highly creative, resourceful, and visually oriented learners. Unlike members of previous generations, they tend not to focus on memorization, because they take for granted that information will always be available at their fingertips (Sladek, 2014).

Though burdened with greater economic uncertainty than many that have come before them, members of this generation appear to be less materialistic in their basic values. Having experienced unprecedented global connections, facilitated by advances in social media and mobile technology, members of this generation are both highly accepting of human diversity and actively engaged in social causes from an early age (Beltramini & Buckley, 2014). Commenting on the national and global crises that have accompanied the birth of Gen Z, Sladek (2014) noted with optimism that

> these dark events have undoubtedly made this generation more cautious and pragmatic, but they have also provided the generation with the inspiration to change the world – and their realistic approach to life is going to allow them to do it.

Based on a national survey of Generation Z, Seemiller and Grace (2016) described its members as "loyal," "compassionate," "thoughtful," "open-minded," "responsible," and "determined" (pp. 8–12). Believing that education is of benefit to both the individual and society, respondents viewed it as an important investment in our nation's future. They expressed concern about both the overall quality of American education, which they saw as being in decline, and the limited opportunities for quality education available to many of today's young people. Likewise, rising tuition and student debt loads have not gone unnoticed by this youngest group of aspiring college graduates.

In comparison to her previous work on Millennials, Twenge (2017) has been more sympathetic in her portrayal of iGen, even taking some comfort in their low rates of engagement in high-risk behaviors that have historically spiked at the transition toward adulthood. This most recent generation of emerging adults has shown lower rates of both teen pregnancy and alcohol consumption than those who have gone before them. Members of this generation are also more likely to postpone sexual activity and even driving. Twenge views these trends as part of a more general slowing of the transition into adulthood, as she notes that iGen'ers also tend to spend more time with their parents and are less likely to hold summer jobs than members of previous generations.

While finding less propensity toward narcissism among iGen'ers than among Millennials, Twenge (2017) found nonetheless a troubling prevalence of various mental health concerns, including anxiety, depression, loneliness, and suicidality, which, in turn, were found to correlate positively with participation in onscreen activities, such as texting, watching television, and browsing the Internet. As a counternarrative, others have highlighted both aggregate statistics and personal accounts that attest to emerging adults' ability to *flourish* in various aspects of their personal development (Padilla-Walker & Nelson, 2017), reinforcing Arnett's (2015) generally optimistic view of this life stage.

Are We Entering a Post-Generational Era?

At first blush unimaginative, the Gen Z moniker may ultimately prove to have been prescient in its finality, as some have suggested that we may soon be entering a post-generational era (Koulopoulos & Keldsen, 2014). Sladek (2014) has even gone so far as to state that the arrival of Gen Z "marks the end of clearly defined roles, traditions and experiences." Koulopoulos and Keldsen (2014) identified six trends that threaten to upend traditional patterns of interaction between generations during the years ahead. First, they projected a more even distribution of the population across generations, replacing the traditional *pyramid* configuration with that of a *skyscraper*. Second, they noted that the *hyperconnectivity* of the digital age has taken hold across all generations, allowing outdated technology to be replaced more quickly than in times past. Third, they pointed to the concept of *slingshotting*, whereby rapid advances in affordability and usability of new devices contribute to their immediate and widespread adoption beyond those segments of the population that are most affluent and technologically proficient. Fourth, they observed that forms of social influence that are accessible to the young hold the potential to offset economic advantages traditionally held by their elders. In particular, they cited six bases of persuasion set forth previously by Cialdini (2009): (1) *reciprocation*, (2) *commitment and consistency*, (3) *social proof*, (4) *liking*, (5) *authority*, and (6) *scarcity*. The fifth trend cited by Koulopoulos and Keldsen (2014) was the expansion of educational opportunities outside the traditional classroom. Finally, they discussed the concept of *lifehacking*, meaning shortcuts taken to produce desired results in unconventional ways.

Koulopoulos and Keldsen (2014) have contended that members of Gen Z, having spent their entire lives developing skills that are uniquely adaptive to the complex world in which all generations will spend their future, are destined to assume leadership roles in helping their elders to navigate this unfamiliar terrain. The authors introduced the term, *reverse mentoring*, to describe this emerging intergenerational dynamic. As educators prepare for the arrival of the next generation of undergraduate students on their campuses, it would seem that longstanding principles of generational theory may themselves require revisiting.

The Significance of Emerging Adulthood

While Arnett's (2015) theory of emerging adulthood is informed by demographic data, his work is distinguished from that of purely demographic theorists insofar as its focus is on characteristics particular to the current life stage of today's traditional aged college students and recent graduates, as opposed to enduring characteristics of their generational cohort. Likewise, his work is distinguished from that of purely psychosocial theorists in that it situates human development in a context that is particular to the current era. Thus, his work exists at the intersection of generational and psychosocial theory, much as the work of constructive developmental theorists, such as Kegan (1994) and Baxter Magolda (2004), exists at the intersection of constructivist learning theory, cognitive developmental theory, and psychosocial theory. Given the student affairs profession's longstanding commitment to the development of the whole student (American Council on Education, 1937/1994), and its increasing embrace of a more integrative view of undergraduate education (American Association for Higher Education, American College Personnel Association, & National Association of Student Personnel Administrators, 1998; American College Personnel Association, 1996; Keeling, 2006; National Association of Student Personnel Administrators & American College Personnel Association, 2004), Arnett's theory of emerging adulthood offers a theoretical foundation for student affairs practice that is uniquely suited to the demands of the 21st century.

References

Alsop, R. (2008). *The trophy kids grow up: How the millennial generation is shaking up the workplace.* San Francisco, CA: Jossey-Bass.

American Association for Higher Education, American College Personnel Association, & National Association of Student Personnel Administrators (1998). *Powerful partnerships: A shared responsibility for learning.* Washington, DC: Author.

American College Personnel Association (1996). The student learning imperative: Implications for student affairs. *Journal of College Student Development, 37,* 118–122.

American Council on Education (1994). The student personnel point of view. In A. L. Rentz (Ed.), *Student affairs: A profession's heritage* (2nd ed.) (pp. 66–77). Lanham, MD: University Press of America. (Original work published 1937.)

Arnett, J. J. (2013). The evidence for Generation We and against Generation Me. *Emerging Adulthood, 1*(1), 5–10.

Arnett, J. J. (2015). *Emerging adulthood: The winding road from the late teens through the twenties* (2nd ed.). New York, NY: Oxford.

Arum, R., & Roksa, J. (2011). *Academically adrift: Limited learning on college campuses.* Chicago, IL: University of Chicago Press.

Arum, R., & Roksa, J. (2014). *Aspiring adults adrift: Tentative transitions of college graduates.* Chicago, IL: University of Chicago Press.

Association of Higher Education Parent/Family Programs Professionals (AHEPPP) (n.d.). *Welcome to AHEPPP!* Retrieved February 24, 2018 from www.aheppp.org/overview.

Baum, S. (2010). Student work and the financial aid system. In L. W. Perna (Ed.), *Understanding the working college student: New research and its implications for policy and practice* (pp. 3–20). Sterling, VA: Stylus.

Baxter Magolda, M. B. (2004). *Making their own way: Narratives for transforming higher education to promote self-development.* Sterling, VA: Stylus.

Beltramini, E., & Buckley, J. (2014). Gen Z: Unlike the generation before. *The Bulletin of the Association of College Unions International, 82*(5), 12–17.

Bessant, J. (2014). *Democracy bytes: New media, new politics, and generational change.* New York, NY: Palgrave Macmillan.

Blimling, G. (2010). *The resident assistant: Applications and strategies for working with college students in residence halls* (7th ed.). Dubuque, IA: Kendall Hunt.

Broido, E. M. (2004). Understanding diversity in millennial students. In M. D. Coomes & R. DeBard (Eds.), *Serving the millennial generation* (pp. 73–85). New Directions for Student Services, n. 106. San Francisco, CA: Jossey-Bass.

Carney-Hall, K. C. (2008). Understanding current trends in family involvement. In K. C. Carney-Hall (Ed.), *Managing parent partnerships: Maximizing influence, minimizing interference, and focusing on student success* (pp. 3–14). New Directions for Student Services, no. 122. San Francisco, CA: Jossey-Bass.

Chickering, A. W., & Reisser, L. (1993). *Education and identity* (2nd ed.). San Francisco, CA: Jossey-Bass.

Cialdini, R. B. (2009). *Influence: Science and practice* (5th ed.). Boston, MA: Pearson.

Cross, K. P. (1992). *Adults as learners: Increasing participation and facilitating learning.* San Francisco, CA: Jossey-Bass.

Daniel, B. V., Evans, S. G., & Scott, B. R. (2001). Understanding family involvement in the college experience today. In B. V. Daniel & B. R. Scott (Eds.), *Consumers, adversaries, and partners: Working with families of undergraduates* (pp. 3–13). New Directions for Student Services, no. 94. San Francisco, CA: Jossey-Bass.

DeBard, R. (2004). Millennials coming to college. In M. D. Coomes & R. DeBard (Eds.), *Serving the millennial generation* (pp. 33–45). New Directions for Student Services, n. 106. San Francisco, CA: Jossey-Bass.

Edmunds, J., & Turner, B. S. (2002). *Generations, culture and society.* Philadelphia, PA: Open University Press.

Erikson, E. K. (1968). Life cycle. In D. L. Sills (Ed.), *International encyclopedia of the social sciences* (pp. 286–292). New York, NY: Macmillan.

Gillon, S. (2004). *Boomer nation: The largest and richest generation ever and how it changed America.* New York, NY: Free Press.

Havighurst, R. J. (1972). *Developmental tasks and education* (3rd ed.). New York, NY: McKay.

Howe, N., & Strauss, W. (2000). *Millennials rising: The next great generation.* New York, NY: Vintage.

Howe, N., & Strauss, W. (2007). *Millennials go to college* (2nd ed.). Great Falls, VA: Life-Course Associates.

Junco, R. (2014). *Engaging students through social media: Evidence-based practices for use in student affairs.* San Francisco, CA: Jossey-Bass.

Junco, R., & Mastrodicasa, J. (2007). *Connecting to the net.generation.* Washington, DC: National Association of Student Personnel Administrators.

Keeling, R. P. (2006). *Learning reconsidered 2: A practical guide to implementing a campus-wide focus on the student experience.* American College Personnel Association, Association of College and University Housing Officers – International, Association of College Unions International, National Academic Advising Association, National Association for Campus Activities, National Association of Student Personnel Administrators, & National Intramural-Recreational Sports Association.

Kegan, R. (1994). *In over our heads: The mental demands of modern life.* Cambridge, MA: Harvard University Press.

Knowles, M. S., Holton, E. F., III, & Swanson, R. A. (2015). *The adult learner: The definitive classic in adult education and human resource development* (8th ed.). New York, NY: Routledge.

Koulopoulos, T., & Keldsen, D. (2014). *The Gen Z effect: The six forces shaping the future of business.* Brookline, MA: Bibliomotion.

Lancaster, L. C., & Stillman, D. (2002). *When generations collide: Who they are. Why they clash. How to solve the generational puzzle at work.* New York, NY: HarperBusiness.

Le Goff, J. (2015). *Must we divide history into periods?* Translated by M. B. DeBevoise. New York, NY: Columbia University Press.

Levine, A. (1980). *When dreams and heroes died: A portrait of today's college student.* San Francisco, CA: Jossey-Bass.

Levine, A., & Cureton, J. S. (1998). *When hope and fear collide: A portrait of today's college student.* San Francisco, CA: Jossey-Bass.

Levine, A., & Dean, D. R. (2012). *Generation on a tightrope: A portrait of today's college student.* San Francisco, CA: Jossey-Bass.

Lowery, J. W. (2004). Student affairs for a new generation. In M. D. Coomes & R. DeBard (Eds.), *Serving the millennial generation* (pp. 87–99). New Directions for Student Services, n. 106. San Francisco, CA: Jossey-Bass.

Marcia, J. E. (1966). Development and validation of ego-identity status. *Journal of Personality and Social Psychology, 3,* 551–558.

Merriam, S. B., Caffarella, R. S., & Baumgartner, L. M. (2007). *Learning in adulthood: A comprehensive guide* (3rd ed.). San Francisco, CA: Jossey-Bass.

Mitstifer, D. I. (Ed.) (2012). *CAS professional standards for higher education* (8th ed.). Washington, DC: Council for the Advancement of Standards in Higher Education.

National Association of Student Personnel Administrators & American College Personnel Association (2004). *Learning reconsidered: A campus-wide focus on the student experience.* Washington, DC: Author.

New Strategist Press (2013). *American generations: Who they are and how they live.* Amityville, NY: Author.

Newton, F. B., & Ender, S. C. (2010). *Students helping students: A guide for peer educators on college campuses* (2nd ed.). San Francisco, CA: Jossey-Bass.

Oldenburg, R. (1989). *The great good place: Cafes, coffee shops, community centers, beauty parlors, general stores, bars, hangouts, and how they get you through the day.* New York, NY: Paragon House.

Padilla-Walker, L. M., & Nelson, L. J. (Eds.). (2017). *Flourishing in emerging adulthood: Positive development during the third decade of life.* New York, NY: Oxford.

Perna, L. W. (2010). Introduction. In L. W. Perna (Ed.), *Understanding the working college student: New research and its implications for policy and practice* (pp. xiii–xxvi). Sterling, VA: Stylus.

Perozzi, B. (Ed.). (2009). *Enhancing student learning through college employment.* Bloomington, IN: Association of College Unions International.

Pryor, J. H., Hurtado, S., DeAngelo, L., Blake, L. P., & Tran, S. (2010). *The American freshman: National norms fall 2010.* Los Angeles, CA: Higher Education Research Institute, UCLA.

Pryor, J. H., Hurtado, S., Saenz, V. B., Santos, J. L., & Korn, W. S. (2007). *The American freshman: Forty year trends, 1966–2006.* Los Angeles, CA: Higher Education Research Institute, UCLA.

Putnam, R. D. (2000). *Bowling alone: The collapse and revival of American community.* New York, NY: Simon & Schuster.

Seemiller, C., & Grace, M. (2016). *Generation Z goes to college.* San Francisco, CA: Jossey-Bass.

Sladek, S. (2014). *Gen Z final white paper.* Association Executives of North Carolina. Retrieved April 10, 2015 from www.slideshare.net/AENC/gen-z-final-white-paper.

Steinhorn, L. (2006). *The greater generation: In defense of the baby boom legacy.* New York, NY: St. Martin's.

Strauss, W., & Howe, N. (1991). *Generations: The history of America's future, 1584 to 2069.* New York, NY: Morrow.

Tapscott, D. (1998). *Growing up digital: The rise of the net generation.* New York, NY: McGraw-Hill.

Tapscott, D. (2009). *Grown up digital: How the net generation is changing your world.* New York, NY: McGraw-Hill.

Taub, D. J. (2008). Exploring the impact of parental involvement on student development. In K. C. Carney-Hall (Ed.), *Managing parent partnerships: Maximizing influence, minimizing interference, and focusing on student success* (pp. 15–28). New Directions for Student Services, no. 122. San Francisco, CA: Jossey-Bass.

Taylor, P., & Keeter, S. (Eds.). (2010). *Millennials: A portrait of generation next.* Washington, DC: Pew Research Center.

Turkle, S. (1984). *The second self: Computers and the human spirit.* New York, NY: Simon and Schuster.

Turkle, S. (1995). *Life on the screen: Identity in the age of the Internet.* New York, NY: Simon and Schuster.

Turkle, S. (2012). *Alone together: Why we expect more from technology and less from each other.* New York, NY: Basic.

Turkle, S. (2015). *Reclaiming conversation: The power of talk in a digital age.* New York, NY: Penguin.

Twenge, J. M. (2006). *Generation me: Why today's young Americans are more confident, assertive, entitled – and more miserable than ever before.* New York, NY: Free Press.

Twenge, J. M. (2013). The evidence for Generation Me and against Generation We. *Emerging Adulthood, 1*(1), 11–16.

Twenge, J. M. (2017). *iGen: Why today's super-connected kids are growing up less rebellious, more tolerant, less happy – and completely unprepared for adulthood (and what that means for the rest of us).* New York, NY: Atria.

Wartman, K. L., & Savage, M. (2008). *Parental involvement in higher education: Understanding the relationship among students, parents, and the institution.* ASHE Higher Education Report, v. 33, n. 6. San Francisco, CA: Jossey-Bass.

Wells, J. B. (Ed.) (2015). *CAS professional standards for higher education* (9th ed.). Washington, DC: Council for the Advancement of Standards in Higher Education.

Wilson, M. (2004). Teaching, learning, and millennial students. In M. D. Coomes & R. DeBard (Eds.), *Serving the millennial generation* (pp. 59–71). New Directions for Student Services, n. 106. San Francisco, CA: Jossey-Bass.

6

CAREER DEVELOPMENT IN EMERGING ADULTHOOD

Lisa Severy

It takes courage to grow up and become who you really are.

e.e. cummings

Love and work are two main constructs that define adulthood and mark key milestones in the lives of emerging adults. Indeed, these two areas are key in understanding the emerging adult stage as distinctly different from late adolescence and early adulthood. Both are defined by identity exploration, instability, a focus on self-independence, a feeling of being in-between, and a sense of optimism and hope moving forward (Arnett, 2015). They are two sides of the same coin. Love determines how individuals relate to and interact with families and their private connections. In our culture, work determines how we interact, engage, and contribute to the rest of the world. Figuring out these internal and external connections can be a roller coaster of positive and negative experiences, emotions, and outcomes. As if the phase were not difficult enough, today's emerging adults may experience long periods of job instability and insecurity created by external factors related to the world of work and internal factors related to continued identity development that make it even more complicated.

The Economics of College Degrees

For college graduates, the world of work looks significantly different than it did for previous generations. As the service and information economy has replaced the manufacturing economy, avenues for attainment of middle class status have become restricted and a college education has become imperative. The percentage of the people over the age of 25 with a bachelor's degree or higher has increased steadily from 1940 to 2015. In 1940, only 5% of adults held a bachelor's degree or higher. By 2015, this percentage had increased more than five times to 33% (Ryan & Bauman, 2016). According to a Gallup-Lumina (2016) poll, 70% of Americans say that it is very important for adults to have a degree or professional certificate beyond high school. In addition, while the majority believe that higher education is available to anyone, only 24% believe it is affordable for all.

Thorough analysis by the Pew Research Center (2014) clearly outlines the lifelong value of a college degree. In looking at pay gap, employment status, attitude about work, advancement opportunities, and satisfaction, young adults ages 25–32 with a college degree significantly outperform peers without a college degree immediately and over their lifespans. For example, these young college graduates annually earn about $17,500 more than their less educated peers do. In addition, more than half of these educated emerging adults describe being "very satisfied" with their current jobs.

Moreover, the economic gap between those with a college degree and those without is more pronounced today than it has been in previous generations. For example, from 1979 to 2013, this gap increased by more than 80% among full-time workers ages 25–32. Among the emerging adult population today, 22% of those with only a high school diploma are living in poverty. In addition to a wage gap, there are also significant gaps in unemployment rates and job satisfaction (Pew Research Center, 2014).

Given rising costs and high levels of student debt, many people have posed questions about the value of a college degree. In addition to the salary, employment and satisfaction measures, Abel and Deitz (2014) examined how long it takes to break even on the cost of the college degree and the years out of wage earning during school. They found that the time required to recoup the cost of a bachelor's degree had fallen significantly over time from more than 20 years in the late 1970s to about ten years in 2013.

School to Work Transitions

With more and more people pursuing college degrees, the increase in educational attainment pushed the completion of education well into individuals' twenties. Paired with the demographic changes in age of marriage and age of first children, this increased length of education has naturally extended the period in which individuals either are under the direction of their parents or committed to adult roles in families and workplaces. Eliason, Mortimer, and Vuolo (2015) describe this as a prevalence of "non-standard" employment situations that do not provide enough stability to start a family.

In the late adolescent stage of development, work is often characterized by low-skill service jobs unrelated to long-term career goals. The goal for these jobs is simple and straightforward—money to be spent now. Emerging adult experiences tend to move toward a more long-term view with some thought to how this experience might be helpful moving forward. This may involve skill development, exposure to a particular field, or simple resume building, but the core desire to make money is partnered with some longer-term implications. As with other aspects of life, this time is marked by two sides of the same coin—exploration and instability.

Emerging adulthood is also a time of significant stress from a wide range of sources including parental pressure to do well in school, multiple changes in living environments, transitioning to college, making career choices, exams, procrastination, lack of sleep, social media pressure, friendships, and romantic relationships (Bland, Melton, Welle, & Bigham, 2012; Dill & Henley, 1998; Peer, Hillman, & Van Hoet, 2015). Although many emerging adults report successful strategies for stress management, this sustained period of turmoil and transition can certainly take a toll. In a cumulative review of research on the prevalence of anxiety disorders, Remes, Brayne, van der Linde, and Lafortune (2016) found that 9.1% of young adults suffered from such disorders.

Expectations of Work

There is no doubt that the emerging adult population has very high expectations for work, especially after graduating from college. In this exploration phase, they desire jobs that allow them to explore and express their identities. As they move from jobs for money only to jobs leading to an adult life, their choices become more serious and more stressful as the perceived stakes are higher. During emerging adulthood, individuals tend to move from school only, to a combination of school and work, to a series of jobs, all with few or no outside obligations such as spouses or children. This pattern allows for a certain amount of flexibility to change jobs often or choose opportunities that may help with exploration but provide little stability in terms of benefits or job security. This flexibility and desire to explore has led to a phenomenon described as "job hopping" or "job surfing." Chao and Gardner (2007a), at Michigan State's Collegiate Employment Research Institute (CERI), conducted a survey of over 10,000 people between the ages of 18 and 28. Almost 65% of respondents indicated they would likely engage in job surfing behaviors early in their careers. The same percentage also indicated that they could move home if they needed to, allowing them the flexibility to seek a wide variety of jobs. More than 50% reported feeling unfocused or very early in their career decision-making, making job surfing a key tool for exploration.

The average college graduate takes about a year and a half to settle into a job that they will stay in for more than three years and about four years to start a job that will last five (Yates, 2005). According to a study by LinkedIn, the number of jobs people have had with different companies or organizations in the first five years after graduation has doubled in the past 20 years (Berger, 2016).

Employers are well aware of this phenomenon. According to one survey, 77% of responding employers report that recent college graduates stay in their first job less than a year, with 10% reporting average stays of only 3–6 months (Funk, 2014). Perhaps these emerging adults are simply continuing their educational pattern of a new challenge each three-month semester, but the transient nature of this age group is a challenge for those who like to hire new college graduates.

Whether the frequency of job changes leads to positive or negative outcomes can be a function of career adaptability. Career adaptability refers to an individual's readiness and comfort in dealing with changes and transition. As described by Rottinghaus, Day, and Borgen (2005), career adaptability relates to a person's abilities to cope with and take advantage of change. High levels of career adaptability have been positively linked to a sense of self-control, social support, self-esteem, career optimism, general and professional well-being, employability skills, and openness (Murphy, Blustein, Bohlig, & Platt, 2010). Career adaptability is predicted when emerging adults exhibit hope, resilience, and optimism (Buyukgoze-Kavas, 2016). As described by Savickas and Porfeli (2012), students who are able to reflect on and prepare for various potential career futures, and take on the risks and responsibilities of making their own career choices, are better able to cope with difficulty and remain flexible in an ever-changing work world. Career counselors, parents, and employers can help emerging adults by incorporating strategies to foster hope, resilience, and optimism. Indeed, in a study by Atzil-Slonim, Reshef, Berman, Peri, and Shulman (2016), they found that career adaptability significantly increased during and after psychotherapy, including levels of career agency and self-fulfillment. Participants in therapy were more confident about their job searching abilities, and thought they would find their work more meaningful and aligned with their wishes and values, which would, in turn, help them to be more authentic.

Each year, Universum conducts a Global Talent Survey to help its employer partners understand what college graduate employees really want from their employers. In results posted in May of 2017, new graduates were looking for a good fit with company culture, work-life balance, advancement opportunities, and a dedication to a greater cause (Clinard, 2017). Respondents indicated that fitting in with an organization and company culture is paramount. They are looking for things like supportive leadership, friendliness, respect, and creativity. There is an impression that small- and medium-sized companies may be better able to provide this type of setting. Universum recommends that employers be proactive and make sure cultural cues that inform candidates about these aspects of their companies—events, fund-raisers, value philosophies, and the like—are featured prominently on recruiting websites and social media.

Work-life balance ranked number one on the Universum survey (Clinard, 2017) in terms of personal values. This work-life balance includes work flexibility and variety in tasks and assignments. This balance does not mean that emerging adults are looking for easy work. In fact, they want the opportunity to learn more, push themselves, and have the opportunity to make good impressions.

Those good impressions lead into the next concern for emerging adults, which is the opportunity to grow and advance. They want to take on a variety of responsibilities in different areas. Universum (Clinard, 2017) recommends employers allow new graduates to try a variety of new tasks so that they stay productive and do not fall into a boring routine, which may press them to move on quickly. Employers should make advancement opportunities and processes very clear so that new graduates feel like they are growing in alignment with the organization.

Regardless of the industry, new graduates are interested in opportunities to contribute to the greater good (Clinard, 2017). This may take the form of philanthropy and volunteering, but also includes innovation, ethics, and inspiration. Arnett (2016) found similar results when comparing attitudes across socioeconomic groups, with all social class categories emphasizing a preference to find employment that contributes to the greater good. Employers need to highlight their efforts to engage in positive change in order to attract new graduates.

The Role of Happenstance

While most emerging adults describe their ideal work setting as one that immediately clicks with the developing identity, the reality is that happenstance comes into play more often than not. In general, there are four pathways in developing a career after college. First, students and recent graduates may discover their paths through experience. Perhaps a student had an on-campus job that led to a permanent position or an internship that sparked a passion. As the primary driver for satisfying employment is a reflection of identity, first-hand experience provides the most valuable information. Second, some students have always known what paths they intend to take. Perhaps they are following their parents' footsteps or have had a particular passion since childhood. Third, and often disappointing, there are those who have been focused on a particular career but have had to rethink those options, like an athlete who experiences injury, a musician who struggles to find gainful employment, or a pre-med student who cannot seem to master organic chemistry classes. Finally, there are those who learn that their dream career is not what they had imagined and begin to reconsider.

Of course, many emerging adults have not found themselves on any of these paths and are still actively exploring. Many of these people will find themselves falling into careers by happenstance. Rather than "exploring," these emerging adults may be described as meandering, drifting, or even floundering. Wilner (in Robbins & Wilner, 1997), coined the phrase *Quarterlife Crisis* after she graduated from college, moved back home, could not figure out what to do with her life, and experienced this identity crisis first hand.

Greenleaf (2014) recommended adopting a "happenstance" approach to career development as a model that fits the ever-changing workplace. Reviewing a rich history of research related to how individuals manage career transitions, Greenleaf concluded that emerging adults who engage in positive career-building behaviors like networking, part-time or internship work experience, and career counseling significantly increase the likelihood of generating opportunities and their chances of meaningful employment. Greenleaf recommends that counselors encourage emerging adults to take action as clients will learn new skills and gain new knowledge, while generating unforeseen employment opportunities.

Managing Expectations

Emerging adults exhibit patterns in their expectations of what their careers will provide, which are significantly different from those they expected as adolescents with jobs just for money. Emerging adults expect careers to be enjoyable, fulfilling, and aligned with their personal identities. Gallup (2016) identified six changes that the organization encourages leaders to make to better engage emerging adults. Rather than simply a paycheck, emerging adults want to connect to the work they are doing with a sense of purpose. Rather than satisfaction, they are seeking development and assessing how their current positions will help them with their next. Supervisors who approach these employees as coaches rather than bosses will be more successful. Emerging adults respond well to constant, ongoing conversations rather than annual performance reviews and would much rather focus on strengths than weaknesses. Most importantly, they are less likely to view personal and work life as separate.

In addition, emerging adults expect that they will be recognized and rewarded for their unique and innovative contributions (Chao & Gardner, 2008). When these expectations are not met, emerging adults have little difficulty moving on to the next opportunity. The established safety net of parental support certainly helps. In exploring this phenomenon with my own students, I will never forget the young woman who described job surfing just like dating. "If it doesn't really click," she said, "why would I hang around for another year just to show people that I can stick it out?"

So, what are the driving characteristics that young job seekers seek? In another report from Chao and Gardner (2007b), young adult respondents focused on six key characteristics of attractive jobs, which remained consistent across gender, ethnicity, and academic major. Starting with interesting and engaging work as the top characteristic, the list also includes good benefits, security, opportunities for promotion, opportunities to learn new skills, and the job location.

Emerging Adult Well-Being

In 2014, Purdue University collaborated with Gallup to understand the lives of new bachelor's degree recipients. More specifically, they examined workplace engagement and overall well-being. The well-being component included *purpose* well-being (liking what one does and feeling motivated to do it), *social* well-being (having strong, supportive relationships), *financial* well-being (effectively managing finances with little stress and good security), *community* well-being (enjoying one's social environment) and *physical* well-being (having good health and energy). The survey was designed to assess respondents' general patterns in each of these components and in three overall categories — *thriving*, *struggling*, or *suffering*. *Thriving* is defined as strong, consistent, and progressing. Key findings of the study included:

- Fifty-four percent of new graduates are thriving in purpose well-being, 49% in social well-being, 47% in community well-being, 42% in financial well-being, and 35% in physical well-being. Only 11% are thriving in all five.
- If these recent graduates are engaged at work, the odds are nearly five times higher that they will be thriving in all five elements of well-being.
- The higher amount of student debt, the worse the sense of well-being.
- Thirty-nine percent of new graduates feel engaged at work. However, if an employed graduate had a professor who cared about them as a person, who made them excited about learning, and had a mentor who encouraged them to pursue their dreams, the odds of being engaged at work more than doubled, thus tying collegiate experience to new graduate work experience in a unique way.
- There was no difference in well-being by race or ethnicity or whether a student was the first in their family to earn a degree (Gallup-Purdue, 2014).

These important findings provide insight into helping emerging adults become fully engaged in their workplaces and achieve an overall sense of well-being in five important areas. In addition to engaged faculty and an encouraging mentor, results of the 2016 Gallup-Purdue Index indicate that strong college or university career services can play a key role. Graduates who visited their career centers and said that visit was very helpful were almost six times more likely to say that their university prepared them well for life outside college (Gallup-Purdue, 2016).

Career Decision Influencers

Understanding that faculty, mentors, and career services influence career development during and after graduation provides insight into how emerging adults approach career decisions. Emerging adulthood is a time in-between: in-between parents or teachers and spouses or children, in-between school and work, in-between jobs or in-between apartments. It is also a time of emerging independence and self-determination wherein people, perhaps for the first time, set their own schedules, decide when and what to eat, make choices related to their health and well-being, and plan other aspects of life that were determined by others and are now self-determined. Living on campus can provide a subtle transition in that area, where there are some adult influences, and while there is certainly a wide range of parental involvement with college students, for the most part, emerging adults are newly independent. Career exploration, therefore, can feel like a solitary pursuit. Colleges and universities often provide career development services, but most of the exploration during this phase is done independently.

In contrast, most career and professional development is accomplished through a social network. Connections are exceedingly important whether they be school, alumni, family, friend, or job related. Utilizing social capital is an essential component of moving into positions that have implications for careers. Being able to see oneself in particular careers through the stories of others—role models, parents, mentors—helps to solidify ideas related to identity and career fit. Many of these connections will provide emerging adults with ideas for what paths may be a good fit, but some may provide just as valuable information about what is NOT a good fit. Students who have seen their parents struggle financially may seek more stable incomes. Students who felt their parents were stressed, overworked, or even absent may seek roles with more work-life balance.

Parental influence on career development in emerging adulthood should not be underestimated. In addition to providing information, psychosocial influence can be very important. Ginevra, Nota, and Ferrari (2015) note that students who report that their parents believe in their career decision-making abilities actually demonstrate a higher level of decision-making ability. Meszaros, Creamer, and Lee (2009) found that students' beliefs about their levels of parental support had positive impacts on their career interests and choices. In this context, support leading to occupational engagement and career agency included two unique types (Jenkins & Jeske, 2016). The first is personal or emotional support, such as encouragement or advice. The second is informational support, such as access to in-depth information about careers. Jenkins and Jeske (2016) found both important in positive career outcomes. Carlson (2014) delved deeper into parental advice for emerging adults and found some interesting results. First, emerging adults in the study both sought and implemented their parents' advice. However, advice was sought most in work-life balance and least in relationship and career categories. In terms of implementation, advice that was practical and supported autonomous decision-making was most frequently implemented. Perhaps not surprisingly, romantic relationship or sexual advice was usually unsolicited.

Career identity, or the meaning a person attaches to their own interests, motivations, strengths, values, and competencies with acceptable career roles, develops over time. As with most growth, the more attention and nurturing it receives, the stronger the end result. Praskova, Creed, and Hood (2015) examined the relationships between career exploration, career planning, career identity, perceived employability, career distress, and career calling. They found that optimal career outcomes were related to career preparation activities such as career exploration and planning, setting personally meaningful career goals, and clarifying who one is and where one wants to be.

Savickas (1997) describes the process of career development as a social construction. The underlying theory examines an individual's life themes and how those themes influence vocational behavior. Unlike traditional models of person-to-position fit related to career choice, Savickas describes integrating career into a grander life narrative. In other words, finding meaningful work that fits into someone's story. Emerging adults use what they are learning about themselves and their identities to adapt to a sequence of job changes while remaining faithful to themselves and recognizable by others. In this sense, the frame of career takes on a different scope from one of simple employment to one in which an emerging adult can identify a problem (personal, local, or global), use work as the solution and eventually be able to contribute to the greater good by using that solution with others. For example, a student who was abused by a parent may find sociology helpful in understanding his story and may eventually pursue social work as means of healing himself and others. Identifying productive themes and patterns can help emerging adults negotiate a series of job changes while developing their sense of self.

The question of independence and self-control provides an interesting avenue for future research on emerging adults. Self-control, or the internal regulation of thoughts, feelings, and behaviors, is an important aspect of many positive outcomes. Converse, Piccone, and Tocci (2014) provided interesting insight into this phenomenon by correlating high levels of adolescent self-control with educational attainment, job complexity, income, and job satisfaction. Konstam, Celen-Demirtas, Tomek, and Sweeney (2015) found that emerging adults with higher levels of self-control and confidence exhibited higher life satisfaction than peers with lower levels. Although more research is needed to further develop this concept, a clear implication for educators, parents, and career counselors is that emerging adults should be taught strategies for increasing self-control.

Although a good deal of research has focused on behaviors that may lead to greater career satisfaction and success for emerging adults, there is also important research into factors that may be hindering success and leading to undesirable outcomes such as anxiety and depression. For example, Lane (2015) examined the Imposter Phenomenon and found an unexpectedly high number of emerging adults exhibiting these feelings. Imposter Phenomenon refers to feelings of incompetence despite evidence to the contrary. It is the latter part of the description, the evidence to the contrary, that differentiates Imposter Phenomenon from other variables. For example, in Lane's qualitative research, he heard from emerging adults who desperately sought external validation but then did not believe any positive feedback they received. This feeling of incompetence makes people feel like frauds, believing that their abilities are overestimated, and in fear that their incompetence will be discovered (Lane, 2015). In a stage of life marked by transition and turmoil, the Imposter Phenomenon can have long-term impacts.

The Reality of Choice

Youth unemployment is not a new phenomenon and not limited to a particular generation. By definition, young workers have less experience, are less knowledgeable, and require training, mentoring, and supervision to thrive. While they may demand lower salaries, the true cost to employers may seem too high, especially with the turnover tendencies described earlier. In this sense, hiring new college graduates is a hopeful investment or even an act of faith. In addition, protections for older workers and job security may limit possibilities for the next generation of workers. No industry reflects that dilemma more effectively than higher education wherein tenured faculty delay retirement for years, limiting the opportunities for emerging faculty seeking tenure-track positions.

These market realities contribute to youth employment challenges like underemployment. In this context, underemployment refers to part-time jobs or jobs that do not require degrees. With limited responsibilities, parental safety nets, and good health, some emerging adults have the flexibility to take positions that might not be acceptable later (no benefits, part-time work, contract work, etc.). As Eliason, Mortimer, and Vuolo (2015) explain, trends in extended education, delayed parenthood, and familial dependence hide a great deal of variation. Youth of higher socioeconomic status groups pursue higher education and postpone starting families while their less-educated peers become parents and start on their professional paths much younger. Greenleaf (2014) summarized it well in saying that career counselors must focus on approaches that help emerging adults to be proactive, flexible, and realistic in their career development.

Ideally, emerging adults should be able to appropriately utilize resources' to determine how to engage and disengage when appropriate to their needs and environmental challenges. Haratsis, Hood, and Creed (2015), describe this as *assimilating*, believing that career goals are attainable and actively engaging with those goals, and *accommodating*, accepting that goals may not be met and, therefore, redefining the desired end goal. This process of assimilating or accommodating is based on the assessment of goals as important, sustainable, and attainable. Haratsis, Hood, and Creed found that individuals generally used one strategy over another except in extreme contextual changes that forced adaptation. In a subsequent study, Haratsis, Creed, and Hood (2016), found that in comparison to accommodation strategies, assimilation strategies were associated with more positive self-perceptions and higher satisfaction with career progress later.

Another interesting factor in career development engagement is emerging adults' beliefs about how higher levels of socioeconomic status are obtained in society. In a study by Shane and Heckhausen (2016), participants who believed that effort, ability, and merit determined level of success were more likely to engage in developing their careers and reported more rapid career success. On the other hand, participants who believed career success is mostly due to factors outside their control, like privilege or luck, were more likely to disengage. This dynamic is important for educators, counselors, and parents as it can become a self-fulfilling prophecy for emerging adults who opt in or out of career development. Those who feel no control and opt out tend to be less successful, confirming their ideas about lack of luck.

As a life stage, emerging adulthood looks very different at the beginning than it does at the end. Emerging adults who successfully transition through this stage have utilized the discussed strategies to progress in their careers and move into young adulthood with a more solidified sense of purpose and focus on pursuits that will help them to continue that progress. Salmela-Aro, Aunola, and Nurmi (2007) note that those nearing the end of emerging adulthood have reduced emphasis and engagement with education, friends, and travelling. Instead, older emerging adults are engaged more in family, health, and career goals. Their observations support a good deal of research on how motivation influences individuals as they move through life stages and adjust their personal goals based on contextual demands (Nurmi, 1992).

Privilege of Choice

One of the challenges of discussing large groups of people such as generations or people experiencing a certain phase of life is oversimplifying or trying to describe a huge range of individual differences with words like "typical." As discussed, there are personal, contextual, and experiential differences that influence an individual's progress through developmental tasks. Even focusing on one subset of the population, those emerging adults pursuing degrees in higher education covers a wide range of individuals. As described by Lee and Waithaka (2017), emerging adults from traditionally underrepresented, low-income, or other marginalized backgrounds may be more likely to experience delayed or accelerated progress or may lack opportunities necessary to transition to the next phase. Understanding how social structures are helping or impeding emerging adults is important for educators and career development professionals who want to be helpful.

In their study, Lee and Waithaka (2017) examined the intersection of race, immigration status, gender, and poverty status in relation to key adult markers including completing school, joining the labor force, establishing independent homes, marriage, and parenthood. They found that poor students were meeting these benchmarks at a slower rate than non-poor students were. While school attendance was about the same by poverty status, entry into the workforce was delayed for poor graduates. While the authors examined various reasons for this difference including higher rates of health problems or other disabilities as well as a lack of career-related network, more research is certainly needed to understand and address these differences. These results supported those found by Blustein, Chaves, Diemer, Gallagher, Marshall, Sirin, and Bhati (2002) in their study of young adults transitioning from school to work. They found that those of high socioeconomic status saw work as a source of personal satisfaction and exhibited higher levels of self-concept crystallization, greater access to external resources, and higher levels of career adaptability than peers in lower socioeconomic levels.

Focus on the Future

As confusing, tumultuous, and uncertain as the emerging adult phase of life can be, it can also be a time of great hope and openness to possibilities. With an active support system of parents, peers, professional networks, and career development professionals, emerging adults can use this time to develop their own self-efficacy and career adaptability that will serve them for a lifetime. Structural life changes such as graduating from college and becoming more independent tend to move emerging adults toward milestones; yet, the more purposeful and meaningful the decisions are along the way, the more likely the possibility of success and satisfaction in future career pursuits. There is a great deal of active research surrounding this unique life phase that should help to answer questions related to how career development professionals can best assist emerging adults as they become the authors of their own life stories.

References

Abel, J. R., & Deitz, R. (2014, September). The value of a college degree. *Liberty Street Economics, Federal Reserve Bank of New York*. Retrieved from http://libertystreeteconomics. newyorkfed.org/2014/09/the-value-of-a-college-degree.html#.VAX6m2Stkgu.

Arnett, J. J. (2015). *Emerging adulthood: The winding road from the late teens through the twenties*. New York, NY: Oxford.

Arnett, J. J. (2016). Does emerging adulthood apply across social classes? National data on a persistent question. *Emerging Adulthood, 4*(4), 227–235.

Atzil-Slonim, A., Reshef, M., Berman, E., Peri, T., & Shulman, S. (2016). Changes in romantic competence and career adaptability among emerging adults in psychotherapy. *Emerging Adulthood, 4*(3), 321–337.

Berger, G. (2016, April). Will this year's college grads job-hop more than previous grads? *LinkedIn Blog*. Retrieved from https://blog.linkedin.com/2016/04/12/will-this-year_s-college-grads-job-hop-more-than-previous-grads

Bland, H., Melton, B. F., Welle, P., & Bigham, L. (2012). Stress tolerance: New challenges for millennial college students. *College Student Journal, 46*(2), 362–375.

Blustein, D., Chaves, A. P., Diemer, M. A., Gallagher, L. A., Marshall, K. G., Sirin, S., & Bhati, K. S. (2002). Voices of the forgotten half: The role of social class in the school-to-work transition. *Journal of Counseling Psychology, 49*(3), 311–323.

Buyukgoze-Kavas, A. (2016). Predicting career adaptability from positive psychological traits. *Career Development Quarterly, 64*, 114–125.

Carlson, C. L. (2014). Seeking self-sufficiency: Why emerging adult college students receive and implement parental advice. *Emerging Adulthood, 2*(4), 257–269.

Chao, G. T., & Gardner, P. D. (2008). *Young adults at work: What they want, what they get, and how to keep them.* East Lansing, MI: Collegiate Employment Research Institute, Michigan State University.

Chao, G. T., & Gardner, P. D. (2007a). *Today's young adults: Surfing for the right job.* East Lansing, MI: Collegiate Employment Research Institute, Michigan State University.

Chao, G. T., & Gardner, P. D. (2007b). *Important characteristics of early career jobs: What do young adults want?* East Lansing, MI: Collegiate Employment Research Institute, Michigan State University.

Clinard, D. (2017). What do graduates look for in an employer? *Universum Talent Survey 2017.* Retrieved from http://universumglobal.com/articles/2017/05/graduates-look-employer/

Converse, P. D., Piccone, K. A., & Tocci, M. C. (2014). Childhood self-control, adolescent behavior, and career success. *Personality and Individual Differences, 59*, 65–70.

Dill, P. L., & Henley, T. B. (1998). Stressors in college: A comparison of traditional and non-traditional students. *Journal of Psychology, 123*(1), 25–32.

Eliason, S. R., Mortimer, J. T., & Vuolo, M. (2015). The transition to adulthood: Life course structures and subjective perspectives. *Social Psychology Quarterly, 78*(3), 205–227.

Funk, R. A. (2014, October). Hired today, gone tomorrow: Recent grads don't stay in first jobs very long. *America Employed: Insights from Express Employment Professionals.* Retrieved from www.expresspros.com/subsites/americaemployed/Recent-College-Grads-10-22-2014.aspx.

Gallup (2016). *How millennials want to work and live: The six big changes leaders have to make.* Washington, DC: Author.

Gallup-Lumina (2016). *Americans value postsecondary education: The 2015 Gallup-Lumina Foundation study of the American public's opinion on higher education.* Washington, DC: Author.

Gallup-Purdue (2014). *Great jobs, great lives: The 2014 Gallup-Purdue index report.* Washington, DC: Author.

Gallup-Purdue (2016). *Great jobs, great lives: The value of career services, inclusive experiences and mentorship for college graduates.* Washington, DC: Author.

Ginevra, M. C. Nota, L., & Ferrari, L. (2015). Parental support in adolescents' career development: Parents' and children's perspectives. *Career Development Quarterly, 63*, 2–15.

Greenleaf, A. T. (2014). Making the best of a bad situation: Career counseling young adults in the aftermath of the great recession. *Journal of Employment Counseling, 51*, 158–169.

Haratsis, J. M., Hood, M., & Creed, P. (2015). Career goals in young adults: Personal resources, goal appraisals, attitudes, and goal management strategies. *Journal of Career Development, 42*(5), 431–445.

Haratsis, J. M., Hood, M., & Creed, P. (2016). Cross-lagged relationships between person-based resources, self-perceptions, and career and life satisfaction in young adults. *International Journal of Education and Vocational Guidance, 16*, 169–188.

Jenkins, L., & Jeske, D. (2016, June 6). Interactive support effects on career agency and occupational engagement among young adults. *Journal of Career Assessment, 25(4),* 616–631.

Konstam, V., Celen-Demirtas, S., Tomek, S., & Sweeney, K. (2015). Career adaptability and subject well-being in unemployed emerging adults: A promising and cautionary tale. *Journal of Career Development, 42*(6), 463–477.

Lane, J. A. (2015). The imposter phenomenon amount emerging adults transitioning into professional life: Developing a grounded theory. *Adultspan Journal, 14*(2), 114–128.

Lee, J. S., & Waithaka, E. N. (2017). The intersections of marginalized social identities in the transition to adulthood: A demographic profile. *Emerging Adulthood, 5*(3), 151–163.

Meszaros, P. G., Creamer, E., & Lee, S. (2009). Understanding the role of parental support for IT career decision-making using the theory of self-authorship. *International Journal of Consumer Studies, 33*, 392–395.

Murphy, K. A., Blustein, D. L., Bohlig, A. J., & Platt, M. G. (2010). The college-to-career transition: an exploration of emerging adulthood. *Journal of Counseling & Development, 88*, 174–181.

Nurmi, J. E. (1992). Age differences in adult life goals, concerns, and their temporal extension: A life course approach to future-oriented motivation. *International Journal of Behavioral Development, 15*, 487–508.

Peer, J. W., Hillman, S. B., & Van Hoet, E. (2015). The effects of stress on the lives of emerging adult college students: An exploratory analysis. *Adultspan Journal, 14*(2), 90–99.

Pew Research Center (2014, February). The rising cost of not going to college. *Pew Research Social & Demographic Trends*. Retrieved from www.pewsocialtrends. org/2014/02/11/the-rising-cost-of-not-going-to-college/

Praskova, A., Creed, P. A., & Hood, M. (2015). Career identity and the complex mediating relationship between career preparatory actions and career progress makers. *Journal of Vocational Behavior, 87*, 145–153.

Remes, O., Brayne, C., van der Linde, R., & Lafortune, L. (2016). A systematic review of reviews on the prevalence of anxiety disorders in adult populations. *Brain and Behavior, 6*(7), 1–33.

Robbins, A., & Wilner, A. (1997). *Quarterlife crisis: The unique challenges of life in your twenties*. New York, NY: Penguin Group.

Rottinghaus, P. J., Day, S. X., & Borgen, F. H. (2005). The Career Futures Inventory: A measure of career-related adaptability and optimism. *Journal of Career Assessment, 13*, 3–24.

Ryan, C. L., & Bauman, K. (2016, March). *Educational attainment in the United States: 2015*. Washington, DC: United States Census Bureau, Department of Commerce.

Salmela-Aro, K., Aunola, K., & Nurmi, J. E. (2007). Personal goals during emerging adulthood: A 10-year follow up. *Journal of Adolescent Research, 22*(6), 690–715.

Savickas, M. L. (1997). The spirit in career counseling: Fostering self-completion through work. In D. P. Block & L. J. Richmond (Eds.), *Connections between spirit & work in career development: New approaches and practical perspectives* (pp. 3–26). Palo Alto, CA: Davies-Black.

Savickas, M. L., & Porfeli, E. J. (2012). The Career Adapt-Abilities Scale: Construction, reliability, and measurement equivalence across 13 countries. *Journal of Vocational Behavior, 80*, 661–673.

Shane, J. & Heckhausen, J. (2016). For better or worse: Young adults' opportunity beliefs and motivational self-regulation during career entry. *International Journal of Behavioral Development, 40*(2), 107–116.

Yates, J. A. (2005). The transition from school to work: Education and work experiences. *Monthly Labor Review, 128*, 21–32.

7

PROBLEMS ASSOCIATED WITH EMERGING ADULTHOOD

Aimee C. Adams and Bruce Sharkin

Emerging adulthood is a stage of life identified by Arnett (2015) that typically occurs during the ages of 18 to 25 years and is characterized by increased independence without traditional adult responsibilities. Given the challenging nature of the developmental tasks encompassed in emerging adulthood, it is not surprising that emerging adults experience struggles and problems associated with this period of "feeling in-between," as aptly described by Arnett. With fewer college students completing their education within four years, many "traditional" age college students are enrolled in studies beyond the age of 22. Thus, we use the terms emerging adult (EA hereafter) and college student interchangeably throughout this chapter.

Researchers suggest that the process of identity development that EAs undergo may account for their experiences of both internalizing and externalizing symptoms. Ritchie et al. (2013) found that the process through which EAs explore and commit to identities is related to such symptoms. For example, identity exploration and commitment were found to be negatively correlated with internalizing symptoms, whereas ruminative exploration was positively correlated with externalizing problems. The associations among externalizing and internalizing symptoms and identity formation processes suggest that these symptoms are important to understanding EAs' experiences.

This chapter will explore several social and psychological problems that can come to the fore in emerging adulthood. Consistent with Arnett's (2015) own work on this subject, this chapter is organized into two general categories: (1) externalizing problems and (2) internalizing problems. In both of these sections, a brief overview of Arnett's work will be provided, followed by an extension of his work that identifies and reviews research on additional problems commonly experienced by EAs. Although this review relies heavily on available research, it is also based, in part, on our many years of combined experience as college counselors. Based on the review, we will identify general principles to guide counselors, advisors, and other professionals who work in colleges or other settings with EAs. The chapter will conclude with a summary of clinical implications and research recommendations.

Externalizing Problems

Arnett (2015) defines *externalizing problems* as the projection of psychological conflicts into the outer world. He identified three externalizing problems commonly experienced by EAs based on an extensive review of research: risky driving, crime, and substance use and abuse. Of these three, we believe that substance use and abuse (particularly binge drinking) is the most critical, and is closely associated with risky driving and crime.

Arnett (2015) provides a thorough discussion of substance abuse among college students and notes the challenge of differentiating between use and abuse in the college student population. Indeed, researchers have shown that a large percentage of college students drink to excess (Hingson & White, 2012) and that such drinking is often associated with specific aspects of the college experience such as spring break, Greek life, and tailgating (Neighbors, Foster, Fossos, & Lewis, 2012). An increase in alcohol use appears to be significantly related to the experience of moving away from home, particularly in combination with going to college, during the period immediately following high school (White et al., 2006).

A review of the research shows that alcohol abuse appears to be significantly linked with the other externalizing problems identified by Arnett (2015), especially for college students. Common alcohol-related legal infractions include underage drinking, driving under the influence, and public intoxication (Dowdall, 2013). It has been well documented that alcohol is often involved in the most serious crimes on campuses, such as sexual violence, physical assault, vandalism, and other problems that can result in police involvement (Dowdall, 2013).

Many negative consequences of alcohol abuse are referred to as "second-hand effects," because they represent unintentional effects that can have an impact on others, ranging from emotional upset to serious injury and sometimes death. The evidence is clear that alcohol abuse not only poses risks to the abuser but is also a major risk factor for college students who do not abuse alcohol (Dowdall, 2013). It has been found that nearly 20% of college students meet criteria for alcohol dependence or abuse (Hingson & White, 2012), and when second-hand effects are factored in, this represents a significant number of students that are directly or indirectly affected.

The problems related to college student alcohol abuse have prompted campuses to explore and implement various harm reduction strategies ranging from individually focused approaches to changes in policies and programs (Kilmer & Logan, 2012). Kilmer and Logan suggest that such harm reduction approaches may be particularly appropriate for EAs who can still benefit from the guidance and assistance of others (e.g., parents, campus programs) as they learn to become more responsible. Common harm reduction interventions include "safe ride" programs and alcohol education. Although research has shown that the use of such strategies is associated with decreases in harm, they do not necessarily result in reductions in alcohol use.

Research suggests that higher parental monitoring prior to college may serve as a protective factor against increases in alcohol use during the transition to college (White et al., 2006). However, problems resulting from the involvement of parents in the lives of their emerging adult children will be the first of three additional externalizing problems we have identified as particularly prevalent among college students. The other two externalizing problems to be discussed include problems in romantic relationship exploration and academics.

Degree of Involvement with Parents

There is vast literature on relationships between emerging adults and their parents, including how earlier parenting styles may influence emerging adults (Nelson, Padilla-Walker, Christensen, Evans, & Carroll, 2011). Here, we focus on externalizing problems that can emerge due to the degree of involvement of parents in EAs' lives and how EAs feel about such involvement. How much or little parents remain involved with their emerging adult children is likely to have a significant influence on how well their sons and daughters handle the challenges of moving toward independent adult status. Additionally, the degree of parental involvement and how emerging adults feel about it can create frustration, stress, conflict, and indecision that can manifest in other problems.

Despite their desire to be responsible for themselves, make their own decisions, and be financially independent, EAs may find it challenging to achieve such independence, especially financially. As a result, many EAs may actively seek their parents' involvement in various forms such as advice, input on critical decisions, or financial assistance. Arnett (2015) noted that it can be difficult for some parents themselves to "let go," which can result in unhealthy forms of over-involvement and control, even when their involvement is enlisted. The involvement of parents in the lives of EAs appears to be trending upward, especially in the wake of increasing student loan debt. In the most recent Pew Research Center (2016) analysis of U.S. Census data, for example, it was found that 32% of Americans between the ages of 18 and 34 were living with their parents.

Although one might assume that over-involvement of parents in the lives of EAs has mostly negative effects, Arnett (2015) concluded that such involvement tends to have more positive than negative effects. Nevertheless, the research findings are, at best, inconsistent. For example, parental over-involvement has been associated with low self-efficacy and mistrust in peers (van Ingen et al., 2015) and less positive views of and anticipated delays in marriage (Willoughby, Hersh, Padilla-Walker, & Nelson, 2015) among college students. In contrast, Fingerman et al. (2012) found that "intense parental involvement" was associated with better psychological adjustment and life satisfaction in a sample of grown children.

Given that financial assistance from parents is a common source of support for EAs, particularly college students (e.g, Lowe, Dotterer, & Francisco, 2015), researchers have specifically examined the effect of this type of parental involvement. Again, the results are inconsistent. For instance, Schoeni and Ross (2005) found that EAs were more successful in establishing themselves financially when they received family-based assistance during their EA years, but Padilla-Walker, Nelson and Carroll (2012) found that the transition to adult-like behavior, including fewer risk behaviors, may be faster for emerging adults who receive little or no financial help from their parents. Attempts to identify optimal levels of parental involvement are further complicated by divergent views of emerging adults and their parents as to what constitutes *adulthood*, as well as gender-related differences in beliefs and expectations across generations (Nelson et al., 2007).

When parental involvement is not wanted to the degree it is given, there may be detrimental effects such as anxiety, depression, self-doubt, indecision, poor self-image, guilt, anger, and developmental delays. As college counselors, we have seen many instances of this in our work with students. Despite their often positive intentions, parents' behavior can stunt the growth and emotional development of students by undermining their sense of confidence in their own decisions. In the more troublesome cases, parents may have extremely poor boundaries and become overly intrusive in students' lives, including unnecessary intrusions into the counseling process. Based on the research, as well as our own clinical experience, we are somewhat more inclined to conclude that over-involvement of parents at this particular stage of life, especially when unwanted, has the potential to do more harm than good.

Having said that, we also acknowledge that the other end of the parenting spectrum (i.e., being completely uninvolved) represents an equally if not more concerning problem for EAs in college. It is interesting to note that research has tended to focus on over-involved parenting, as opposed to under-involved or uninvolved parenting. In one study, Nelson et al. (2011) identified *uninvolved* parenting as one parenting style that was associated with negative outcomes, but which was perhaps not as problematic as an over-involved or controlling style. However, in our own clinical experience, we have found it quite difficult to assist students with serious mental health problems without the benefit of parental assistance or support, particularly in cases where students need higher levels of care, such as inpatient or intensive outpatient treatment. It should be noted that it is sometimes the choice of students to keep parents out of their lives completely, oftentimes for good reason (e.g., a history of abuse) rather than parents making the decision to be uninvolved. However, in cases where students would welcome their parents' involvement, parental unavailability can have troubling effects on problems that already exist.

Ideally, parents of emerging adults should maintain a healthy balance of being available while still allowing for autonomy in the lives of their emerging adult children (Nelson et al., 2011). The attachment theory concept of secure base, wherein the parent or caregiver (the attachment figure) provides a sense of security that enables exploration, risk-taking, and self-development (Ainsworth, 1991) provides a model for this ideal balance. Whereas this balance is often not a reality for EAs, and despite concerns about the potential negative effects of over-involved parenting, we find that over-involved rather than uninvolved parents are more effectively managed when counseling college students. Although over-involved parents' intrusiveness can be challenging to handle, it at least represents something to work with and manage, clinically speaking.

Clinicians and other professionals working with college students should be aware of the potential for parental relationships to represent an externalizing problem. The degree of parental involvement and how it is experienced by the student can provide guidance on interventions. For example, treatment approaches such as Dialectical Behavior Therapy (DBT) provide resources in developing healthy interpersonal boundaries and interpersonal effectiveness skills. For EAs with under-involved or uninvolved parents, treatment approaches may take on more of a social work-type approach in which the EA is assisted in developing self-care skills and accessing resources to meet their needs. Regardless of level of involvement, family therapy may be indicated for those EAs who present with parental relationships as a concern. For college students with uninvolved or under-involved parents, such an approach may prove challenging. Nonetheless, family systems approaches, such as Bowenian family therapy, which works with one individual to create change within the family system, may be beneficial.

Future research on parental involvement as an externalizing problem for EAs should aim to clarify the aspects of involvement that are associated with positive and negative mental health outcomes. Further, the mediating effects of factors such as degree of agreement on expectations for involvement would shed light on why certain parental relationships are more helpful or harmful than others. Finally, based on previous research demonstrating that age and gender have an influence on involvement outcomes, the moderating effects of these and other cultural variables should be examined in future research.

Romantic and Sexual Relationships

Romantic and sexual relationships represent another crucial challenge for emerging adults. According to a recent national survey, relationship issues represent the third highest presenting concern among EAs seeking counseling at university centers (AUCCCD, 2016). It is important to note upfront that a limitation of the current research is that most of it pertains to heterosexual relationships and may not be applicable to same-sex relationships. One of the most well-documented aspects of the challenge of dating and exploring relationships during emerging adulthood is the apparently increasing trend of marriage postponement (Arnett, 2015; Carroll et al., 2009; Shulman & Connolly, 2013). Arnett used the phrase "meandering toward marriage" to capture the trepidation of the current generation of emerging adults in regard to marriage. Carroll et al. (2009) found evidence to suggest that the growing number of EAs (particularly college students) who are not ready for marriage may be a reflection of their need to first accomplish certain tasks that they believe can only be accomplished when single. This often includes milestones such as completing college and attaining advanced degrees, acquiring full-time employment, and ultimately achieving total financial independence. For some EAs, it is only after one has made the transition from being taken care of by others (namely, parents) to being able to care for oneself, that they can transition to being able to care for others (namely, a spouse or partner and children).

Similarly, Shulman and Connolly (2013) proposed a new transitional romantic stage for EAs to account for the postponement of marriage, relationship instability, and hesitancy to commit that are now common among EAs, particularly those who attend college. They argue that while EAs may be "psychologically ready" for a committed relationship, they may feel less confident about their ability to support themselves and, thus, their ability to support others. Much of this can be attributed to the changing societal and economic conditions of the past 20 or more years, which have made it more challenging for young people to establish themselves professionally and financially. One example of this is the burden that student loan debt places on so many EAs who choose to attend college.

Shulman and Connolly (2013) believe that emerging adulthood poses more developmental tasks and life decisions than may be faced at any other life stage. Perhaps this sense of individual instability explains why "relationship churning" (i.e., a pattern of repeatedly breaking-up and reconciling) is commonly observed among emerging adult couples. As would be expected, relationships with a churning pattern typically display minor conflicts such as arguing and reduced levels of relationship commitment (Halpern-Meekin, Manning, Giordano, & Longmore, 2012). More seriously, however, relationships with a churning pattern may also be more prone to verbal and physical abuse as compared to more stably committed relationships (Halpern-Meekin, Manning, Giordano, & Longmore, 2013). Unfortunately, violence and abuse within dating and romantic relationships is not uncommon among college students and has raised concern on college campuses (Aspy, 2007; Hays, Michel, Bayne, Colburn, & Myers, 2015).

Another often discussed aspect of relationship exploration during emerging adulthood, especially among college students, is the prevalence of *casual sexual relationships and experiences* (CSREs) (Claxton & van Dulmen, 2013). Claxton and van Dulmen present research showing that a majority of EAs (especially college students) are likely to experience one or more CSREs. They suggest that CSREs can be seen as somewhat normative during emerging adulthood because they serve to fulfill the developmental task of relationship exploration.

Claxton and van Dulmen (2013) found several predictors of CSREs, including attachment styles, personality characteristics, personal values, religious values, and situational factors. Not surprisingly, they found that the most cited reason that college students gave for engaging in CSREs was alcohol use. As Arnett (2015) noted, alcohol use and sex are a common combination among college students, and Dowdall (2013) identified unsafe sex as one of the consequences of college student drinking.

In addition to physical risks such as sexually transmitted infections and unplanned pregnancies, CSREs may have negative effects on mental health, including feelings of anger, depression, guilt, regret, shame, and diminished self-esteem (Claxton & van Dulmen, 2013). Claxton and van Dulmen found that these negative psychological outcomes may be more pronounced for women than for men. Although there can certainly be positive outcomes from CSREs (e.g., physical pleasure), the risks are high and the potential for negative outcomes appear to outweigh the benefits.

One final issue regarding relationship exploration during emerging adulthood has to do with the possible fallout from the use of Internet pornography. As discussed by Arnett (2015), this has been identified as a problem primarily for emerging adult males. Indeed, a condition known as *pornography-induced erectile dysfunction*, which reportedly results from addiction to pornography that can begin in early adolescence, has been garnering attention as a contributing factor in sexual performance difficulties in young men, particularly during emerging adulthood (Luscombe, 2016). Hence, clinicians may now see increasing numbers of otherwise healthy young men who seek help with such concerns.

What can be concluded from the available research on relationship exploration during emerging adulthood is that it is perhaps more complicated and fraught with risk today than ever before, and therefore, may reflect an externalizing problem for many EAs. There are many roadblocks for EAs to navigate in their quest for healthy, stable relationships that may ultimately lead to marriage or another form of partnership. The research suggests that one of the primary challenges may be to firmly establish oneself as an independent and stable individual before making any serious commitment to another, especially for recent college graduates. We often see romantic relationship struggles as a primary presenting concern in our counseling work with college students. Consequently, we see the developmental dynamics of relationship exploration play out before us, such as conflicted feelings of wanting but fearing intimacy and wanting to be accepted and loved but fearing rejection. For EAs, relationship exploration seems to represent both excitement and anxiety simultaneously.

Clinicians and other professionals working with EAs should be aware that romantic relationships can be an externalizing concern, given their reciprocal impact on the challenges inherent to this developmental period. As with parental relationships, the type and nature of relationships should be assessed and problematic issues addressed within a clinical setting as indicated. In addition to direct intervention, EAs can benefit from psychoeducation on healthy relationships. Presentation of such information needs to be offered in a manner that is respectful of individuals' personal and cultural identities and their choices about sexual behavior and relationships. Research on interventions that are helpful in addressing this externalizing issue is needed, as is research that pertains to a wider range of sexual orientations than the current literature reflects.

Academic Distress

For emerging adults who choose to attend college, much of their sense of identity and accomplishment is on the line during this time. In addition to the expected challenges, there are other obstacles that can hinder or prevent one from successfully completing college. For example, mental health problems such as anxiety and depression can interfere with the demands of academic life (Sharkin, 2006). Such mental health problems can translate into poor class attendance, diminished concentration and motivation, lack of persistence, poor study habits, and poor overall academic performance. Similar negative effects on academic performance have been found for alcohol use (Dowdall, 2013; Hingson & White, 2012). Thus, as challenging as college is, it can be made more challenging by nonacademic problems and distractions. When students experience problems that interfere with their academics, they are often forced to spend more time on their studies, which can result in their feeling even more stressed and possibly more burdened by debt.

Both externalizing and internalizing problems are sometimes intertwined with college students' academic functioning. For example, much has been written about how parents often interject themselves into aspects of their emerging adult children's academic experiences, such as decisions about choosing a major (Arnett, 2015; van Ingen et al., 2015), though it is not always clear if and when such parental involvement interferes with student success. It has also been found that students with lower GPAs may use Facebook as a way to cope with their academic frustrations (Michikyan, Subrahmanyam, & Dennis, 2015).

Navigating college represents one of the key ways that many young people first transition into emerging adulthood, and for those who graduate, this can subsequently pave the way for their transition to adulthood. However, when things go awry in the academic realm, this can be a tremendous setback for those who see college as the stepping stone to adulthood, particularly in terms of establishing a career path. In counseling students, we note how non-academic problems such as anxiety, family-related distress, and financial stress can result in academic distress. Likewise, poor academic performance can result in nonacademic problems such as depression and low self-esteem. There are many cases in which students have to temporarily leave school due to academic concerns; some of these students are able to subsequently resume their studies and others cannot.

Given the available empirical and clinical evidence, it is important to include academic distress as an externalizing problem for emerging adults who pursue a college degree because it can be a critical factor in some emerging adults' ability to achieve a successful transition from emerging adulthood to adulthood. Clinicians and other professionals working with EAs should assess for this externalizing issue and address it directly or by referring to academic support services as indicated. In some cases, EAs in college may benefit from basic interventions such as tutoring and study skills instruction, while others may need to utilize accommodations available to those with documented learning and other disorders. More research is needed on how best to help EAs with academic distress, particularly when it is comorbid with other presenting issues.

Internalizing Problems

Arnett (2015) highlights three internalizing problems that are prevalent among EAs. He notes that depression, anxiety disorders, and eating disorders are all common within this population and deserve consideration when assessing, treating, and researching their mental health needs. Anxiety and depression are the two most frequently reported presenting concerns of college student EAs seeking counseling (50.61% and 41.23%, respectively) and eating disorders are also reported as a concern by 7.37% of students (AUCCCD, 2016). The following overview expands on Arnett's findings and details four additional internalizing problems that are common among EAs: posttraumatic stress disorder, nonsuicidal self-injury, suicide, and low self-esteem.

Post-Traumatic Stress Disorder

One internalizing problem that is critical to consider when working with EAs is exposure to traumatic events and associated post-traumatic symptoms. There is evidence that more than half of all EAs in college have had exposure to at least one traumatic event in their lifetime (Boyraz, Granda, Baker, Tidwell, & Waits, 2016). Further, rates of posttraumatic stress disorder (PTSD) among college-enrolled EAs are higher than for noncollege students.

Students may arrive to college already having experienced a traumatic event, such as sexual assault, witnessing domestic violence, and exposure to community violence. Veterans are at elevated risk for PTSD, due to possible combat-related trauma exposure. Of particular concern is evidence that college students, particularly first-year students, are at greater risk than their noncollege and more advanced student counterparts for experiencing the trauma of sexual assault.

Further, certain cultural groups are at risk for discrimination, which is also associated with PTSD symptoms. Carter, Forsyth, Mazzula, and Williams (2005) suggest that experiences of racism can be perceived as traumatic, and may explain higher rates of PTSD among non-Whites in some studies. Although the fifth edition of the *Diagnostic and Statistical Manual of Mental Disorders* (DSM-5; American Psychiatric Association, 2013) defines trauma as life-threatening, Carter et al. (2005) argue that this definition fails to capture the significance of racism as a stressor for people of color and propose using an alternative model of traumatic stress, such as that posited by Carlson (1997). Carlson defines trauma as an experience that is negative, sudden, and uncontrollable, but does not require the person's life to be threatened as is required by the DSM-5.

Among college students, PTSD has been found to be positively related to smoking, drinking, poor academic performance, dropping out, and other undesirable outcomes (Bachrach & Read 2012; Boyraz et al., 2016; Klanecky, Woolman, & Becker, 2015). Of particular importance is the finding that PTSD symptoms mediate the relationship between trauma exposure and such outcomes. Among PTSD symptoms, hyperarousal is often one of the strongest predictors of negative mental health outcomes. Avoidance behaviors are also strongly associated with negative outcomes. It is therefore imperative that interventions targeting problems with drinking, smoking, and academic performance also screen for hyperarousal, avoidance, and other PTSD symptoms and provide appropriate treatment interventions or referrals as indicated. Outreach programs targeted at reducing these behaviors could also be strengthened by adding information on their links to trauma and the role that hyperarousal and avoidance play in their adoption. Such information could help students gain insight into factors affecting their behavior and provide motivation to address these factors.

Although trauma exposure is typically viewed as a risk factor for college students, there is evidence that some individuals experience a phenomenon known as posttraumatic growth (PTG) following trauma exposure. PTG is characterized as an increased sense of meaning, purpose, and connectedness among trauma survivors. Interventions aimed at facilitating PTG on the individual and group level may serve to ameliorate trauma exposure (Tedeschi & Calhoun, 2004). This may be particularly important for universities and other organizations where emerging adults are exposed to trauma on a large scale, such as campus shootings or natural disasters.

Clinicians working with EAs should regularly assess for PTSD symptoms. There is evidence that individuals who have been exposed to events that they perceive as traumatic can experience PTSD symptoms, even if the event does not meet DSM-5 criteria for a traumatic event. With regard to assessing traumatic reactions to racism, Bryant-Davis and Ocampo (2005) suggest that counselors assess the conditions surrounding racist incidents. They argue that clients who experience repeated racist incidents, who are traumatized by someone they knew and trusted, or are publicly humiliated are all at risk for more severe trauma reactions. There is also evidence that clients report trauma history significantly more when specifically asked about it (Freedy, Monnier, & Shaw, 2002), suggesting that trauma history screening questions should be included in assessment of all EAs.

Research on interventions for PTSD indicates that exposure treatments provide the most consistently positive outcomes (Nemeroff et al., 2006). Exposure approaches can be direct (i.e., processing the trauma verbally and through writing in individual therapy) or indirect (i.e., through approaches such as EMDR). There is also evidence that encouraging trauma survivors to process a disaster event immediately can be counterproductive and may actually increase the prevalence of PTSD symptoms. Instead, mental health professionals are encouraged to facilitate the use of natural supports and coping strategies among individuals exposed to large-scale traumatic events. Unfortunately, there are limited data on trauma interventions specifically for EAs; more research is needed to determine whether these interventions are effective for this age group and their needs. In one promising study, Van Dusen, Tiamiyu, Kashdan, and Elhai (2015) found that gratitude was negatively correlated with a number of PTSD symptoms in college students, suggesting that gratitude-based interventions may help to alleviate such symptoms.

The current literature on PTSD in college students provides abundant information on its prevalence, its links to numerous outcome variables, and mediation and moderation of these relationships. These findings provide substantial information to professionals who work with EAs on possible areas of intervention. A significant gap in the literature pertains to validation of interventions with this population. Future research should explore the most effective ways to reduce PTSD symptoms and promote posttraumatic growth among EAs. Interventions should also aim to reduce students' exposure to new trauma in college, for example, by preventing sexual assault, relationship violence, and discrimination. A second issue with existing literature on PTSD in EAs is the wide variability in operational definitions of trauma and measures used to assess PTSD symptoms. More consistent definitions, as well as measures that are validated for use with EAs, would allow for meta-analytic studies that provide greater insight into the problem of PTSD in this population.

Nonsuicidal Self-Injury (NSSI)

NSSI, or intentional injury of body tissue without suicidal intent, is another internalizing problem that can occur among emerging adults. NSSI was recently identified as a condition for further study in the DSM-5 (American Psychiatric Association, 2013). It is important to distinguish NSSI from suicidal behavior, as they are shown to be correlated by distinct constructs. NSSI is typically viewed as a coping strategy that is utilized to manage negative emotions and thoughts. NSSI can take various forms, including cutting, burning, skin picking, head banging, and hitting or punching oneself.

Although this internalizing problem is not unique to EAs, there is evidence that college age students are at particularly high risk for it. Noncollege student EAs, who are still coping with the developmental tasks and stressors that adolescents face, are also at risk for engaging in NSSI. Rates of NSSI among EAs vary across studies. Whitlock, Eckenrode, and Silverman (2006) reported a prevalence rate of 17% in their college student sample, whereas Whitlock et al. (2011) reported a lifetime prevalence rate of 15.3% in their sample. Among those who engage in NSSI, cutting is reported as the most frequent method (Brausch, Williams, & Cox, 2016). Whitlock, Prussien, and Pietrusza (2015) note that EA college students in their sample who reported current NSSI perceived themselves as "self-injurers" more than those with a past history of NSSI, but no current self-injury. This suggests that as EAs engage in identity formation, they may take on the identity of self-injurer rather than viewing NSSI as simply a behavior in which they engage to cope with stressors.

Wester and Trepal (2010) found that college students who engaged in NSSI were more likely to seek counseling services than their non-NSSI counterparts, but that only 21.6% of self-injurers were currently in counseling. Of concern, EAs who engage in NSSI report low rates of disclosure about their NSSI, especially to mental health professionals (Whitlock et al., 2011); those who do disclose are more likely to do so to peers and romantic partners (Armiento, Hamza, & Willoughby, 2014). Thus, clinicians working with EAs need to be aware that clients may be unlikely to voluntarily self-disclose their NSSI, so direct assessment methods may be needed.

According to the DSM-5, NSSI must serve at least one of three functions: (1) relieve negative thoughts or feelings, (2) resolve an interpersonal problem, or (3) cause a positive feeling or emotion (American Psychiatric Association, 2013). Brausch, Muehlenkamp, and Washburn (2016) found that differences in undergraduate students' frequency of NSSI were not associated with differences in function. Therefore, interventions aimed at reducing NSSI should take function into account regardless of the frequency of NSSI.

NSSI may co-occur with other mental health issues such as depression, anxiety, and eating disorders (Whitlock et al., 2006) but may also occur independent of other mental health conditions (Whitlock, Muehlenkamp, & Eckenrode, 2008). Of particular concern is evidence that NSSI predicts concurrent and subsequent suicidal thoughts and behaviors (Whitlock et al., 2013). Additionally, difficulty with emotion regulation is greater among EAs who engage in NSSI than those who do not (Heath, Toste, Nedecheva, & Charlebois, 2008). Despite earlier findings suggesting a direct link between abuse history and NSSI (Whitlock et al., 2006), more recent research indicates that after controlling for psychiatric risk factors, childhood sexual abuse and childhood trauma are not significantly associated with NSSI (Klonsky &

Moyer, 2008; Heath et al., 2008). Thus, it appears that the manner in which individuals cope with distress rather than the etiology of the distress may be a critical factor in the development of NSSI in EAs.

Although limited, there is some evidence on factors that protect against the occurrence of NSSI for EAs. Kress, Newgent, Whitlock, and Mease (2015) found that spirituality/religiosity, life satisfaction, and life meaning were significantly negatively predictive of NSSI among college students, but the regression co-efficients were small. More research is needed on the specific aspects of these constructs that serve as protective factors against NSSI, as well as on additional protective factors that could be enhanced in treatment. Whitlock et al. (2013) found that the risk for suicidal thoughts and behaviors that is associated with NSSI is decreased by the presence of meaning in life and supportive parents. Although EAs may seek support for dealing with NSSI online, researchers caution that on-line representations of NSSI may normalize or reinforce the behavior, minimize its consequences, and trigger the behavior (e.g., Lewis & Baker, 2011).

Clinicians and other professionals who work with EAs should assess for vari-ous forms of NSSI currently and in the client's past, and should be mindful that many clients may not voluntarily self-report symptoms. Information about the context and function of the behavior for the individual should be obtained via clinical interview and/or self-report assessments (Lewis & Arbuthnott, 2012). Suicidality is important to assess given the elevated risk among those who en-gage in NSSI. Given the evidence that NSSI is typically a coping strategy, alter-native healthy coping strategies need to be developed via therapy. Specifically, active coping strategies, rather than inactive techniques, have been shown to be helpful (Nock, Prinstein, & Sterba, 2009). Additionally, it is important to improve emotion regulation skills, regardless of the specific treatment approach that is utilized. With regard to specific approaches, DBT (DBT; Linehan, 1993) and problem-solving therapy have been shown to reduce the occurrence of NSSI and associated symptoms among college student EAs (Pistorello, Fru-zzetti, MacLane, Gallop & Iverson, 2012; Townsend et al., 2001). Clinicians should also be mindful that NSSI may be perceived by others in the client's life as attention-seeking. Therefore, providing psychoeducation about the causes and functions of NSSI to members of clients' support system may be beneficial. The finding that individuals may adopt a "self-injurer" identity (Whitlock et al., 2015) has implications for practice, as clinicians may need to explore ways to challenge and modify this identity in addition to helping clients develop alternative coping skills. Qualitative research by Gelinas and Wright (2013) on college students' reasons and strategies for NSSI cessation and on barriers to cessation suggest that clinicians must attend to the specific motives, strategies, and barriers to cessation that are salient for their clients rather than utilizing a universal approach. Wester and Trepal's (2010) finding that nearly 80% of students who engaged in NSSI were not in counseling indicates that direct ser-vices may not be sufficient to reduce NSSI in this population. They suggest that outreach on the topic of NSSI and factors related to it could also be effective in reducing NSSI. The finding that disclosure of NSSI is more likely to peers and romantic partners (Armiento et al., 2014) suggests that gatekeeper training designed to assist peers to respond effectively may be beneficial. Additional research on non-college student EAs could further clarify the prevalence of NSSI, associated variables, and effective treatments.

Suicide

Suicide is the second leading cause of death among EAs, and this age group reports more frequent suicidal thoughts and plans than other age groups. Females have a greater incidence of suicidal thoughts, whereas males are four times more likely to complete suicide (Centers for Disease Control, 2015). Clinicians and other professionals working with EAs must be aware of risk factors for suicide and treatments that reduce risk.

In addition to general risk factors for suicide, there are factors particular to EAs. Depression and hopelessness have been found to predict suicidal thoughts in college students (Konick & Gutierrez, 2005). Nadorff, Nazem, and Fiske (2013) found that college students who reported having nightmares were at greater risk for suicidal ideation, after controlling for depression, anxiety, and PTSD symptoms. Comorbid Attention Deficit Hyperactivity Disorder symptoms (combined type) have been shown to increase the risk of suicide among college students with depression (Patros et al., 2013). Sexual minority EAs show higher levels of suicidal ideation and attempts (Silva, Chu, Monahan, & Joiner, 2015), whereas college student military personnel and veterans report levels similar to the general college student population (Bryan & Bryan, 2015).

Professionals who work with EAs should screen for risk factors when determining suicide risk for EAs. Additionally, current and past suicidal ideation, plans, intent, and attempts should be assessed in order to plan treatment accordingly. Treatment aimed at reducing suicide risk must address underlying mental health issues such as depression. As with NSSI, DBT has been shown to be effective in reducing suicidality among college students (Pistorello et al., 2012). Unfortunately, EAs who are suicidal frequently do not seek psychological help (Garlow et al., 2008). Thus, working to reduce suicide among EAs requires approaches outside of traditional clinical settings, such as mental health screenings and outreach. King et al. (2015) found that college students who screen positive for suicide risk are more willing to seek psychological help if offered motivational interviewing approaches via online counseling rather than text-only feedback. Given the popularity of online screenings in college counseling settings, this evidence suggests that they should be accompanied by interactive counseling in order to ensure that suicidal students actually access psychological help. Online gatekeeper training programs such as QPR have been shown to be effective in increasing the self-reported self-efficacy, knowledge, and behavioral intentions about recognizing and responding to suicide risk (Lancaster et al., 2014). Unfortunately, data on the effectiveness of these programs in reducing suicide rates are limited.

Low Self-Esteem

Self-esteem generally increases throughout emerging adulthood (Galambos, Barker, & Krahn, 2006). This positive change is likely due in part to EAs' accomplishment of developmental tasks related to their identities, careers, and relationships, thereby increasing positive feelings about themselves. However, there is evidence that some struggle with low self-esteem during this period. For example, Galambos et al. (2006) found that individuals who experience longer periods of unemployment report lower self-esteem. Given its association with other mental health outcomes, self-esteem is an important internalizing issue to consider within this population. Self-esteem is typically conceptualized as the global level of positive or negative feelings one has about oneself. However, some researchers argue that type of self-esteem is also important. Contingent self-esteem depends upon meeting the standards of oneself and others (e.g., Crocker & Wolfe, 2001).

Most of the research on self-esteem and other mental health issues affecting EAs has been conducted with college students. Self-esteem has a significant, negative relationship with depression (Galambos et al., 2006; Lakey, Hirsch, Nelson, & Nsamenang, 2014), suicide risk (Lakey et al., 2014), and maladaptive perfectionism (Taylor, Papay, Webb, & Reeve, 2016). In contrast, self-esteem has a significant, positive relationship with academic and overall adjustment (Pasha & Munaf, 2013). While there is evidence that both level and contingency of self-esteem are linked to depression (Lakey et al., 2014), level appears to be the stronger predictor (Wouters et al., 2013). Further, Nordstrom, Goguen, and Hiester (2014) found that specific forms of self-esteem varied in their association with aspects of adjustment, which suggests that interventions aimed at improving adjustment and retention of college-enrolled EAs must take into account self-esteem in its various forms.

Self-esteem has been studied in relation to identity development among EAs. Research by Rueng, Kroger, and Martinussen (2013) suggests that identity commitment is positively associated with self-esteem. Further, Soenens, Berzonsky, and Papini (2016) found that college students' approaches to identity development were influenced by their levels of self-esteem. Specifically, low self-esteem was found to predict an avoidant style, whereas contingent self-esteem predicted both informational and normative styles of identity development. The findings suggest that in order to assist EAs in reflective and autonomous identity development, professionals may work toward increasing self-esteem. In particular, clinicians may assist clients in focusing more on their own standards, as this aspect of contingent self-esteem is most closely associated with the normative style (Soenens et al., 2016). Interventions aimed at increasing self-compassion (Neff, 2003) may also be beneficial. Given that experiences and perceptions of discrimination and their relationship with psychological distress have been linked to self-esteem (Nadal, Wong, Griffin, Davidoff, & Sriken, 2014; Wei, Chao, Su, Yeh, & Carrera, 2013), support for minority students remains important as well.

Conclusions

The literature on problems in emerging adulthood suggests that professionals working with this population must be cognizant of how membership in this age group places them at high risk for such issues. Several of the problems reviewed are unlikely to be disclosed by clients voluntarily, so clinicians must include various and specific forms of assessment in their work with EAs. The research suggests specific treatment approaches such as study skills and tutoring for academic distress, DBT and family therapy for parental issues, exposure therapy for PTSD, and DBT for NSSI and suicidality. Self-compassion interventions may be useful for shifting self-esteem from more pathological contingent self-esteem to more beneficial noncontingent self-esteem.

The research on problems in emerging adulthood provides information on their prevalence, etiology, and function. A primary limitation of the literature is that the vast majority of studies utilize EAs who are ages 18 to 22, Caucasian non-Hispanic, and enrolled in college. This literature may not generalize further. Another concern is that more research is needed on treatment approaches applied to this specific age group. Many studies highlight the role of identity development in internalizing and externalizing problems, but there is a dearth of research on how clinicians can help EAs navigate identity development while improving their well-being. Future research should incorporate measures of identity when investigating which treatment approaches are most beneficial for EAs in reducing such problems.

References

Ainsworth, M. D. S. (1991). Attachments and other affectional bonds across the life cycle. In C. M. Parkes, J. Stevenson-Hinde, & P. Marris (Eds.), *Attachment across the lifecycle* (pp. 33–51). New York, NY: Routledge.

American Psychiatric Association. (2013). *Diagnostic and statistical manual of mental disorders* (5th ed.). Arlington, VA: American Psychiatric Publishing.

Armiento, J. S., Hamza, C. A., & Willoughby, T. (2014). An examination of disclosure of nonsuicidal self-injury among university students. *Journal of Community & Applied Social Psychology, 24,* 518–533.

Arnett, J. J. (2015). *Emerging adulthood: The winding road from the late teens through the twenties* (2nd edition). New York, NY: Oxford.

Aspy, C. B. (2007). When dating relationships go bad: Counseling students in relationship violence. In J. A. Lippincott & R. B. Lippincott (Eds.), *Special populations in college counseling: A handbook for mental health professionals* (pp. 117–128). Alexandria, VA: American Counseling Association.

The Association for University and College Counseling Center Directors Annual Survey (AUCCCD; 2016). The AUCCCD Annual Survey. Retrieved from www.aucccd.org/director-surveys-public.

Bachrach, R. L., & Read, J. P. (2012). The role of posttraumatic stress and problem alcohol involvement in university academic performance. *Journal of Clinical Psychology, 68*, 843–859.

Boyraz, G., Granda, R., Baker, C. N., Tidwell, L. L., & Waits, J. B. (2016). Posttraumatic stress, effort regulation, and academic outcomes among college students: A longitudinal study. *Journal of Counseling Psychology, 63*, 475–486.

Brausch, A. M., Muehlenkamp, J. J., & Washburn, J. J. (2016). Nonsuicidal self-injury disorder: Does Criterion B add diagnostic utility? *Psychiatry Research, 244*, 179–184.

Bryan, C. J., & Bryan, A. O. (2015). Sociodemographic correlates of suicidal thoughts and behaviors among college student service members/veterans. *Journal of American College Health, 63*, 502–507.

Bryant-Davis, T., & Ocampo, C. (2005). The trauma of racism: Implications for counseling, research, and education. *The Counseling Psychologist, 33*, 574–578.

Carlson, E. B. (1997). *Trauma assessments: A clinician's guide*. New York, NY: Guilford.

Carroll, J. S., Badger, S., Willoughby, B. J., Nelson, L. J., Madsen, S. D., & Barry, C. M. (2009). Ready or not? Criteria for marriage readiness among emerging adults. *Journal of Adolescent Research, 24*, 349–375.

Carter, R. T., Forsyth, J. M., Mazzula, S. L., & Williams, B. (2005). Racial discrimination and race-based traumatic stress: An exploratory investigation. In R. T. Carter (Ed.). *Handbook of racial-cultural psychology and counseling, Vol 2: Training and practice* (pp. 447–476). Hoboken, NJ: Wiley.

Centers for Disease Control (2015). *Suicide facts at a glance 2015*. Retrieved from www.cdc.gov/violenceprevention/pdf/suicide-datasheet-a.pdf.

Claxton, S. E., & van Dulmen, M. H. M. (2013). Casual sexual relationships and experiences in emerging adulthood. *Emerging Adulthood, 1*, 138–150.

Crocker, J., & Wolfe, C. T. (2001). Contingencies of self-worth. *Psychological Review, 108*, 593–623.

Dowdall, G. W. (2013). The role of alcohol abuse in college student victimization. In J. J. J. Sloan, & B. Fisher (Eds.), *Campus crime: Legal, social, and policy perspectives* (pp. 184–210). Springfield, IL: Thomas.

Fingerman, K. L., Chang, Y. P., Wesselmann, E. D., Zarit, S., Furstenberg, F., & Birditt, K. S. (2012). Helicopter parents and landing pad kids: Intense parental support of grown children. *Journal of Marriage and Family, 74*, 880–896.

Freedy, J. R., Monnier, J., & Shaw, D. L. (2002). Trauma screening in students attending a medical university. *Journal of American College Health, 50*, 160–167.

Galambos, N. L., Barker, E. T., & Krahn, H. J. (2006). Depression, self-esteem, and anger in emerging adulthood: Seven-year trajectories. *Developmental Psychology, 42*, 350–365.

Garlow, S. J., Rosenberg, J., Moore, J. D., Haas, A. P., Koestner, B., Hendin, H., & Nemeroff, C. B. (2008). Depression, desperation, and suicidal ideation in college students: Results from the American Foundation for Suicide Prevention College Screening Project at Emory University. *Depression and Anxiety, 25*, 482–488.

Gelinas, B. L., & Wright, K. D. (2013). The cessation of deliberate self-harm in a university sample: The reasons, barriers, and strategies involved. *Archives of Suicide Research, 17*, 373–386.

Halpern-Meekin, S., Manning, W. D., Giordano, P. C., & Longmore, M. A. (2012). Relationship churning in emerging adulthood: On/off relationships and sex with an ex. *Journal of Adolescent Research, 28,* 166–188.

Halpern-Meekin, S., Manning, W. D., Giordano, P. C., & Longmore, M. A. (2013). Relationship churning, physical violence, and verbal abuse in young adult relationships. *Journal of Marriage and Family, 75,* 2–12.

Hays, D. G., Michel, R. E., Bayne, H. B., Colburn, A. A. N., & Myers, J. S. (2015). Counseling with HEART: A relationship violence prevention program for college students. *Journal of College Counseling, 18,* 49–65.

Heath, N. L., Toste, J. R., Nedecheva, T., & Charlebois, A. (2008). An examination of nonsuicidal self-injury among college students. *Journal of Mental Health Counseling, 30,* 137–156.

Hingson, R. W., & White, A. M. (2012). Prevalence and consequences of college student alcohol use. In C. J. Correia, J. G. Murphy, & N. P. Barnett (Eds.), *College student alcohol abuse: A guide to assessment, intervention, and prevention* (pp. 13–25). Hoboken, NJ: Wiley.

Kilmer, J. R., & Logan, D. E. (2012). Applying harm-reduction strategies on college campuses. In C. J. Correia, J. G. Murphy, & N. P. Barnett (Eds.), *College student alcohol abuse: A guide to assessment, intervention, and prevention* (pp. 146–165). Hoboken, NJ: Wiley.

King, C. A., Eisenberg, D., Zheng, K., Czyz, E., Kramer, A., Horwitz, A., & Chermack, S. (2015). Online suicide risk screening and intervention with college students: A pilot randomized controlled trial. *Journal of Consulting and Clinical Psychology, 83,* 630–636.

Klanecky, A. K., Woolman, E. O., & Becker, M. M. (2015). Child abuse exposure, emotion regulation, and drinking refusal self-efficacy: An analysis of problem drinking in college students. *The American Journal of Drug and Alcohol Abuse, 41,* 188–196.

Klonsky, E. D., & Moyer, A. (2008). Childhood sexual abuse and non-suicidal self-injury: Meta-analysis. *The British Journal of Psychiatry, 192,* 166–170.

Konick, L. C., & Gutierrez, P. M. (2005). Testing a model of suicide ideation in college students. *Suicide and Life-Threatening Behavior, 35,* 181–192.

Kress, V. E., Newgent, R. A., Whitlock, J., & Mease, L. (2015). Spirituality/religiosity, life satisfaction, and life meaning as protective factors for nonsuicidal self-injury in college students. *Journal of College Counseling, 18,* 160–174.

Lakey, C. E., Hirsch, J. K., Nelson, L. A., & Nsamenang, S. A. (2014). Effects of contingent self-esteem on depressive symptoms and suicidal behavior. *Death Studies, 38,* 563–570.

Lancaster, P. G., Moore, J. T., Putter, S. E., Chen, P. Y., Cigularov, K. P., Baker, A., & Quinnett, P. (2014). Feasibility of a web-based gatekeeper training: Implications for suicide prevention. *Suicide and Life-Threatening Behavior, 44,* 510–523.

Lewis, S. P., & Arbuthnott, A. E. (2012). Nonsuicidal self-injury: Characteristics, functions, and strategies. *Journal of College Student Psychotherapy, 26,* 185–200. doi:10.1080/87568225.2012.685853

Lewis, S. P., & Baker, T. G. (2011). The possible risks of self-injury web sites: A content analysis. *Archives of Suicide Research, 15,* 390–396.

Linehan, M. M. (1993). *Cognitive-behavioral treatment of borderline personality disorder.* New York, NY: Guilford.

Lowe, K., Dotterer, A. M., & Francisco, J. (2015). 'If I pay, I have a say!': Parental payment of college education and its association with helicopter parenting. *Emerging Adulthood, 3,* 286–290.

Luscombe, B. (2016, April 11). Porn and the threat to virility. *Time, 187*, 40–47.

Michikyan, M., Subrahmanyam, K., & Dennis, J. (2015). Facebook use and academic performance among college students: A mixed-methods study with a multi-ethnic sample. *Computers in Human Behavior, 45*, 265–272.

Muise, A., Christofides, E., & Desmarais, S. (2009). More information than you ever wanted: Does Facebook bring out the green-eyed monster of jealousy? *Cyberpsychology and Behavior, 12*, 441–444.

Nadal, K. L., Wong, Y., Griffin, K. E., Davidoff, K., & Sriken, J. (2014). The adverse impact of racial microaggressions on college students' self-esteem. *Journal of College Student Development, 55*, 461–474.

Nadorff, M. R., Nazem, S., & Fiske, A. (2013). Insomnia symptoms, nightmares, and suicide risk: Duration of sleep disturbance matters. *Suicide and Life-Threatening Behavior, 43*, 139–149.

Neff, K. D. (2003). Self-compassion: An alternative conceptualization of a healthy attitude toward oneself. *Self and Identity, 2*, 85–101.

Neighbors, C., Foster, D. W., Fossos, N., & Lewis, M. A. (2012). Events and contexts associated with extreme drinking. In C. J. Correia, J. G. Murphy, & N. P. Barnett (Eds.), *College student alcohol abuse: A guide to assessment, intervention, and prevention* (pp. 42–56). Hoboken, NJ: Wiley.

Nelson, L. J., Padilla-Walker, L. M., Carroll, J. S., Madsen, S. D., Barry, C. M., & Badger, S. (2007). "If you want me to treat you like an adult, start acting like one!" Comparing the criteria that emerging adults and their parents have for adulthood. *Journal of Family Psychology, 21*, 665–674.

Nelson, L. J., Padilla-Walker, L. M., Christensen, K. J., Evans, C. A., & Carroll, J. S. (2011). Parenting in emerging adulthood: An examination of parenting clusters and correlates. *Journal of Youth and Adolescence, 40*, 730–743.

Nemeroff, C. B., Bremner, J. D., Foa, E. B., Mayberg, H. S., North, C. S., & Stein, M. B. (2006). Posttraumatic stress disorder: A state-of-the-science review. *Journal of Psychiatric Research, 40*, 1–21.

Nock, M. K., Prinstein, M. J., & Sterba, S. K. (2009). Revealing the form and function of self-injurious thoughts and behaviors: A real-time ecological assessment study among adolescents and young adults. *Journal of Abnormal Psychology, 118*, 816–827.

Nordstrom, A. H., Goguen, L. S., & Hiester, M. (2014). The effect of social anxiety and self-esteem on college adjustment, academics, and retention. *Journal of College Counseling, 17*, 48–63.

Padilla-Walker, L. M., Nelson, L. J., & Carroll, J. S. (2012). Affording emerging adulthood: Parental financial assistance of their college-aged children. *Journal of Adult Development, 19*, 50–58.

Pasha, H. S., & Munaf, S. (2013). Relationship of self-esteem and adjustment in traditional university students. *Procedia - Social and Behavioral Sciences, 84*, 999–1004.

Patros, C. G., Hudec, K. L., Alderson, R. M., Kasper, L. J., Davidson, C., & Wingate, L. R. (2013). Symptoms of attention-deficit/hyperactivity disorder (ADHD) moderate suicidal behaviors in college students with depressed mood. *Journal of Clinical Psychology, 69*, 980–993.

Pew Research Center (2016). Analysis of Census Data. Retrieved from www. Pewsocialtrends.org.

Pistorello, J., Fruzzetti, A. E., MacLane, C., Gallop, R., & Iverson, K. M. (2012). Dialectical behavior therapy (DBT) applied to college students: A randomized clinical trial. *Journal of Consulting and Clinical Psychology, 80*, 982–994.

Ritchie, R. A., Meca, A., Madrazo, V. L., Schwartz, S. J., Hardy, S. A., Zamboanga, B. L.,… Lee, R. M. (2013). Identity dimensions and related processes in emerging adulthood: Helpful or harmful? *Journal of Clinical Psychology, 69*, 415–432.

Ryeng, M. S., Kroger, J., & Martinussen, M. (2013). Identity status and self-esteem: A meta-analysis. *Identity: An International Journal of Theory and Research, 13*, 201–213.

Schoeni, R., & Ross, K. (2005). Material assistance received from families during the transition to adulthood. In R. A. Settersten Jr., F. F. Furstenberg Jr., & R. G. Rumbaut (Eds.), *On the frontier of adulthood: Theory, research and public policy* (pp. 396–416). Chicago, IL: The University of Chicago Press.

Sharkin, B. S. (2006). *College students in distress: A resource guide for faculty, staff, and campus community.* Binghamton, NY: Haworth.

Shulman, S., & Connolly, J. (2013). The challenge of romantic relationships in emerging adulthood: Reconceptualization of the field. *Emerging Adulthood, 1*, 27–39.

Silva, C., Chu, C., Monahan, K. R., & Joiner, T. E. (2015). Suicide risk among sexual minority college students: A mediated moderation model of sex and perceived burdensomeness. *Psychology of Sexual Orientation and Gender Diversity, 2*, 22–33.

Soenens, B., Berzonsky, M. D., & Papini, D. R. (2016). Attending to the role of identity exploration in self-esteem: Longitudinal associations between identity styles and two features of self-esteem. *International Journal of Behavioral Development, 40*, 420–430.

Taylor, J. J., Papay, K. A., Webb, J. B., & Reeve, C. L. (2016). The good, the bad, and the interactive: Evaluative concerns perfectionism moderates the effect of personal strivings perfectionism on self-esteem. *Personality and Individual Differences, 95*, 1–5.

Tedeschi, R. G., & Calhoun, L. G. (2004). Target Article: 'Posttraumatic Growth: Conceptual Foundations and Empirical Evidence'. *Psychological Inquiry, 15*, 1–18.

Townsend, E., Hawton, K., Altman, D. G., Arensman, E., Gunnell, D., Hazell, P., & Van Heeringen, K. (2001). The efficacy of problem-solving treatments after deliberate self-harm: Meta-analysis of randomized controlled trials with respect to depression, hopelessness and improvement in problems. *Psychological Medicine, 31*, 979–988.

Van Dusen, J. P., Tiamiyu, M. F., Kashdan, T. B., & Elhai, J. D. (2015). Gratitude, depression and PTSD: Assessment of structural relationships. *Psychiatry Research, 230*, 867–870.

van Ingen, D. J., Freheit, S. R., Steinfeldt, J. A., Moore, L. L., Wimer, D. J., Knutt, A. D.,… Roberts, A. (2015). Helicopter parenting: The effect of an overbearing caregiving style on peer attachment and self-efficacy. *Journal of College Counseling, 18*, 7–20.

Wester, K. L., & Trepal, H. C. (2010). Coping behaviors, abuse history, and counseling: Differentiating college students who self-Injure. *Journal of College Counseling, 13*, 141–154.

White, H. R., McMorris, B. J., Catalano, R. F., Fleming, C. B., Haggerty, K. P., & Abbott, R. D. (2006). Increases in alcohol and marijuana use during the transition out of high school into emerging adulthood: The effects of leaving home, going to college, and high school protective factors. *Journal of Studies on Alcohol, 67*, 810–822.

Whitlock, J., Eckenrode, J., & Silverman, D. (2006). Self-injurious behaviors in a college population. *Pediatrics, 117*, 1939–1948.

Whitlock, J., Muehlenkamp, J., & Eckenrode, J. (2008). Variation in nonsuicidal self-injury: Identification and features of latent classes in a college population of emerging adults. *Journal of Clinical Child and Adolescent Psychology, 37*, 725–735.

Whitlock, J., Muehlenkamp, J., Eckenrode, J., Purington, A., Baral Abrams, G., Barreira, P., & Kress, V. (2013). Nonsuicidal self-injury as a gateway to suicide in young adults. *Journal of Adolescent Health, 52*, 486–492.

Whitlock, J., Muehlenkamp, J., Purington, A., Eckenrode, J., Barreira, P., Baral Abrams, G.,... Knox, K. (2011). Nonsuicidal self-injury in a college population: General trends and sex differences. *Journal of American College Health, 59,* 691–698.

Whitlock, J., Prussien, K., & Pietrusza, C. (2015). Predictors of self-injury cessation and subsequent psychological growth: Results of a probability sample survey of students in eight universities and colleges. *Child and Adolescent Psychiatry and Mental Health, 9* doi:10.1186/s13034-015-0048-5

Willoughby, B. J., Hersh, J. N., Padilla-Walker, L. M., & Nelson, L. J. (2015). "Back off"! Helicopter parenting and a retreat from marriage among emerging adults. *Journal of Family Issues, 36,* 669–692.

Wouters, S., Duriez, B., Luyckx, K., Klimstra, T., Colpin, H., Soenens, B., & Verschueren, K. (2013). Depressive symptoms in university freshmen: Longitudinal relations with contingent self-esteem and level of self-esteem. *Journal of Research in Personality, 47,* 356–363.

8

THE ROLE OF PARENTS IN EMERGING ADULTHOOD

*Richard Mullendore, Christina Daniel,
and Michael Toney*

The lens of emerging adulthood creates an important opportunity for student affairs practitioners to reconceptualize how we work with family members in supporting their college students. As student populations evolve and diversify, it is increasingly important for us to understand the impact of family in creating effective learning environments. The college years become some of the most important for an emerging adult as students begin to navigate and negotiate adulthood and the intersection of this new state with their parental relationships. Students, many for the first time, have diminished parental supervision, test independent decision-making, and take on more personal and financial responsibilities. Utilizing Arnett's theory as a backdrop, this chapter will explore the five features of emerging adulthood as they relate to the student-family relationship and provide recommendations for practitioners to consider and implement in their work.

It is important to note at the outset that the term "parents" is being used in this chapter as a generic descriptor of the relationship between the emerging adult and other significant adults, including, but not limited to single parents, step-parents, grandparents, same sex parents, etc.

In 1975, Head Resident Advisors at Michigan State University received multiple sets of instructions regarding fall semester move-in day. One of those instructions clearly indicated that parents may assist students with moving in their belongings and initial room set up; they were then to be strongly encouraged to leave immediately. And they did! No trips to Walmart or Target; no dinner in a fine local restaurant; no picnic with the president; no parent/family orientation program; and no invitation to return for a weekend in the fall.

As parents left the campus, they did so trusting their student's ability to navigate the college bureaucracy, and they trusted the college to operate in the best interest of their student. "Students valued the responsibility to speak for themselves and solve their own problems, and were uniformly mortified by any suggestion of an alternative arrangement" (Jackson & Murphy, 2005, p. 53).

Twenty years later, some colleges were beginning to understand that parents were not the enemy; instead, they could be helpful as retention agents and financial contributors (Mullendore, 1998). Parent-student relationships were changing and evolving into partnerships as the cost of higher education increased rapidly and customer service became an important issue. Parents started to intervene on behalf of their students regarding financial aid, academic, and disciplinary issues. Parent orientation programs were developed, parent associations and parent councils were in the early stages of formation, and parent-family weekends were becoming common.

Between 1995 and 2005, it seems that everything changed. Parents not only joined their students on precollege tours but also enrolled their students in test-prep courses, assisted with completing college applications, attended orientation sessions, negotiated financial aid packages, sat in on academic advising sessions, and contacted the college if there was a roommate conflict. Students communicated frequently with their parents as the cell phone gained popularity, leading one student affairs vice president to call the cell phone the "world's longest umbilical cord" (Shellenbarger, 2005).

New terms were developed to describe parents (helicopters, lawn mowers, stealth bombers, etc.) who intervened on behalf of their students. But the reality was that students and their parents were closer than previous generations, combined with the fact that college was a major financial investment, "too important to risk it being sidetracked or undermined by a novice" (Mullendore, Banahan, & Ramsey, 2005, p. 2). True, some parents stepped over the invisible line; for example, one mother rented an apartment in Paris so she could monitor her daughter's study abroad experience. Another mother attended the college's career fair and distributed her son's resume since he was "too busy" to attend. Many parents have contacted faculty members (and still do) to demand explanations for grades their students received.

During the college years, traditional age students, as emerging adults, struggle with Arnett's (2015) three cornerstones for becoming adults: accepting responsibility for oneself, making independent decisions, and becoming financially independent. Students today do not mind, and in fact, encourage parent involvement in academic, financial, or personal conflicts. In one study, 71% of parents who contacted the college on their student's behalf did so at the student's request (King, Watson, & Mullendore, 2009). According to the National Survey of Student Engagement (NSSE, 2007), students whose parents intervened on their behalf exhibited greater gains on a host of desired outcomes and greater satisfaction with their educational experience. And, somewhat surprisingly, parent involvement (advice, assistance, intervention) actually supports student development (Mullendore, King, Watson, Rissmeyer, & Peralta, 2012).

To date, there is no evidence that parenting styles are changing to be less in-trusive; in fact the parent-emerging adult relationships appear to be strengthening throughout the 18–29 year age bracket. Financial, residency, and communication issues have become even more critical as the economy and traditional social values remain in transition. Student loan debt, low starting salaries, the high cost of renting, and the struggle for a home down payment have caused over 40% of emerging adults to move in with family members (Kirkham, 2016; Bleemer, Brown, Lee, & van der Klaauw, 2014). Millennials are staying single longer than any previous generation, as they decide what type of future they desire financially and romantically.

An exploration of the parent-emerging adult relationship through the college years confirms Arnett's (2015) features of emerging adulthood (identity exploration, instability, self-focus, feeling in-between, and possibilities/optimism). Two of the authors of this chapter are masters-prepared student affairs professionals who, at the time of this writing, are within the emerging adult age group. As they expand on the five features, they will do so with personal stories to bring Arnett's theory to life.

Identity Exploration

> I thought I had a diverse high school experience until my first week of classes at my undergraduate institution. Suddenly, multiple languages I could not understand filled my ears, different opinions challenged my perspective, and my understanding of personal identity changed every day. At the beginning, I tried to stay grounded in my previous conceptions of identity, mostly influenced by upbringing and family environment. Slowly, however, I started to meet more people and develop deep relationships that informed how I perceived others and myself. Indeed these interactions had a profound impact on who I am today, both personally and professionally.

The college experience, a significant component of most emerging adulthood processes, is uniquely linked to a period of personal development for students. This central question of "Who am I?" permeates changing relationships, interests, and involvements. As the first time many of our students are spending a significant amount of time away from home, the college environment significantly shapes their identity development and the evolving relationships with family. Even so, family members can carry substantial influence in the college decision-making process and what students choose to do post graduation.

Theoretical Foundations

Identity is socially constructed and reconstructed, with a significant influence of context and environment on identity (Torres, Jones, & Renn, 2009). Parents and family members are often significant players in a student's environment and can substantially impact their development throughout the college experience. Peer groups, athletics teams, and other clusters also constitute important pieces of students' environments, and thereby, their identity development.

Abes, Jones, and McEwen's (2007) exploration into students' meaning-making capacity also provides a useful lens to understanding the role of family members. Their reconceptualized Model of Multiple Dimensions of Identity specifically lists family members as a contextual influence on how individuals make meaning of their identities. The model posits a meaning-making filter that illustrates the degree to which these contextual influences impact self-perceptions of identity dimensions such as race, sexual orientation, gender, and socioeconomic status. Students just starting their college journey may have a less dense meaning-making filter that allows a lot of parental influence, whereas a graduating senior may have developed a more complex filter that limits family sway.

Now that we have frameworks in which to view identity exploration for emerging adults, there are four areas to focus on in more depth: college selection, transition, personal identity exploration, and major and career exploration. As student affairs professionals, we want students to discover who they are with and apart from their family members—while understanding the interconnectedness between those two positions.

College Selection

College selection greatly impacts the development of students and the environments in which they find themselves. Involvement from families can have an effect on continuation of current norms or branching out into something totally different. According to the Cooperative Institutional Research Program (CIRP) survey, 17.6% of students rated "my parents/relatives wanted me to come here" as very important in their college decision. In 2000, only 7.8% of students rated this factor as very important. (Eagan, Stolzenberg, Bates, Aragon, Suchard, & Rios-Aguilar, 2016). There is a clear and increasing amount of family influence in the college decision-making process as financial contributions and post-graduate career opportunities become a more significant determinant in selection criteria. The distance students move away from home or how often they visit home can also have an impact on identity exploration. The degree to which families have a role in the college selection process may continue to influence how students make meaning of their experience, as their enrollment at the institution is closely tied to a decision made with their families.

Transition

Family members often serve as an important support system for students in college and this can be especially true in the first-year transition. Given the central role technology plays in communication efforts, students and family members are more connected than ever. Students can request and receive guidance about course scheduling, roommate issues, and classroom concerns in the matter of seconds. While the common assumption is that this closer connection to families is detrimental for students' development, research shows that these relationships are often beneficial for emerging adults (Arnett, 2015). The proliferation of family weekends and dedicated family engagement offices are an institutional acknowledgement that family members are critical members in the transition and persistence of students. Throughout the college journey, students develop more microsystems that will "share space" with their families. This may lead to conflict as parents recognize some decreasing influence in their student's decision-making and identity. Indeed, students are not the same persons that left home after high school.

Personal Identity Exploration

The central question raised earlier of "Who am I?" is paramount to the personal identity exploration students pursue during emerging adulthood and their college experience. Issues of race, sexuality, gender identity, socioeconomic status, faith, political beliefs, and values are all shaped in the college crucible. Some identity development theories have included interactions with family into their frameworks. For instance, D'Augelli's (1994) theory of lesbian, gay, and bisexual development includes a stage about becoming an LGB offspring. Abes, Jones, and McEwen's (2007) model is a valuable lens to understand the shifting role families play in this exploration. Students who grow up in a rural, faith-oriented community may find that attending an institution with increased faith diversity impacts how they view religion. Their parents' faith view may not shift, but increased density of the student's meaning-making filter could limit the influence of parental values as students develop their own sense of faith identity.

Major and Career Exploration

Beyond personal identity components, emerging adults also work to clarify their career interests. In the college environment, this is most exemplified in the major selection process. Most universities articulate a belief that students should broadly explore their interests to find a major area they want to pursue deeply. But as Arnett (2015) notes, "some emerging adults enter college with a major that has been influenced strongly by their parents, only to discover it does not fit at all with their own identity" (p. 146). Today's emerging adults defy norms regarding jobs and careers. Undergraduate majors may or may not be related to employment desired, sought, or gained. And, changing jobs (even careers) on a regular basis is commonplace. Parents, many of whom worked in a single environment or career, struggle to understand the instability of their children. Higher education professionals must acknowledge the familial and financial pressures that influence a student's decision-making environment.

Instability

College students can be considered modern-day nomads: year to year, they wander from residence to residence with baskets and bins overflowing with free t-shirts and other worldly possessions. This physical change in location is symbolic of the instability during the four (or five, or six...) years of college. As residence changes, so might the plan, driven by interests/passions, worldviews, and goals that are in flux as emerging adults explore. Parents are both coauthors and co-managers of the plan as they walk closely alongside their emerging adults as they move toward adulthood. During these important college years, the plan is challenged, revisited, and adjusted as students experiment, negotiate identity, embark on new experiences, and meet obstacles. The so-called helicopters, lawn mowers, and stealth bombers are nearby to assist and intervene when problems arise.

Theoretical Foundations

College student instability is in direct relation to the first feature of emerging adulthood, identity exploration. While taking time to develop a response to the question, "Who am I?" students shift course direction many times. As we understand identity exploration through changing roles and players in the microsystem (Bronfenbrenner, 1993) and parental influence on the complexities of their student's meaning-making filter (Abes, Jones, & McEwen, 2007), it is also helpful to understand how student support through instability can be predicted and expected.

Emerging adults and their parents are in more regular communication than college students ever before. More than half (55%) communicate nearly every day with convenient means like texting, emails, and phone calls available 24/7 (Arnett & Schwab, 2013). It is evident that parents are first responder, correspondent, and a main source of support for college students. Support is one of the four main contributors to a person's ability to cope in a transition (Schlossberg, Waters, & Goodman, 1995) and for parents of emerging adults facing an abundance of transition, the role to help, love, and provide feedback is available and accessible. Students continue to experience transition after the initial adjustment to college: the very nature of the instability of emerging adulthood leads to change as a constant for students.

Understanding the increased support parents offer college students today, we can also utilize Sanford's work on challenge and support to work with students. Many college students have not practiced adult behaviors colleges and universities expect, like making their own doctor's appointments or reading instructions and completing processes, because they have had parents to take the lead. Recalling Sanford's use of readiness is distinctly applicable here, too. Some students may not be ready immediately to take personal ownership, but the transition should encourage their behavior in this direction (Sanford, 1966).

From our work with college students, we know it takes time, trial, and error for emerging adults to discover and nurture their interests, skills, and road ahead. Parent understanding of the uncertainty is key as they support their student's transition to college and numerous changes in direction thereafter. As student affairs practitioners, we should seek to partner with parents to anticipate and support student exploration.

Changing Goals

Emerging adults feel pressure to stick to the parent-approved plan and avoid disappointment. As students work toward goals and execution of the cocreated plan, they seek parental support and guidance and view the input as a positive norm (Fingerman & Yahirun, 2016). With each change of major, shifted goal, and failed experiment, emerging adults gain an additional experience necessary to piece together the end result. However, parents may view each changed or failed plan less as learning and more filled with financial burden or negative consequence. For the first time since 2010, parent contributions exceeded scholarships and grants in paying for college (Sallie Mae, 2015), thereby increasing parental stake and expected return on investment. As student affairs professionals, we understand the need for exploration and support of instability; however, parents paying for the experience may view study abroad or organization dues as another line item on a bill, not a place where their student will explore interests and potentially rewrite the plan for a better fit as their identity develops.

In addition, we know approximately 80% of college students change their major at least once, according to the National Center for Education Statistics (Wine, Janson, & Wheeless, 2011). Preparing parents for the potential major change that could result from failed coursework or newly developed interests can make for powerful partnerships with student affairs professionals. Sharing our expertise and understanding of college students through parent and family orientation or robust resources better equips parents to assist their student on the road to emerging adulthood and trust the investment in college.

Assisting expectations

Between the ages of 18–24 I moved thirteen times; my parents loaded the truck and trailer to accommodate each. Some were simple moves from the residence hall to their home for the summer (about an hour away), while others involved more advanced planning for a move several states away. While unstable in residence, each move had purpose and supported personal discovery of both success and failure in love, work, and educational goals. In the first few changes of address, parents were necessary to grant permission, pay the down payment, and actively participate in decision-making. In later decisions, conversations evolved to seeking counsel and input prior to more independent decision-making. As parent financial contribution waned, the personal responsibility and autonomy increased.

The role of the student affairs professional is to help parents expect changes to the plan and equip them to provide the necessary support and guidance as a first responder. Especially in the early college years, students have just been introduced to more independent decision-making and may not be ready to make housing, internship, or other decisions that may affect the plan without parent input. Recently, a student reneged on his student leader position to pursue an alternative summer internship. In that conversation, he offered that he wanted to tell his supervisor that he planned to quit sooner, likely before signing an employment contract, but heeded the advice of his parents who encouraged him against saying anything. In college, parent persuasion can still trump a supervisory conversation or reasonable job expectations.

Physical proximity to and instructions from the supervisor were both outdone by parent input from over six hours away. This first-year student communicated more frequently with and relied more directly on parent counsel. As student affairs professionals, we can acknowledge the important role families play in decision-making and offer dissonance and alternative perspective to students in similar situations. After the decision, our conversation can encourage emerging adults to consider more than parent guidance and an insular view of the situation.

Self-Focus

For me (and likely all of the authors), college presented the first time I could exercise autonomy over my daily actions and decisions. The first winter break, however, is often where the shift in self-focus begins to reveal changing norms. I lived within an hour's distance from my hometown, so I could come home for a weekend here and there or have dinner with my family on occasion. With a break's longer time frame, though, I was suddenly back into a home environment that seemed incredibly restrictive compared to the freedom of the college residence hall. Whether true or not, I felt all my actions were questioned or pressured by the presence of my parents. In a matter of months, my increase in self-focus created some tension in the relationship. Over the years, we have had (and continue) to renegotiate the parent-child dynamic in a way that honors the patterns of emerging adulthood.

Emerging adulthood presents many challenges similar to this one—how to navigate becoming you in and around the constraints of your environment.

Student affairs professionals can play a critical support role in helping our students and families develop new relationships and realities. Given the significant amount of development occurring in the college years, it is natural for there to be a high degree of self-focus during the emerging adulthood process. More or less released from the parent-monitored and structured routine of school prior to college, emerging adults are deciding what they want to do, who they are, and where they want to go—all before the perceived constraints of older age, career, and marriage limits their ability to explore. It is critical for student affairs educators to create space for students to prioritize their own sense of self, wellness, and exploration during college.

Each of our functional areas shares in this responsibility in distinct and interconnected ways. For example:

- Orientation programs help to prepare family members to let go and support students from afar, while priming students to take ownership of their own affairs
- Residence Life staff members are on the ground working with students on a daily basis to make healthy choices
- Career Services practitioners help students to reflect on their personal interests and passions and create professional opportunities
- Counseling professionals guide our students through their experiences to support their personal wellbeing

There is a wealth of literature related to the role of self-focus during the college experience. One of the seminal student development texts, *Education and Identity* (Chickering & Reisser, 1993), highlights the process of moving through autonomy toward interdependence. This includes being able to function without constant reassurances and approval from others, while also self-directing actions. The authors further discuss vectors that range from establishing identity to developing integrity—all strengthened by a focus on the self during the college experience. Baxter Magolda's (1992) work on self-authorship deepens this research. The key components of self-authorship emphasize the process of developing an individual's internal voice, learning to cultivate it, trust it, and act in alignment with it. These voices are often honed and clarified during the college experience, and Baxter Magolda provides recommendations for educators looking to help students in their self-authorship journeys.

It is important, however, to discuss how this particular feature (like most) is impacted by cultural contexts. Our high regard for independence and individuality is deeply embedded in American culture. International students or students from nonmajority ethnicities may find that our insistence on self-focus clashes with what was taught and valued in their households. This degree of self-focus can also look different for students who identify as first-generation or low-income. These students may have to balance finding themselves while maintaining close ties to their families and home environments. Some low-income students may have to send money home to help their families with finances. First-generation students may struggle negotiating the college environment that promotes independence and a family environment that values closeness and shared decision-making. We might find similar struggles with our commuting students, physically and mentally moving through environments that may offer different messages on a daily basis.

Feeling In-Between

Both students and parents can feel the push-pull of students establishing themselves as adults—then reverting to say "not *yet*"—during the college years. The in-between is especially noticed as boundaries are tested and students have sights set on experimentation toward adulthood. While finances play the largest role, college programs and experiences like study abroad, internships, and student leadership positions seek to teach emerging adults how to tackle all three of Arnett's cornerstones of adulthood: personal responsibility, independent decision making, and financial independence. Institutions provide information about and access to experiences that create opportunities for dissonance and movement toward adulthood, but students often hand the bill to parents to fund these experiences.

> I can recall sitting at our family desktop computer, in the early 2000s, frustrated and upset that I was expected to fill out my FAFSA form and plug in my parents' financial information. I had no exposure to this type of financial information, had never earned a paycheck, struggled to answer the questions, and irresponsibly wrote down parent salary and social security numbers on a Post-It that my mother probably scolded me for and then appropriately shredded. From my interactions with college student parents now, in these short ten years, the process has stayed a partnership, but responsibility has tilted further, and in some cases completely, to parents.

Prior to students reaching 18 years of age, parents play a huge role in assisting new emerging adults to college doors. They navigate college application and admission, decide which school(s) and career path(s) offer the best return on investment (ROI), advocate for scholarships, assist with financial aid applications, and travel with students to visit, tour, and deposit at their future homes. This process has cumbersome forms and strict deadlines, and uses a language familiar to insiders to the institution, but not always welcoming to first-generation parents, parents who are years removed, or distracted students focused on high school sports, proms, and graduations. Some parents of emerging adults coddle, hand-hold, and, maybe, take on too active a role in this process.

Playing such an active role in high school (through parent portals, and easily accessible teachers and administrators) and in the application process (through guidance counselors and college fairs), parents meet the college years with resistance, and we label them as helicopters and bulldozers interrupting our work with their students. The Family Educational Rights and Privacy Act (FERPA) calls for a complete "180" from how parents have parented for 18 years. They are expected to finance their student's future, but the institution communicates the details directly with the student. This does not account for many students' lack of preparation and, again as Sanford (1966) would identify, readiness to be responsible for something they are not financing. This push-pull is clear when independent decision-making can be stifled by the investors (parents) who are perceived as the ultimate decision-makers.

Shedding further light on the impact of parental financial contributions on successful navigation to adulthood, Hamilton (2016) provided thought-provoking insight and possible conclusions for today's approach to college parenting. She identified five parenting approaches characterized by varying levels of financial support and parental influence. In general, she concluded that parenting styles that provide complete funding and high contact with the student can inhibit growth in responsibility and progress toward adulthood. Conversely, a completely hands-off (low contact) approach with little to no funding saw students taking greater ownership of their decisions, but with lower academic performance and diminished financial returns. The conclusions Hamilton draws suggest that socioeconomic status might be a factor in the role of parents in college students' lives. True to this feature of emerging adulthood, an *in-between* approach to college parenting, in which parents provided some financial support and were available to provide timely guidance when needed, increased students' likelihood of persisting in college, effectively managing debt, and valuing parental support, as they tested and moved toward independence.

Emerging adults have repackaged how to navigate the in-between into the colloquial term "adulting" and redefined these once assumed behaviors (paying bills, grocery shopping, operating an iron, etc.) as taxing and unnecessarily burdensome. Emerging adults have even created how-to books with "468 easy(ish) steps" to figure out what to do after dining halls no longer provide dinner, takeout every night conflicts with financial independence, and parents are no longer available to serve dinner (Brown, 2013).

> When I think of my advisors and supervisors in college, these were the student affairs professionals who became an additional sounding board— for decisions related to jobs or student organizations, but also for my personal relationships, finances, and major post-graduation decisions. I viewed them as armed with the wisdom of *real* adults, but without the burden of heavy expectations and guilt that could come from disappointing my parents with mistakes made, changes of direction, or decisions

that affected them financially. Often, these advisors and mentors provided counsel, support, and encouragement for my decision-making.

Providing company for students as they figure out how to "adult" is a daily responsibility for student affairs professionals (Baxter Magolda, 2002). As students find themselves negotiating the in-between, student affairs professionals should provide the space for reflection and guidance through various learning labs (student organizations, study abroad trips, etc.) that allow students to take ownership of a specific role or responsibility, decide how to manage and allocate resources, or make decisions.

Possibilities/Optimism

Emerging adulthood is filled with a sense of possibilities that can simultaneously energize and overwhelm. In the college setting, we capitalize on this notion of possibility in our signature entry and exit points. College orientation and welcome week programs bring in students with big fanfare and speeches about what they can expect and explore over the next four years. Commencement ceremonies look to graduates' *next* future and predict the achievements that will come. For most students, family members are present at both of these points—integral partners that help shape possible futures.

Context is important in examining possibilities and optimism. We have seen drastic shifts in what emerging adults look to do with their lives in just the past 50 years. One of the coauthors who attended college in the late sixties reflects on his own emerging adulthood in order to compare experiences of today's youth:

> For students who left home for college, parents were distant encouragers and enforcers. It was not unusual for parents to drop the student off at the residence hall, and head back home the same day. College orientations were NOT for parents. Communication generally occurred once or twice a month via a pay phone and a collect call home. Once, when this writer's grades were not "up to standard," his parents refused to accept the charges for the obligatory Sunday phone call after mid term grades were sent to the student's permanent home address and were therefore intercepted.
>
> As students became college graduates, corporations had multiple job offers awaiting those who did not have to enter the armed services. The economy was in great shape, student debt was virtually non-existent, and the future (beyond the war) looked wonderful. Graduates got married and bought homes or traveled and worked at a variety of jobs while they were "finding themselves." The idea of moving home with parents wasn't a desirable or viable option for either party. During three years of traveling much of the US after college in an old VW van, picking up interesting hitchhikers provided unforgettable memories for this

writer; and eventually (somehow) led to graduate degrees and a wonderful 41-year career in college student affairs administration.

College wasn't an option for most emerging adults, however, but manufacturing and other job opportunities remained stable. These youth could make a decent living, afford a home, and seemed to be optimistic and idealistic when looking toward the possibilities of the future as society, education and corporations were changing in some exciting ways.

Fast forward to today's emerging adults and the similarities and differences from the 60s are sharp. Everyone is encouraged to attend college, and colleges are being held accountable for their graduation rates. Mental health providers, career counselors, academic advisors, activities programmers and health professionals, among others, are available to assist students over every hurdle. Parents are in constant contact with their student and the college to help navigate the collegiate bureaucracies. Upon graduation, many emerging adults choose to return home short or long term for a variety of reasons, and today's parents are supportive of the move.

For another coauthor who completed his undergraduate degree in the early 2010s, the role of family enormously impacted his sense of optimism in emerging adulthood. Financial support throughout college allowed him to graduate with little financial obligation post graduation. While his parents were skeptical of his plans to enter into graduate school for a master's degree in education, they mostly supported him—and challenged when appropriate. With their support, this author was able to create his own path that diverged from the one initially set out, but ultimately ended up a successful one.

For many, college is the turning point for those in emerging adulthood to take ownership of their lives and begin exploring opportunities to develop their authentic selves. Surrounded by supportive peers and professionals, students can explore interests and identities that were perhaps previously disregarded in their home environment. Moreover, student activism is once again on the rise on numerous college campuses. Their protests are rooted in an idealism that things can change with active engagement in disrupting discriminatory systems.

Our current employment climate has shifted the role of college for some families. While admissions officers and faculty members will espouse the importance of learning and investing in a "traditional" college experience, 60.1% of first-time freshmen indicated that the ability of graduates to obtain good jobs was very important in their college decision (Eagan et al., 2016). Student debt concerns are at an all-time high as well. These anxieties can cause students to reshape their possibilities through college choice, major choice, involvements, and career exploration.

Recent research indicates that

> rising income inequality has eroded the ability for American children to grow up to earn more than their parents.... . The research...estimates that

only half the children born in the 1980s grew up to earn more than their parents did (at age 30), after adjusting for inflation.

(Tankersley, December 11, 2016, p. A21)

These data show the impact that the current employment climate has on emerging adults. At an age when idealism is usually the norm, how will today's emerging adults maintain their optimism about the possibilities for the future?

Student affairs professionals certainly have a role to play as students consider their possibilities. What is the role of student involvement in and outside the classroom in helping students prepare for life after college? How can students be counseled regarding debt obligations? What role does the debt play in decisions to live at home after college and take jobs that are unfulfilling in order to have a paycheck? And will this generation remain optimistic?

Conclusion

In preparing this chapter, it has become clear that Arnett's (2015) theory of emerging adulthood has tremendous relevance to student affairs administrators and educators. The authors are excited that the emerging adult conceptualization will now be entering the student affairs arena of literature. Practitioners and professors are encouraged to examine Arnett's theory, specifically the five features of emerging adulthood to see how they can utilize awareness of these features in their work and/or their classrooms.

Each of the five features (identity explorations, instability, self-focus, feeling in-between, and possibilities/optimism) should resonate with anyone who works with the traditional age (and beyond) college student population. The brief personal stories shared in this chapter were but a few of what could have been a lengthy document in and of itself, and readers hopefully can relate to these stories and reflect on their own transitions through emerging adulthood.

The impact of parent/family involvement in the lives of college students cannot be underestimated. The trend that began slowly, as student retention emerged as a consideration for those colleges that (financially) needed to retain students, has blossomed into an entirely new functional area for all colleges to embrace. Orientation, counseling, career services, housing, health services, financial aid, admissions, academic advising, classroom teaching, and other institutional functions have all been greatly impacted by parents and their desire to see their students succeed. Parents are not helicopters, lawn mowers, stealth bombers, or kamikaze pilots; they are strong advocates in their children's journey through life. What is different today is the length and depth of their involvement and the willingness for professionals to embrace the partnership.

In this chapter, we have referred to the significant advocates for today's emerging adults as parents and family members. The impact of the extended family cannot, however, be overstated. Changing family dynamics can place college officials in uncomfortable legal arenas regarding who can communicate with whom. Continuous education regarding FERPA/HIPAA/Title IX, etc., is critical as parents and others approach the college with questions, concerns, or information.

- We recommend that an institutional philosophy for working with parents be developed and clearly communicated to all campus constituencies. It should be adaptive in understanding the cultural contexts for family relationships as well as the developmental differences of students, from incoming first-year students to graduation seniors.
- Not all students have close connections to any family members, and may have to serve as their own advocates. Faculty and administrators must not forget the legitimate needs of all students.
- If the institution does not have an office devoted full time to parent services, it should identify a point person to handle parent issues and concerns.
- Faculty and staff should be educated regarding the positive impact that parents can have on the college environment. Because their work to prepare orientation programs involves communication and collaboration with virtually every office on campus, orientation professionals are well equipped and positioned to educate the campus community.
- Utilize emerging adults employed as professional staff or graduate students to provide their perspectives, experiences, and recommendations for communication.
- Finally, we recommend that Arnett's theory of emerging adulthood serve as a framework for sharing with parents and college staff and faculty why we encourage certain programs or have certain processes.

References

Abes, E. S., Jones, S. R., & McEwen, M. K. (2007). Reconceptualizing the model of multiple dimensions of identity: The role of meaning-making capacity in the construction of multiple identities. *Journal of College Student Development, 48*, 1–22.

Arnett, J. J. (2015). *Emerging adulthood* (2nd ed.). New York, NY: Oxford University Press.

Arnett, J. J., & Schwab, J. (2013). *The Clark University poll of parents of emerging adults.* Worcester, MA: Clark University.

Baxter Magolda, M. B. (1992). *Knowing and reasoning in college: Gender-related patterns in students' intellectual development.* San Francisco, CA: Jossey-Bass.

Baxter Magolda, M. B. (2002). Helping students make their way to adulthood: Good company for the journey. *About Campus, 6*(6), 2–9.

Bleemer, Z., Brown, M., Lee, D., & van der Klaauw, W. (2014, November 1). Debt, jobs or housing: What's keeping millennials at home? FRB of New York Staff Report No. 700.

Bronfenbrenner, U. (1993). The ecology of cognitive development: Research models and fugitive findings. In R. H. Wozniak & K. W. Fischer (Eds.), *Development in context: Acting and thinking in specific environments* (pp. 3–44). Hillsdale, NJ: Erlbaum.

Brown, K. W. (2013). *Adulting: How to become a grown-up in 468 easy(ish) steps*. New York, NY: Grand Central.

Chickering, A. W., & Reisser, L. (1993). *Education and identity* (2nd ed.). San Francisco, CA: Jossey-Bass.

D'Augelli, A. R. (1994). Identity development and sexual orientation: Toward a model of lesbian, gay, and bisexual development. In E. J. Trickett, R. J. Watts, and D. Birman (Eds.), *Human diversity: Perspectives on people in context*. San Francisco, CA: Jossey-Bass.

Eagan, K., Stolzenberg, E. B., Bates, A. K., Aragon, M. C., Suchard, M. R., & Rios-Aguilar, C. (2016). *The American freshman: National norms fall 2015*. Cooperative Institutional Research Program. Chicago, IL: HERI.

Fingerman, K. L., & Yahirun, J. J. (2016). Emerging adulthood in the context of family. In J. J. Arnett (Ed.), *The Oxford handbook of emerging adulthood* (pp. 163–176). New York, NY: Oxford.

Hamilton, L. T. (2016). *Parenting to a degree: How family matters for college women's success*. Chicago, IL: The University of Chicago Press.

Jackson, M. L., & Murphy, S. (2005) Managing parent expectations: My how times have changed. In K. Keppler, R. H. Mullendore, & A. Carey (Eds.), *Partnering with the parents of today's college students* (pp. 53–60). Washington, DC: NASPA.

Kirkham, C. (2016, December 21). Percentage of young Americans living with parents rises to 75-year high. *Wall Street Journal*.

King, S., Watson, A., & Mullendore, R. (2009, January 14). *The impact of parent involvement on college student development: A longitudinal study, Part II. NASPA Net Results*. Retrieved February 18, 2009 from www.naspa.org/membership/mem/pubs/nr/default.cfm?id=1669

Mullendore, R. H. (1998). Including parents and families in the orientation process. In R. H. Mullendore (Ed.), *Orientation planning manual*. Bloomington, IN: National Orientation Directors Association.

Mullendore, R. H., Banahan, L. A., & Ramsey, J. L. (2005). Developing a partnership with today's college parents. In K. Keppler, R. H. Mullendore, & A. Carey (Eds.), *Partnering with the parents of today's college students* (pp. 1–10). Washington, DC: NASPA.

Mullendore, R., King, S., Watson, A., Rissmeyer, P., & Peralta, A. (2012, March). Parent involvement and student development: A four-year study. Presentation to NASPA Annual Conference, Phoenix, AZ.

National Survey of Student Engagement (NSSE). (2007). Report from the Center for Postsecondary Research, Indiana University School of Education. Bloomington, IN: Indiana University.

Sallie Mae. (2015). *How America pays for college*. Newark, DE: Report.

Sanford, N. (1966). *Self and society: Social change and individual development*. New York, NY: Atherton Press.

Schlossberg, N. K., Waters, E. B., & Goodman, J. (1995). *Counseling adults in transition: Linking practice with theory* (2nd ed.). New York, NY: Springer.

Shellenbarger, S. (2005, July 29). Colleges ward off overinvolved parents. *Wall Street Journal Online*. Retrieved July 2, 2018, https://www.wsj.com/articles/SB112250452603298007

Tankersley, J. (2016, December 11). *American dream collapses for young*. Wilmington, NC: *Wilmington Star News*.

Torres, V., Jones, S. R., & Renn, K. A. (2009). Identity development theories in student affairs: Origins, current status, and new approaches. *Journal of College Student Development, 50*(6), 577–596.

Wine, J.S., Janson, N. & Wheeless, S.C. (2011). 2004/09 Beginning postsecondary students longitudinal study. NCES handbook of survey methods. Washington, DC: U.S. Department of Education.

9

STRATEGIC ENROLLMENT MANAGEMENT FOR EMERGING ADULTS

An Organizational and Equity-Based Perspective

Jarrett B. Warshaw and James C. Hearn

The transition into emerging adulthood for many young people coincides with embarking on postsecondary plans. As they turn 18, high school graduates face a number of decisions about their educational futures and, in turn, their prospects for who they want to become and the careers they want to have. They must choose, for example, whether to attend college, the institutions to which they want to apply, the majors and cocurricular opportunities to pursue, the mechanisms for financing their education, and where, ultimately, to enroll. When they head to college, emerging adults may encounter other questions such as whether to persist to graduation, and perhaps, too, to advance to graduate programs or enter the job market. Each choice does not determine the paths and plans that unfold thereafter, but can indeed shape—and magnify—the process of moving toward adulthood.

Arnett's (2015) theory of emerging adulthood may illuminate the decisions that students make about college. As he suggests, emerging adulthood entails five main features: identity explorations, instability (in work, relationships, geographic location, etc.), self-focus, feeling in-between (e.g., no longer an adolescent but not yet an adult), and optimism for the future amid an "age of possibilities." Young people tend to experience emerging adulthood for about a decade or more, from when they turn 18 and into their early 30s. Interestingly, during a developmental stage in which they seek autonomy, more than half of emerging adults engage in daily contact by phone, e-mail, and text with their parents, and many rely on their parents for ongoing financial support and return home after college to live with them (Fingerman & Yahirun, 2016). To emerging adults, as Arnett further observes, the arrival into adulthood means taking self-responsibility, making independent decisions, and achieving financial independence. The contexts in which their development takes root, from family to institutional influences, may thus be paradoxical and empowering but also constraining life possibilities and decisions.

Not all emerging adults attend college, but participation rates in U.S. post-secondary education have grown nationally (Perna & Finney, 2014). In turn, questions arise for college leaders and practitioners about how to work with and help emerging adults and their families. The college search, enrollment, and academic support and retention processes may be especially poignant for emerging adults and merit close consideration from a campus-oriented, organizational perspective. For example, many institutions have formed divisions of strategic enrollment management (SEM) that tie together once-functionally separate operations and services of admissions, financial aid, registration, and retention (Hossler, 2015). SEM entails identifying and marketing institutional strengths and goals (Dixon, 1995), and it also reflects a substantive organizational change that can influence key decisions of emerging adults about applying to and enrolling in college, financing attendance, and persisting to graduation.

Our chapter focuses on the relationship between enrollment management and emerging adults. Additionally, it seeks to advance an equity-based perspective. College choice, enrollment, academic outcomes, and retention vary widely by socioeconomic status (SES) (e.g., Bastedo & Jaquette, 2011; Hearn, 2013; Hillman, 2013, 2014; McDonough, 1997; Perna, 2006). We emphasize, here, the *organizational constraints and contexts* that shape the various pathways within the developmental stage of emerging adulthood. Arnett (2015) suggests that a main critique of the theory of emerging adulthood centers on what observers perceive as its lack of sensitivity to SES (see also Arnett & Tanner, 2011; Silva, 2013). By including an equity-based dimension, our chapter may contribute conceptually to the application of the theory to higher education and student affairs and practically to considerations for campus-level policy and practice.

First, we focus on college choice, enrollment, selection of academic majors, and the future aspirations of students from the perspective of emerging adults. Then, we turn attention to the organizational development and characteristics of SEM, highlighting its connection to decision-points about and financial factors for college for emerging adults, and emphasize the campus perspective in this arena. Building on our discussion of SEM, we subsequently discuss implications for institutional policy and practice in the domains of enrollment management, academic advising and support, and retention. By way of conclusion, we offer closing remarks about emerging adulthood and SEM and raise questions to inform future research.

Emerging Adults' Decisions about College

There are several key factors that may influence college choice among high school graduates. At the individual level, emerging adults may have particular preferences, motivations, and future ambitions and goals that shape their postsecondary aspirations and plans (DesJardins & Toutkoushian, 2005). Financial considerations are important as well. A number of students pursue college degrees no matter how much they cost because of anticipated benefits in the labor market from their investment in education. Another faction of high school graduates may choose to enter work and careers directly without attending college and may still not prefer to seek college degrees even if they were free. In between, however, lies a group of students "on the margins" who are likely considering college but who perhaps could benefit from college guidance, academic preparation, and financial resources to encourage enrollment.

High school context, including college counseling resources and opportunities, and peer groups can inform the knowledge base that students have about college as well as college-going norms and expectations (e.g., Perna, 2006). The cues and guidance from parents and family members may be influential as well, with differing participation rates in higher education based on parents' educational attainment (Hearn, 2013). What is more, SES in terms of available financial resources and social class can limit the range of college options for students toward either end of the class spectrum.

While emerging adults perceive a nearly unlimited range of possibilities for themselves and their futures, their postsecondary opportunities are often delimited. Students from low-SES backgrounds are often concentrated in less well-funded high schools, which may limit their academic preparation and access to adequate college counseling, and they may not be able to afford to attend college without significant financial aid (Hillman, 2013). High school graduation rates across income groups have equalized nationally, but low-SES students are more likely to enroll at private, for-profit, public two-year, and non-elite public four-year institutions (College Board, 2016). Indeed, there is evidence to suggest less direct forms of involvement of low-SES families in the school and educational lives of students (e.g., Lareau, 2011). Such dynamics may restrict considerably the window of options available to low-SES students.

High-SES students may face strong *normative* constraints that pressure them to attend the "right" college. As McDonough (1997) observes of high-SES students and families,

> Many parents and students alike are cued in to attending the 'right college,' and believe that the best investment in college will come from acceptance at a well-known, elite institution. Parents also are aware that going to a selective college increases one's social standing, contacts, and income potential. This knowledge, however tacit, is chilling to suburbia, where downward mobility is dreaded.
>
> *(p. 120)*

To this end, researchers and analysts suggest, the very lives of high-SES high school students, from formal schooling to involvement in activities and clubs, seem to center on strategies to achieve the penultimate goal of going to competitive, selective colleges (e.g., Avery, Fairbanks, & Zeckhauser, 2003).

College choice entwines students, families, and institutions, and can thus represent expressions of individual identity and class status. For example, high-ability low-SES students (and particularly those who are the first in their families to attend college) tend to "undermatch." That is, they may not apply to institutions whose quality and selectivity match their qualifications, and if they do apply, they enroll at less competitive colleges whose profiles are below their academic achievement levels. Undermatching could be related to financial aid, lack of clear, helpful information about the cost of attendance, and cultural mismatches between students and the campus climate and culture (see, for example, Hoxby & Turner, 2013). High-ability low-SES students could potentially benefit the most from attending selective colleges and universities, but are likely to enroll in institutions that keep them "running in place" in terms of social mobility (Bastedo & Jaquette, 2011).

On the other hand, high-SES students tend to gain disproportionate access to college in general and to elite institutions in particular (Karabel, 2005; Hearn & Rosinger, 2014; Warshaw, Henne-Ochoa, & Murray, 2017). High-ability high-SES students may have the scholastic skills to receive admittance to top colleges and universities, but even those who are not as academically talented may still have the pedigree, college-related knowledge and guidance, and financial means for access (Golden, 2006). While access to college has broadened among different student populations nationally, SES-related constraints are still associated with differentiated—and increasingly stratified—types of educational opportunities for students (Belasco, Rosinger, & Hearn, 2015).

It may be helpful to clarify the relationship between families and institutions, especially around admissions and the daily college experiences of students. There has been growing attention in the higher-education research literature to "parental involvement," defined as family members' engagement in the curricular and cocurricular activities of students and the expressed interest in their day-to-day lives and overall well-being (Wartman & Savage, 2008; Wolf, Sax, & Harper, 2009). The popular press tends to portray extreme cases of parental involvement, in which parents' involvement in college students' lives becomes counterproductive (Joyce, 2014). However, contrary to such depictions, academic researchers have maintained that the interactions between parents and institutions and between parents and students are usually helpful and constructive (Harper, Sax, & Wolf, 2012; Shoup, Gonyea, & Kuh 2009).

One context in which emerging adults work through their own preferences and family and institutional influences is in their choice of academic majors. As Arnett (2015) observes, the first two years of college, prior to declaration of a major, often serves as a period of identity exploration for emerging adult undergraduates. Such a perspective suggests that the very structure of college allows for an extended period of exploration of curriculum to test various academic possibilities and, by extension, individual identities. Some students may select majors and formulate career paths aligned with family influences only to realize that another program may be better suited to their interests and goals. Indeed, many students switch their majors multiple times throughout college. The percentage of students who switch majors in college may vary by campus, but, over the years, observers suggest that about 75% of first-time, full-time degree-seeking undergraduates change majors at least once (Gordon, 1995), and the average student will change majors about three times while in college (Ramos, 2013).

Even as students resolve their academic explorations by choosing their majors, persistence to graduation poses another hurdle. Issues of motivation, as well as inadequate or unhealthy coping mechanisms, may in part preclude student success. Given the rising costs of attending college, both in the public and private, nonprofit sectors, affordability and finances may shape decisions about persistence as well (Hillman, 2013). Additionally, students may find that they do not fit their institutions based on campus curricular and cocurricular opportunities, culture, and climate (Tinto, 1993) and lack meaningful contact with faculty both in and beyond the classroom (Tinto, 2006). Some may leave college due to family circumstances, such as needing to care for their parents or siblings, or for their own health reasons.

Organizational dynamics inform the contexts and constraints within which emerging adults make decisions about applying to and enrolling in college, finding a major, and persisting to graduation. Colleges and universities are adapting in structure, operations, programs, and finances and in ways that respond to, but that may also intensify, student experiences of emerging adulthood. Next, we discuss the core aspects of SEM, an organizational reform that carries implications for emerging adults in relation to admissions, financial aid, registration, and retention.

Strategic Enrollment Management

As colleges and universities work to meet their enrollment and financial goals, many have developed deliberate, targeted approaches to guide their decision-making. Organizational reforms in this arena suggest the increasing adoption and utilization of SEM (Kraatz, Ventresca, & Deng, 2010). As Hossler (2004, 2015) has observed, SEM entails coordinated efforts to streamline and integrate once-functionally separate domains of admissions, financial aid, and registration and retention. The maneuver suggests a *structural component* of folding distinct departments into a single division, typically under the purview of a Vice President for Enrollment Management, and an *operational dimension* of facilitating the sharing of student information and files and coordinating efforts around core institutional interests.

The specific features and characteristics of SEM may vary among campuses, but tend to concentrate on four overarching objectives. As Dixon (1995) suggests, SEM focuses on:

- Defining and marketing the distinctive purposes and characteristics of one's institution to compete for students;
- Incorporating relevant campus constituencies into marketing planning and actions;
- Making strategic decisions on critical financial-aid policies; and
- Using restructuring and budgeting reforms to create the organizational conditions for success in these efforts.

By implementing SEM-oriented initiatives, institutional leaders have marketed to broad student populations and shaped the distribution of enrollment and financial resources to improve access and equity. SEM has thus become a prominent institution-level approach to mitigating postsecondary barriers for low-SES students (Hearn, Warshaw, & Ciarimboli, 2016), but its financial aspects, of optimizing both the distribution of financial aid and also tuition and fee revenues, can be difficult to balance effectively.

Consider the erosion of "need blind" admissions policies that coincides with SEM. "Need blind" admissions refers to policies to admit and fund students without consideration of families' financial means to pay for college. With SEM, however, the proportion of institutional resources allocated as merit instead of need-based aid has risen and often targets high-achieving, high SES-students who are already likely to attend college but whose scholarship awards may sway enrollment decisions (Hossler, 2004). By favoring merit over need-based aid, institutions may thus seek to gain advantage in the highly competitive market for students who add academic prestige to the campus and whose tuition revenues offset the aid deployed to entice their enrollment.

A closely related financial aspect of SEM entails tuition-discounting practices that tend to favor a higher-tuition, higher-aid model, which increases the sticker price and also the pool of subsidies to allocate to students. As they aim to spur enrollment by offsetting their published prices, enrollment managers can leverage SEM to calibrate tuition discounts to each individual student and family by way of institutional grants (e.g., gift aid) that students and families do not have to repay. Grant aid, whether from institutions or federal and state sources, is associated with strong increases in enrollment, and especially among the most financially needy students and families (e.g., Hillman, 2013).

Over time, institutions have increased the amount of grant aid that they offer and expanded the proportion of students who receive this type of support. Yet because of the rising costs of providing educational services (Winston, 1999), they may not be able to discount tuition and fee prices as sharply as they may like or meet full financial need of students and families. With grant aid less favored at the state and federal levels, and constraints on tuition discounting at the institutional level, many students and families use loans to pay for college (Hearn et al., 2016). In a study of factors associated with student loan defaults, Hillman (2014) observed that "where students enroll and whether they earn a degree or gain employment after leaving college are the strongest factors predicting students' default status" (p. 187) and that "lower-income students, minoritized students, and students who care for dependents face greater odds of defaulting when compared to their White and upper-income peers who do not care for dependents" (p. 190).

The effective use of SEM can provide important financial opportunities for low-SES students, reducing the cost and debt associated with attending college. But it may not be enough to offset the heavy loan-orientation within the postsecondary system nationally or buffer low-SES students from further cycles of debt that can be prevalent among working-class families. For example, Silva (2013) suggests that the use of credit cards and debt is prominent among working-class youth and families who take financial risks to "purchase" flexibility for themselves, but who are often, instead, victims of predatory lending and deepening financial burden. Whether working-class emerging adults are, as Silva argues, stuck in the present and precluded from future social mobility may be debatable, but they do face steep disadvantages that can limit their educational opportunities.

SEM has notable enrollment and financial implications, and it also wields considerable influence on the scope and types of academic programs that students pursue. At some colleges and universities, students are required to declare in their applications for admission the specific school or major into which they seek entrance. As such a scenario suggests, institutional officials determine whether to admit students to their colleges and to specific programs of study. Broadly considered, attending college is associated with positive cognitive and noncognitive outcomes (e.g., Mayhew et al., 2016). But individual campuses—and public systems of higher education—may sort students into various levels, academic programs, and honors colleges that can shape their developmental outcomes and prospects, potentially, for social mobility (Bastedo & Gumport, 2003).

Despite such variation in access, it may be naïve to suggest that colleges and universities are outright reproducers of stratification for society as a whole. The most stratified sectors of postsecondary education, the elite private colleges and selective public flagship universities, tend to educate only a relatively small proportion of the overall student population, indicating their roles perhaps as *facilitators* of life prospects and social status (Hearn, 1990, 2013). As McDonough, Korn, and Yamasaki (1997) found, about 3% of college-bound students employ private admissions counselors, outside of school, to assist with the application and admissions process. Despite these small numbers, highly selective colleges and universities provide important pathways into socioeconomic success, and they maintain strong and persistent barriers to access for low-SES students (Bastedo & Jaquette, 2011; Hearn & Rosinger, 2014).

Emerging adults may genuinely perceive unlimited possibilities for themselves and their futures, and their postsecondary aspirations and plans, especially for low-SES students, may affirm such optimism. Arnett and Tanner (2011) found, for example, that

> the primary reason for the optimism of emerging adults from lower social class backgrounds was that they were confident that they would receive more education than their parents had received, and consequently they would exceed their parents in income and occupational success
>
> *(p. 38)*

Such a perspective seems to emphasize a paradox of postsecondary education: college may represent opportunities for social mobility, and can indeed help individuals progress toward that goal, but it can also perpetuate inequity.

The relationship between retention and socioeconomic diversity suggests inequality as well. SEM includes the efforts of institutional leaders to manage retention as part of revenue goals, reputational benefits, and student development outcomes. More than half of all full-time, first-year students typically leave college before the start of their second year, and the stop-out and drop-out rates vary considerably by institutional sector and Carnegie classification, SES, and other demographic factors such as gender and race/ethnicity (Hossler, Bontrager, & Associates, 2015; Perna, 2006). More generally, about 56% of full-time degree-seeking college students graduate in six years (Arnett, 2015), with unevenness in terms of which students persist to graduation. Overall, the research-literature points toward structural barriers to success among low-SES students, and it also indicates some variation in the academic success of high-SES students who may flounder in college (see, for example, Martin & Spenner, 2009).

SEM can be helpful to institutional leaders and practitioners for its emphasis on planning, creating operational efficiencies, and mitigating barriers to postsecondary education and success for underserved students. For institutional leaders and practitioners, how might they leverage SEM to meet the developmental needs of emerging adults? Which approaches can or should be taken, especially in light of commitments to access and equity? We turn to these considerations next.

Implications for Institutional Policy and Practice

Institutional leaders and practitioners could pursue, as they work with emerging adults, strategies and initiatives in the domains of admissions, academic advising and support, and retention. In this section, we do not highlight or aim to advance proven "best practices" per se, but rather to emphasize what we perceive as potentially helpful organizational mechanisms for change. In so doing, we focus on select, but increasingly prominent, points for consideration for higher education and student affairs.

Enrollment Management

In recent years, a number of private liberal arts colleges have adopted "test-optional" admissions policies. Standardized tests, such as the SAT and ACT exams, are intended to measure students' scholastic abilities, but their scores are often associated with race/ethnicity and socioeconomic status and favor White, high-SES students. By going test-optional, institutions may lessen the barriers for underserved students to admission and enrollment. But empirical research suggests that test-optional policies do not always lead to more diverse student populations on campuses (Belasco et al., 2015). Instead, the policies allow institutions to increase the size of their applicant pools, enhance their selectivity, and report higher average SAT and ACT scores of admitted and enrolled students than prior to implementing the policies (thus serving to strengthen their academic profiles and prestige).

Some institutions have reformed "early admission" programs as part of their diversity initiatives and to ease the time-pressure on students for enrollment decisions. A number of institutions offer applicants the option of applying "early decision," where students apply in the fall of their senior year of high school, sign a binding commitment with their parents to enrolling at the institution if they are admitted, and learn of their admission status later in the fall and often before December. Another set of institutions offer "early action" in which students follow a timeline analogous to early decision, but do not have a binding commit to enrolling if admitted. Early admission programs tend to have favorable acceptance rates, more generous than what may be the case for other applicants (Levy, 2017), and favor high-SES students who know the game (Avery et al., 2003) and whose resources preclude them from needing financial aid or having to compare aid offers from other institutions (Jaschik, 2007). Enrollment managers have made anecdotal success claims, noting expanded recruitment efforts across an increasingly broad range of high schools, while others have reinstated nonbinding early admissions as part of their competitive recruitment strategy (Steinberg, 2010).

A notable SEM-focused, financial innovation has entailed the advent of no-loan programs. Hillman (2013), for example, reported on 69 colleges and universities that had implemented no-loan financial aid packages to students and families whose incomes fell below a particular threshold. The replacement of loans with institutional grants, Hillman suggests, may have strong influences on socioeconomic diversity by providing "an effective way for colleges to help low-income students make educational choices based on their academic achievement rather than their ability to pay" (p. 823). As noted earlier in this chapter, the leveraging of institutional grants, within a context of increasing tuition and fees, may have limited purchasing power. What is more, some institutions may not be able to sustain their no-loan programs in periods of economic constraint that, in turn, hit their endowments. But many of these institutions still deploy discounting strategies to *limit*, though not remove, loans from aid packages (Censky, 2010).

An emphasis on the work of admissions counselors may be warranted here as well. As McDonough et al. (1997) suggest, the sheer competition to recruit students has coincided with a shift among admissions counselors toward marketing and sales. What would happen if admissions counselors returned to their initial focus on counseling? In such a scenario, admissions officers would continue to recruit students to their institutions, but their contact and interactions with students and families would center, more so, on helping them ask questions and find information helpful to their finding the right college fit. Relatedly, in making admissions decisions, sensitivity to students' high school contexts may be especially helpful. Bastedo and Bowman (2017) found that when admissions counselors evaluated applications "holistically," that is, considering closely the types of curricula, programs, resources, and support available to students in their specific high schools, they made decisions that enhanced the diversity of the admitted student pool.

The adoption of gap-year programs in college admissions suggests an intriguing institutional direction of relevance to emerging adults. As Arnett (2015) suggests, a gap year entails the intentional delay of high school graduates from beginning their postsecondary education. There are potential benefits for emerging adults. They may take time to travel, and thus, broaden their perspectives and experiences. Others may pursue employment opportunities. Some, as Arnett reports, may watch daytime television and regret the wasted year. On the whole, however, emerging adults who take gap years may potentially enter college with focus, maturity, and experience helpful to them in college and also valued, later on, by employers. About 2% of American emerging adults take a gap year (see Arnett, p. 164): "After all that labor and stress centered on getting into college," Arnett observes, "who would want to go through the whole thing again the next year?" (p. 165). But most colleges and universities now allow and even encourage accepted students to take a gap year. Colleges and universities could fold into SEM specific programs and guidance for students who take gap years and consider gap-year students more deliberately in their enrollment projections and revenue models.

Academic Advising and Support

On the academic-support side, there has been growing attention among student affairs scholars and practitioners to the concept of academic coaching. The coaching framework entails the steps of self-assessment, reflection, and goal setting, helping students to "identify their interests, motivations, and resources" (Robinson & Gahagan, 2010, p. 27). Moreover, the approach consists of identifying and mapping not only daily study habits and levels of campus engagement (self-assessment) but also aspects of college that students enjoy and have found positive and meaningful (reflection) and strategic steps and plans to move forward (goal setting). Depending on the campus, academic coaches may only work with students who self-select into their programs and offerings, or who may be required to seek their assistance due to academic probation. Yet coaching, with its emphasis on concrete planning, strategy, and positive psychology, could potentially help resolve a dilemma that some emerging adults face in college of having too much freedom and flexibility (Arnett, 2015).

The college environment offers a number of "surrogate" parents to students such as faculty and staff. They may provide important, transitional relationships for students who seek autonomy from family but who also value positive, supportive connections with adults. Surrogates could help to guide students, steering them toward undergraduate research opportunities or service and outreach that matches their interests and goals as well as needs for family-like affiliations (Warshaw et al., 2017). Both through formal and informal mentoring, faculty and staff could also potentially help to support and challenge students as they choose majors and develop career plans. Some students may select majors that reflect their families' influences and experiences, and their surrogates, on campus, could help them determine whether their choice-sets might be expanded and are true to who they are and who they want to be. The work of academic advisors may be especially critical to students who are thinking about leaving their institutions, and an emphasis on helping students identify what they enjoy and encounter positively on campus can be helpful dimensions of supportive practice (Bloom, Hutson, He, & Konkle, 2013). As we have suggested throughout this chapter, both low- and high-SES students may benefit from affirmation and also expansion of their perceived ranges of academic majors.

Retention

An important aspect of SEM concentrates on retention and the fit between institutions and students. From an organizational perspective, an increase in retention rates could help institutions optimize tuition and fee revenues and also meet performance goals of interest to institutional leaders and policy makers. At the same time, retention carries implications for student development and the overall campus culture and climate. Tinto (2006) suggests that interactions between students and faculty, both in and beyond the classroom, may be especially impactful for retention. Yet there may also be an opportunity to engage families, channeling and lending some structure to parental involvement, to support efforts in this arena.

As noted earlier in this chapter, parental involvement can benefit students by enhancing their campus engagement and satisfaction in college. In response to the changing relationships between students and families, a number of institutions have launched parent programs. According to Wartman and Savage (2008, p. 80), a parent program

> with the purpose of student development is designed to provide advice on parenting a college student, relieve parents' common fears, proactively address issues and expect preemptive phone calls and e-mails, promote campus events and activities, and open dialogue between parents and students.

While such programs are not necessarily new to higher education, there has been striking growth in the number of parent-focused offices, with nearly half opening between 2000 and 2007. An important consideration for institutional leaders and practitioners is the cost associated with developing and sustaining parent programs and offices (see Wartman & Savage, p. 90). Additionally, parental involvement in primary and secondary education suggests differences by SES with more direct contact between high-SES families and schools than between low-SES families and schools. How to make college and university parent programs accessible and beneficial across the SES spectrum deserves further attention.

A crucial factor in addressing retention is financial aid. The utilization of no-loan programs is associated with substantial gains in student persistence to graduation among low-SES students (Hillman, 2013). Arnett (2015) suggests that the U.S. should make higher education free to students analogous to postsecondary systems abroad. Unfortunately, it appears that federal and state governments are increasingly moving toward privatization of higher education, favoring nongovernmental sources of funding, such as private-capital loans (rather than grants), and deferring most of the costs of education to institutions and students and families (Hearn et al., 2016). Though perhaps an obvious strategy, increasing and leveraging grants for low-SES students, especially during the first two years of college when students are most susceptible to leaving, could be critical for success.

Conclusion

As emerging adults make decisions about college, they encounter organizational contexts that influence the range of options available to them. Our chapter has aimed to shed some light on the relationship between SEM and emerging adulthood, underscoring the constraints that shape fundamental choices and financial aspects pertaining to enrollment in postsecondary education, selection of academic major, and retention. It has also sought to emphasize an equity-based perspective to add nuance to the application of the theory of emerging adulthood to higher education and student affairs. In this section, we offer several possibilities for future research in this arena.

College student development occurs within specific campus contexts, structures, and resources. In what ways, then, do organizational reforms such as SEM shape college student development? As we have noted, SEM can open educational opportunities for underserved students. But, within the context of enrollment management, institutions may admit students into particular segments of programs and activities on campus and offer financial support tailored to individual students and families. In this way, SEM could be associated with the increasing *atomization* of the college experience for students. Yet what does atomization, of access to specific pieces of college campuses for particular prices for select students, mean for engagement and related student-level outcomes? Such a question should not be taken to imply stratification per se, but rather to suggest that SEM can differentiate—and perhaps privilege—which students receive which opportunities, resources, and support on campuses. Thus, the incentives and effects of SEM merit attention.

Perhaps more central to issues of equity, the postsecondary system may reflect some structured disadvantages for low-SES students and advantages for high-SES students. For example, working-class emerging adults in Silva's (2013) study expressed "a sense of powerlessness and mystification toward the institutions that order their lives," often leading them to believe "that choice is simply an illusion" (p. 46). In particular, at all levels of the educational system, her research participants often found themselves struggling to navigate the same institutional environments in which they had invested their hopes for a better future. Such a perspective brings to mind a long-standing area of interest to researchers and analysts: the role of social institutions, and of higher education specifically, in facilitating social mobility.

Insofar as some select private, nonprofit colleges and universities have made notable gains in socioeconomic diversity on their campuses (e.g., Hearn & Rosinger, 2014), much can be learned from studying conditions that have enabled such institutions to expand access and equity, as well as factors that have slowed or limited such progress. Whereas only a small proportion of students (and available seats in higher education) are located in private, nonprofit institutions, calling attention to ways that institutions in the public sector (e.g., selective state flagship universities) have worked toward access and equity goals may also prove to be informative.

But do organizational developments on individual campuses, and in the postsecondary system generally, help emerging adults become adults? Recall that, as Arnett (2015) observes, emerging adults perceive adulthood in terms of taking self-responsibility, making independent decisions, and achieving financial independence. Though the college experience may provide students with an extended period of time to explore and make decisions about what they want to do and who they want to be, it may limit their future financial autonomy. Most students who attend college and persist to graduation have some form of financial debt and can thus be tied to their lenders for many years after graduation. Increasing levels of college debt, along with diminished prospects for retention and graduation, raise questions as to how organizational and financial aspects of higher education can be retooled and reconfigured to support students' development toward adulthood.

Finally, the relationship between parents and both students and institutions is receiving the increasing attention of researchers, campus stakeholders, and the general public. Emerging adulthood suggests an entwinement of parents and students that, if healthy, constructive, and balanced, can help students to transition into independent adults. The college environment may offer students a number of "surrogates" who become, to them, symbolic and transitional family members. As students work to distance themselves from their families, they turn to faculty and staff and transfer onto them family-like needs of support, guidance, and mentorship. These dynamics overlap with deliberate institutional outreach to parents and efforts to fold them into the work and messaging of campuses. In this arena, who or what is a "parent"? Who or what is a "family member"? In the era of emerging adulthood, the way that institutions "parent" students (and their families by way of formal programs and outreach) warrants our careful examination.

References

Arnett, J. J. (2015). *Emerging adulthood: The winding road from the late teens through the twenties* (2nd ed.). New York, NY: Oxford.

Arnett, J. J., & Tanner, J. L. (2011). Themes and variations in emerging adulthood across social classes. In J. J. Arnett, M. Kloep, L. B. Hendry, & J. L. Tanner (Eds.), *Debating emerging adulthood: Stage or process?* (pp. 31–50). New York, NY: Oxford.

Avery, C., Fairbanks, A., & Zeckhauser, R. (2003). *The early admissions game: Joining the elite*. Cambridge, MA: Harvard University Press.

Bastedo, M. N., & Bowman, N. A. (2017). Improving admissions of low-SES students at selective colleges: Results from an experimental simulation. *Educational Researcher, 46*(2), 67–77.

Bastedo, M. N., & Gumport, P. J. (2003). Access to what? Mission differentiation and academic stratification in U.S. public higher education. *Higher Education, 46*, 341–359.

Bastedo, M. N., & Jaquette, O. (2011). Running in place: Low-income students and the dynamics of higher education stratification. *Educational Evaluation & Policy Analysis, 33*(3), 318–339.

Belasco, A. S., Rosinger, K. O., & Hearn, J. C. (2015). The test-optional movement at America's selective liberal arts colleges: A boon for equity or something else? *Educational Evaluation & Policy Analysis, 37*(2), 206–223.

Bloom, J. L., Hutson, B. L., He, Y., & Konkle, E. (2013). Appreciative education. In P. C. Mather & E. Hulme (Eds.), *Positive psychology & appreciative inquiry in higher education: New directions for student services, no. 143* (pp. 5–18). San Francisco, CA: Jossey-Bass.

Censky, A. (2010, April 9). No loans! Major colleges pledge aid without debt. *CNN Money*. Retrieved March 3, 2017, from http://money.cnn.com/2010/04/09/pf/college/no-loan_financial_aid/

College Board. (2016). *Trends in student aid: 2016*. Washington, DC: Author. Retrieved from https://trends.collegeboard.org/student-aid

DesJardins, S. L., & Toutkoushian, R. K. (2005). Are students really rational? The development of rational thought and its application to student choice. In J.C. Smart (Ed.), *Higher education: Handbook of theory and research, volume XX* (pp. 191–240). Dordrecht, The Netherlands: Springer.

Dixon, R. R. (Ed.). (1995). *Making enrollment management work*. New Directions for Student Services No. 71. San Francisco, CA: Jossey-Bass.

Fingerman, K. L., & Yahirun, J. J. (2016). Emerging adulthood in the context of family. In J. J. Arnett (Ed.), *The Oxford handbook of emerging adulthood* (pp. 163–176). New York, NY: Oxford.

Golden, D. (2006). *The price of admission: How America's ruling class buys its way into elite colleges—and who gets left outside the gates*. New York, NY: Crown.

Gordon, V. N. (1995). *The undecided college student: An academic and career advising challenge* (2nd. ed.). Springfield, IL: Thomas.

Harper, C. E., Sax, L. J., & Wolf, D. S. (2012). The role of parents in college students' sociopolitical awareness, academic, and social development. *Journal of Student Affairs Research and Practice, 49*(2), 137–156.

Hearn, J. C. (1990). Pathways to attendance at elite colleges. In P. W. Kingston & L. S. Lewis (Eds.), *The high status track: Studies of elite schools and stratification* (pp. 121–145). Albany: State University of New York Press.

Hearn, J. C. (2013). Commotion at the gates: Higher education's evolving role in U.S. inequality. In J. R. Thelin (Ed.), *The rising costs of higher education* (pp. 163–173). Santa Barbara, CA: ABC-CLIO.

Hearn, J. C., & Rosinger, K. O. (2014). Socioeconomic diversity in selective private colleges: An organizational analysis. *Review of Higher Education, 38*(1), 71–104.

Hearn, J. C., Warshaw, J. B., & Ciarimboli, E. B. (2016). Privatization and accountability trends and policies in U.S. public higher education. *Education and Science, 41*(184), 1–26.

Hillman, N. W. (2013). Economic diversity in elite higher education: Do no-loan programs impact Pell enrollments? *Journal of Higher Education, 84*(6), 806–833.

Hillman, N. W. (2014). College on credit: A multilevel analysis of student loan default. *Review of Higher Education, 37*(2), 169–195.

Hossler, D. (2004). How enrollment management has transformed – or ruined - higher education. *Chronicle of Higher Education, 50*(34), B3–B5.

Hossler, D. (2015). Origins of strategic enrollment management. In D. Hossler, B. Bontrager, & Associates (Eds.), *Handbook of strategic enrollment management* (pp. 3–17). San Francisco, CA: Jossey-Bass.

Hossler, D., Bontrager, B., & Associates. (Eds.). (2015). *Handbook of strategic enrollment management*. San Francisco, CA: Jossey-Bass.

Hoxby, H., & Turner, S. (2013). Expanding college opportunities for high-achieving, low income students. (SIEPR Discussion Paper No.12–014). Stanford, CA: Stanford Institute for Economic Policy Research.

Jaschik, S. (2007, September 27). Subtleties and ethics of early decision. *Inside Higher Ed*. Retrieved March 3, 2017, from www.insidehighered.com/news/2007/09/27/early

Joyce, A. (2014, September 2). How helicopter parents are ruining college students. *Washington Post*. Retrieved March 28, 2016, from www.washingtonpost.com/news/parenting/wp/2014/09/02/how-helicopter-parents-are-ruining-college-students/

Karabel, J. (2005). *The chosen: The hidden history of admission and exclusion from Harvard, Yale, and Princeton*. Boston, MA: Houghton Mifflin.

Kraatz, M. S., Ventresca, M. J., & Deng, L. (2010). Precarious values and mundane innovations: Enrollment management in American liberal arts colleges. *Academy of Management Journal, 53*(6), 1521–1545.

Lareau, A. (2011). *Unequal childhoods: Class, race, and family life* (2nd ed.). Berkeley: University of California Press.

Levy, H. O. (2017, January 12). The discrimination inherent in early-admissions programs (essay). *Inside Higher Ed*. Retrieved March 3, 2017, from www.insidehighered.com/views/2017/01/12/discrimination-inherent-early-admissions-programs-essay

Martin, N. D., & Spenner, K. L. (2009). Capital conversion and accumulation: A social portrait of legacies at an elite university. *Research in Higher Education, 50*(7), 623–648.

Mayhew, M. J., Rockenbach, A. N., Bowman, N. A., Seifert, T. A., & Wolniak, G. C., with Pascarella, E. T., & Terenzini, P. T. (2016). *How college affects students: Volume 3: 21st Century evidence that higher education works*. San Francisco, CA: Jossey-Bass.

McDonough, P. M. (1997). *Choosing colleges: How social class and schools structure opportunity*. Albany, NY: State University of New York Press.

McDonough, P. M., Korn, J., & Yamasaki, E. (1997). Access, equity, and privatization of college counseling. *Review of Higher Education, 20*(3), 297–317.

Perna, L. W. (2006). Studying college access and choice: A proposed conceptual model. In J. C. Smart (Ed.), *Higher education: Handbook of theory and research, vol. XXI* (pp. 99–157). Dordrecht, The Netherlands: Springer.

Perna, L. W., & Finney, J. E. (2014). *The attainment agenda: State policy leadership in higher education*. Baltimore, MD: Johns Hopkins University Press.

Ramos, Y. (2013, March 13). College students tend to change majors when they find one they really love. *Borderzine*. Retrieved March 3, 2017, from http://borderzine.com/2013/03/college-students-tend-to-change-majors-when-they-find-the-one-they-really-love/

Robinson, C., & Gahagan, J. (2010). Coaching students to academic success and engagement on campus. *About Campus, 15*(4), 26–29.

Shoup, R., Gonyea, R. M., & Kuh, G. D. (2009). Helicopter parents: Examining the impact of highly involved parents on student engagement and educational outcomes. Paper presented at the annual meeting of the Association for Institutional Research, Atlanta, GA.

Silva, J. M. (2013). *Coming up short: Working class adulthood in an age of uncertainty*. New York, NY: Oxford.

Steinberg, J. (2010, November 23). University of Virginia explains its return to early-admissions arena. *The New York Times*. Retrieved March 3, 2017, from https://thechoice.blogs.nytimes.com/2010/11/23/virginia/?_r=0

Tinto, V. (1993). *Leaving college: Rethinking the causes and cures of student attrition* (2nd ed.). Chicago, IL: University of Chicago Press.

Tinto, V. (2006). Research and practice of student retention: What next? *Journal of College Student Retention: Research, Theory & Practice, 8*(1), 1–19.

Warshaw, J. B., Henne-Ochoa, R., & Murray, J. L. (2017). Institutional generativity or reproduction of privilege? How campus context and parental involvement affects legacy students. *Journal of Student Affairs Inquiry, 2*(1).

Wartman, K., & Savage, M. (2008). Parental involvement in higher education: Understanding the relationship among students, parents, and the institution. *ASHE Higher Education Report, 33*(6), 1–125. San Francisco, CA: Jossey-Bass.

Winston, G. (1999). Subsidies, hierarchy and peers: The awkward economics of higher education. *Journal of Economic Perspectives, 13*(1), 13–36.

Wolf, D., Sax, L., & Harper, C. (2009). Parental engagement and contact in the academic lives of college students. *NASPA Journal, 46*(2), 325–358.

10

CREATING CAMPUS ENVIRONMENTS FOR EMERGING ADULTS

C. Carney Strange

That the transition from childhood to adulthood is both dynamic and power-fully developmental is an insight long established in the literature on college students and young adults. From the pioneering work on youth culture, for example, by Keniston (1960, 1971) to the seminal research on life transitions by Levinson (1978) and others, it is clear that becoming a mature young adult is a challenging stage of life, full of complexities and choices that yield answers neither simple nor certain. Within the context of going to college, Chickering and Reisser (1993) described this period as a time of prelimi-nary resolution of vectors of development (e.g., identity, relationships, and purposes) that establish the foundations for maturity. Parks (2000, 2011) also underscored the tenuous quality of this stage, which she characterized as one of "probing commitment," suggesting that a cautious testing is inevita-ble as both promise and vulnerability shape individuals' choices that define what it means to be an adult. All of this is to recognize that while Arnett's (2015) work on emerging adulthood adds further nuance to the psychology and sociology of young adulthood, it does so within a substantial scholarship that has already mapped out many of the fundamental aspects of this devel-opmental period. What Arnett has accomplished though in his analysis is to draw further attention to the puzzling years that often follow the college experience for many young adults. In doing so, he has articulated a frame-work of understanding that focuses on these aspects as they continue to evolve in the 20s through the 30s transition. Arnett (2015) characterized this period as a "winding road" for many, as choices are made and revisited, options are included or released, and directions are pursued to establish a viable structure for ensuing adulthood.

Emerging Adulthood

Although the characteristics and tenets of emerging adulthood are clarified else-where (see Chapter 2), a restatement of them here serves to ground the discussion that follows. According to Arnett (2015), emerging adults are distinguished by (a) their exploration of questions of identity and pursuit of options in love and work; (b) their inherent instability in terms of relationships, job opportunities, and where they choose to live; (c) the balance of their focus being on self rather than others; (d) their strong sense of being in-between life phases, no longer adolescent but not yet adult; and (e) their optimism about the possibilities that lie ahead for them. Collectively, these features portray "twenty-somethings" (Hassler, 2008, 2010; Heath & Cleaver, 2003; Pooley, 2005; Robbins & Wilner, 2001), who are at once seemingly bold and hesitant, certain but unsure, both committed and tentative, and hoping and doubting while immersed-in but removed-from life's tasks and challenges. Just as Levinson (1978, 1997) described this early-life journey through the segues of occupational and relational dreams, Arnett's emerging adults are all dressed up and ready to go, with questions of where, with whom, and how to get there yet to be discerned. In that sense, although confusing for some, these years frame a very creative time, properly coded as "emerging" and ripe for what opportunities life has to offer. For a significant number of individuals, the opportunities of the college experience offer an unmatched environment for pursuing and resolving, at least initially, the challenges of young "adulting" (Brown, 2013).

The Power of Campus Environments

Decades of research have documented the power of the postsecondary experi-ence to effect changes along a variety of dimensions and outcomes (Mayhew, Rockenbach, Bowman, Seiffert, & Wolniak, 2016; Pascarella & Terenzini, 1991; 2005). Commonly referred to as "impacts of college," such changes range from improvements in verbal, quantitative, and subject matter competence to broad shifts in cognitive, psychosocial, attitudinal, and moral development. Collec-tively, such outcomes form a critical resource for many emerging adults as they approach the complex of decisions and choices that await their selection in the process of maturation. Just how well they acquire these skills and achieve these outcomes depends much on the quality of developmental environments they engage along the way. The college experience has proven to be one of the more powerful venues in that respect, as individuals encounter generative conditions of community in a purposeful educational setting, a point explored by Strange and Banning (2015) in their articulation of the components and purposes of powerful learning environments.

Accommodating students in their developmental journey is a matter of both individual and institutional success. Although students can succeed only by

Community

Engagement

Inclusion & Safety

FIGURE 10.1 Hierarchy of environmental design. Strange, C. C. & Banning, J. H. (2015). Designing for learning: Creating campus environments for student success. San Francisco: Jossey-Bass.

accomplishing the tasks that lead to their goals, institutions have an equal responsibility to understand and respond to students' needs so that their success is more probable. This involves the resolution of several critical steps in a hierarchy of institutional designs (Strange & Banning, 2015) (see Figure 10.1).

Researchers and observers of higher education have argued that powerful learning, and ultimately, student success, is achieved best under conditions of community. Palmer (1987) averred a similar claim that "community must become a central concept in ways we teach and learn" (p. 25). Building a community of learners requires that institutional "goals, structures, values, people, and resources come together in a seamless experience for purposes of self-actualization and fulfillment" (Strange & Banning, 2015, p. 141). Thus, community building and its correlates have become a major focus in recent years in how we discuss the goals of higher education and the means to achieve them.

However, achieving conditions of community entails several fundamental prerequisites. First, students must feel like they belong in our institutions and that who they are does not place them at undue risk in these settings. This first crucial step is about achieving a sense of inclusion and security among students. If either of these conditions is in doubt, for whatever reasons, it is not long before students check out psychologically, and soon thereafter, physically; that is, they leave the institution. Colleges and universities must understand what it takes to welcome to campus students of all groups, especially those who differ from the institution's dominant enrollment profile. Furthermore, members of nondominant groups (e.g., students of color, LGBT students, adult learners, first-generation students) might inherently experience a sense of risk in such places, if for no other reason than little is familiar to them, and at practically every turn, the presumed potential for failure lurks. For example, for students of differing ethnic origins (e.g., Native American), the absence of like mentors among faculty and staff might inadvertently discourage them at a time when they are questioning their own choice to pursue such a goal as higher learning in the first place. Similarly, students with various disabilities (e.g., deafness) inevitably encounter hurdles, in addition to their own steps to negotiate, in sensitizing the campus to the basic requirements of such success. With every pioneer, so to speak, comes an extra burden to create new and more accessible pathways for those to follow.

Although feeling welcomed and secure are necessary first steps toward the ultimate experience of a learning community, they are insufficient in and of themselves to achieve such an end. Satisfaction and comfort alone do little to advance students toward their educational goals. There is an additional critical step in the process: becoming an engaged student. Engagement or involvement in active learning is the principal mechanism for educational success. Students who become engaged in learning take on a degree of responsibility that challenges their capacities to achieve beyond theirs' and others' expectations. Well established in the literature some time ago, this theory of involvement (Astin, 1985) claims that:

> Involvement refers to the amount of physical and psychological energy that the student devotes to academic experience. A highly involved student is one who, for example, devotes considerable energy to studying, spends a lot of time on campus, participates actively in student organizations, and interacts frequently with faculty members and other students. Conversely, an uninvolved student may neglect studies, spend little time on campus, abstain from extracurricular activities, and have little contact with faculty members or other students.
>
> *(p. 134)*

Thus, involvement is most clearly manifested in actions such as joining, participating, attaching, committing, immersing, and volunteering.

Although a person's motivation is a potentially important dimension of involvement, Astin (1985) also contended that "it is not so much what an individual thinks or feels but what he or she does that defines and identifies involvement" (p. 135). Similarly, Pace (1984) suggested, "what counts most is not who [students] are or where they are but what they do" (p. 44). Since this basic tenet was first articulated, however, a wealth of new understandings has appeared in the higher education literature to suggest that a revision of such a claim is in order. Who a student is *does* matter, and various subgroup attributes examined in the literature over the past two decades offer a starting point for exploring how such differences "count" in the matter of student engagement. Regardless, the experience of a full learning community remains out of reach if conditions for student engagement are not in place. For adult learners, this may mean the institution's recognition and accrediting of their prior experiences; for students of color, this may entail the establishment of relevant cultural centers on campus; and for students of a differing sexual orientation or expression, it may mean extending a sense of legitimacy to their status through readings and observations inclusive of authors so identified. Students who are engaged in learning see themselves as integral to the setting, whether a classroom, student club or society, residence hall, or advocacy organization, such that without their participation, the setting's goals and outcomes are jeopardized. Active involvement or engagement is the engine of student success.

Over time, as included, secured, and engaged students actively carry out the activities of learning, something very special happens. Individual efforts soon give way to a collective sense of achievement in creating a powerful and memorable experience. Some students might consider this to be the experience of an especially powerful class; some may associate this with their planning and implementation of a significant event (e.g., institution-wide festival or campaign); and others might recognize this as the outcome of having lived together with a special group of peers (e.g., residential learning community). Whatever the case, the standard rises to that of an experience of community, where "unifying purposes and values, traditions and symbols of belonging and involvement, and mutuality of care, support, and responsibility encourage a synergy of participation and worth, checking and cross-checking, to create a positive learning environment" (Strange & Banning, 2015, p. 214). The ultimate test of having achieved such a quality of experience is that, when students leave it, they are missed; the community of learning no longer exists without them, at least in the form it once did. In an age driven by economies of scale, especially in the beginning years of postsecondary education (e.g., large lecture classes), experiences of community are becoming rarer in our colleges and universities, but nonetheless remain critical for assuring maximum impact of what they have to offer. The experience of community is the capstone of postsecondary learning, one that capitalizes on students having felt like they belonged and were safe on our campuses, were motivated to embrace engaging possibilities, and sustained their efforts to the point where some level of synergy and achievement was apparent for all. Students who look back on their postsecondary years with fond memories and a deep sense of accomplishment are those most likely to have been included, secured, engaged, and invited into the learning community of higher education.

In the context of this analysis and discussion of emerging adults, the above conditions (inclusion, safety, engagement, and community) are purported to form an essential hierarchy of institutional designs appropriate for nurturing the development of these students. To effect such conditions, basic components of the environment must be arranged accordingly. Thus, the natural and synthetic physical layout and design (the "physical" components), the collective characteristics of people within the environment (the "human aggregate" components), the structures facilitating purposes and goals of the environment ("organizational" components), and the collective impressions and cultural artifacts associated with the setting (the "socially constructed" components) must lend themselves first to the attraction, satisfaction, and retention of participants in the environment. When arranged appropriately, each of these four components has the potential for contributing to the inclusion, security, engagement, and community experience of students. For example, homogeneous human aggregates of common interests (e.g., a themed learning community) are most attractive to and strengthen the sense of inclusion and security experienced by those who share those same characteristics and interests. In fact, over time, an accentuation effect occurs when the dominant characteristic is strengthened by their participation. The challenge becomes when those who are dissimilar seek entry and inclusion in the group. Heterogeneous aggregates, on the other hand, are disparate and pliable in character, and consequently, struggle to attract and retain members who find it difficult to identify sources of satisfaction and stability within. So it is with the other environmental aspects, as flexible physical components invite the imprint of members, dynamic ("organic") organizational components encourage engagement of participants in significant roles and responsibilities, and distinctive socially constructed components confirm the experience of community over time in an affirming and memorable way (Strange & Banning, 2015). Of particular importance in the present analysis is the potential of these components and designs for tapping the explorative creative processes of emerging adults at a time when and place where they are most vulnerable, but also most ready to pursue the path of this period of life. For that, I turn the focus to the nature of "mentoring environments" (Parks, 2011) and their role in facilitating the development of emerging adults in the college setting.

Mentoring Environments

In her seminal work on "mentoring emerging adults in their search for meaning, purpose, and faith," Parks (2000, 2011) mined the literature on human development to articulate a progression of young adulthood, exploring in particular the phase she associated with the college years and beyond, identifying it as one of "probing commitment" (Parks, 2011, p. 88). This is an in-between time in one's life when the fragile sense of inner-dependence encounters a myriad of possibilities and choices. Environments best suited for facilitating this stage of life are what Parks (2011) identifies as "mentoring communities" that offer "the gifts of recognition, support, challenge, and inspiration" and that "distinctively honor and animate the potential of emerging adult lives" (p. 176). According to Parks, mentoring communities are distinguished by seven qualities or hallmarks, inasmuch as they offer (a) a network of belonging; (b) big-enough questions; (c) encounters with otherness; (d) vital habits of mind; (e) worthy

FIGURE 10.2   Hierarchy of environmental design & characteristics of mentoring communities. Adapted from Strange, C. C. & Banning, J. H. (2015). Designing for learning: Creating Campus environments for student success. San Francisco: Jossey-Bass. & Parks, S. D. (2011). Big questions, worthy dreams: mentoring emerging adults in their search for meaning, purpose, and faith (2nd ed.). San Francisco: Jossey-Bass.

dreams; (f) access to images; and (g) opportunities for practicing hearth, table, and commons. For purposes of this analysis, I have re-ordered their sequence and embedded them within the hierarchy of environmental design discussed previously (see Figure 10.2). At each level of the hierarchy are specific mentoring qualities articulated in Parks's (2011) model that contribute to each step in Strange and Banning's (2015) design framework.

In effect, mentoring communities offer the environmental conditions deemed essential for personal development, as they include, secure, engage, and invite students into the learning community of higher education. College and university campuses are replete with opportunities and resources, in Parks's words—for animating the potential of emerging adults. I address each dimension or hallmark as it relates to the context of postsecondary education, with attention given to the kinds of policies, practices, experiences, and resources available for achieving its ends.

Network of Belonging

A mentoring community offers a "network of belonging that constitutes a spacious home for the potential and vulnerability of the young adult imagination in practical, tangible terms" (Parks, 2011, p. 176). It serves both "to reassure and to encourage the development of inner-dependence" (p. 177). Going to college is inherently a "joining experience." In due time, as students matriculate, their sense of belonging manifests in attachments to a friendship group, an institution, a department, a major, a class, a residence, a floor, a cultural center, an organization, a club, a committee, and a "favorite place" on campus. Achieving this sense and the relationships that nurture it is the "necessary precondition" to a successful college experience, as a recent ten-year study of the student experience at one liberal arts college concluded:

> Relationships are central to a successful college experience. They are the necessary precondition, the daily motivator, and the most valuable outcome.... Relationships shape in detail students' experience: what courses they take or majors they declare; whether they play a sport or join an extracurricular activity; whether they gain skills, grow ethically, or learn whatever is offered in various programs. Relationships are important because they raise or suppress the motivation to learn; a good college fosters the relationships that lead to motivation.
>
> *(Chambliss & Takacs, 2014, p. 155)*

As the hierarchy of environmental design presented previously suggests, failure to achieve this basic sense of belonging and security jeopardizes subsequent involvement in the form of student engagement, itself a requisite for the experience of community.

From the perspective of policies and practices, any programs and interventions that build relationships around common interests and connection to others can promote this sense of belonging and security, and the earlier the better. Front-loading events such as orientation, campus welcome week, convocation and induction ceremonies, departmental picnics, student organization fairs, open houses, and even sports pep rallies can go a long way in initiating student attachment to the institution, especially within the first six weeks of the college experience. Specialized events that target nontraditional groups (e.g., adult learners, students of color, LGBT students, and international students) are critical for students who differ from or don't identify with the prevailing campus culture and who may be at risk because of who they are (Strayhorn, 2012). Inclusion and security must be a priority for such groups. Among the early signs of having done so for some students may appear in the form of institutional swag-wear, as they begin to acknowledge their identification with their new environment while letting go of their past. Ultimately achieving a sense of home place is an important first step toward exploring the kinds of big questions colleges offer as agents of change and growth in the journey toward emerging adulthood. In addition to questions, they also offer opportunities for encountering otherness, developing critical habits of mind, accessing images of goodness and truth, and pursuing worthy dreams. These next five hallmarks of mentoring communities form a powerful agenda of student engagement.

Encounters with Otherness

By definition, this feature of a mentoring environment encourages constructive encounters "with those outside one's own tribe, those generally regarded as *them* instead of *us*," resulting in an "empathic bond" that recognizes others' suffering and "capacity for hope, longing, love, joy, and pain." The effect of such an encounter is deeply rooted in the human adventure of perspective-taking, as

> the ability to imagine the experience of the other by drawing on our own well of experiences and blending it with the particular features of the other's experience makes it possible to see through another's eyes, to feel through another's heart, to know something of another's understanding.
>
> *(Parks, 2011, p. 181)*

Being able to see another's perspective has multiple benefits, generating a degree of compassion recognizing that "my well-being and the well-being of the other are linked" (p. 182). In the course of an encounter with otherness, both the self and the other emerge with a greater sense of clarity about what one understands, what one believes, and where one stands in a world of diverse views and experiences. This is at once an opportunity for affirmation and reconsideration, as the familiar is contrasted with the unfamiliar and new ways of thinking and being appear plausible.

In many ways, achieving the sense of belonging discussed above is dependent on successful encounters with otherness, and vice versa; at the very least, the one contributes to the other. In a diverse world, a sense of belonging dependent only on the familiar is inevitably at risk without the capacity to understand and appreciate the experience of a different other. This underscores the critical importance of our institutions' multicultural mission, a policy provision that warrants explicit statement and direction. In the first edition of her work, Parks (2000) noted that a mentoring environment is a place where "hospitality to otherness is prized and practiced" (p. 141). From initial orientation groups and first day move-ins, to introductory class sessions and onset meetings of clubs and organizations, opportunities for early encounters with otherness abound on most campuses. Whether students recognize these as occasions for learning or not, colleges and universities bear responsibility for identifying and encouraging such experiences as pivotal to the educational mission of academic and student affairs on campus. Students, in turn, should be held accountable for such expectations, inasmuch as they contribute to the broadening of their views and their capacity for adapting to the diverse dynamics of a complex world. Failure to achieve comfort with otherness is to fall short of the goals of a liberal education. While technical knowledge within most fields becomes obsolete in relatively short time, the deep lessons of encounters with otherness have lasting effect well beyond the college years and offer a base from which to discover self and others along the path of emerging adulthood.

With a basic sense of belonging established and encounters with others initiated, the first steps of environmental design (inclusion and security) make more probable the challenging work of engaging in big questions, developing critical habits of mind, accessing images of goodness and truth, and pursuing worthy dreams. Together, these qualities of mentoring communities constitute the second level of design—encouraging involvement of students in their own learning.

Big Enough Questions

Once acclimated to the initial maze of new faces and spaces, familiar and unfamiliar, college students are almost immediately immersed in the challenges of big questions. Whether through introductory courses in the disciplines or opportunities for late-night peer sessions, the emergence of ultimate questions about identities, relationships, and purposes are inevitable among young explorers in a setting dedicated to discovery, understanding, and the critical process. In that regard, colleges and universities are ideal institutions for this essential feature of mentoring environments, to the extent that they have the "capacity to extend hospitality to big questions," that is, those that "stretch us...reveal the gaps in our knowledge, in our social arrangements, in our ambitions and aspirations." Big questions are "ones that ultimately matter" (Parks, 2000, p. 137).

Each student's weekly schedule of classes comprises a potential agenda of discipline-based questions that range from the particular to the general, the immediate to the eventual, and from the incidental to the ultimate. Insights about stimulus and response from a course in psychology might become questions of "What worth and value am I?" or "How can I be a better person?" From courses in sociology, economics, and communications, may come concerns such as "How do I experience community in life?" or "What does it mean to be forgiven, faithful, or productive?" Finally, "What compels or orients me in life?" or "For what and whom am I willing to die?" are questions that might arise from an immersion in philosophy and ethics or introductory courses to various fields and occupations to which students are attracted (e.g., education, social work, business). Whether about self-definition and understanding, relationships with others, or life's purposes and directions, such questions form the warp and woof of learning, as the wisdom of the ages is examined and sampled for relevance and application should the opportunity present itself. For students fortunate enough to attend college full-time and experience living in residence, such questions spill seamlessly into the cocurricular where they are revisited and revised in action with mentors, advisors, and peers who comprise the chorus of trusted others they seek for guidance and comparison.

Access to Images

Closely related to the big questions that arise from the disciplines and out-of-class encounters, are the "images of truth, transformation, positive images of self and of the other, and images of interrelatedness" (Parks, 2000, p. 148) that derive from the very same sources. These are images of truth that offer a complete picture, incorporating the "realities of suffering [as well as] the awe of wonder"; they are images of transformation that distill a "hope for renewing the world"; they are affirming images of self "that convey a faithful corre-spondence between [one's] own aspirations and positive reflection in the eyes of another whom [one] values and trusts"; they include "images of the other as both similar and unique" and "images of interrelatedness and wholeness" about "institutions that work" (p. 151). From the creative imaginings of a Homer, Faulkner, Machiavelli, DuBois, Jefferson, Dostoevsky, Friedan, Darwin, Picasso, Sartre, Dewey, Thompson, Baldwin, Mozart, Marx, and Wright, to honor just a few, come a catalog of potential ideals about what it means to be good, honest, anxious, faithful, sad, caring, frightened, fair, helpful, creative, loyal, confused, and loving, to name some. Such images are there for the tak-ing to shape vicariously students' experiences of goodness and truth. Learning communities and interdisciplinary courses offer special opportunities to exam-ine a multitude of images worthy of admiration and aspiration for the emerging adult. "What is at the core of these images?" "How would one explain these images to someone else?" and "Why are some images more important than others?" are all questions that should be posed by advisors and peers alike as their answers slowly take shape, exacting personal commitments.

Big questions and images of goodness and truth in combination underscore the real importance of general education requirements and the value they deliver through their distribution across the disciplines. The power of learning becomes clear as students gain in breadth and depth in the kinds of questions they can ask and the range of images they can access in addressing the complexity of the world around them. Integral to all this is their acquiring the habits of mind nec-essary for examining, critiquing, and applying what they absorb in the process.

Habits of Mind

Parks discusses this feature of mentoring environments as a "gift" that makes "it possible for emerging adults to hold diversity and complexity, to wrestle with moral ambiguity, and to develop deeper wells of meaning, purpose, and faith." Aligning with the very purposes of higher education, the challenge and support of mentoring communities "assist in creating habits of discourse and inclusions that invite genuine dialogue, strengthen critical thought, encourage connective-holistic awareness, and develop the contemplative mind" (Parks, 2011, p. 185). In a world of sound-bites, slogans, and fact-free claims, nothing seems more critical than the kinds of capacities and skills identified in this feature. While options and choices abound, the means to sort through them all, to exchange relevant questions and images, to compare, to evaluate, and to arrive at a synthesis that works becomes even more urgent. The proper role of dialogue is illustrated:

> When one speaks, and then is heard – but not quite, and therefore tries to speak yet more clearly – and then listens to the other – and understands, but not quite, and listens again – one becomes actively engaged in sorting out what is true and dependable within oneself and about one's world. How one makes meaning is composed and recomposed in this process.
>
> *(Parks, 2011, p. 186)*

Nash, Bradley, and Chickering (2008) extolled the value of "moral conversation," especially urgent in the current context of fundamental religious differences and worldviews about many things. As a form of dialogue, moral conversation:

> Is a way for people to communicate peacefully and empathically with one another across an array of competing and, at times, conflicting worldviews. Its ultimate objective is not guilt-mongering, conversion, argumentation or ridicule. Rather this communication process posits as its primary ideal the need to arrive at a compassionate understanding of the differences that exist among diverse belief systems and contending groups before moving to critique and challenge.
>
> *(Nash & Murray, 2010, p. 283)*

Deconstruction and critical examination of ideas are of course important, but eventually they must be reassembled in a manner that contributes to the evolving perspectives of the emerging adult; this requires a capacity for connective-systemic-holistic thought and contemplation. Such advanced habits of mind provide the tools for engaging and interpreting the meaning of all that is gained in the process of formal learning, and once again the college environment is an ideal place for doing so. Lectures, presentations, debates, discussions, reflections, journaling, and demonstrations are the usual fare for emerging adults on the college campus. Both in-class and out-of-class opportunities for exercising these habits of mind abound and institutions would do well to emphasize them more explicitly across the curriculum within a framework of learning goals and outcomes.

Worthy Dreams

From the earliest days on campus to the walk across the commencement stage, a fundamental question of any college student's experience is: "What's your major?" Although many students change how they answer that question multiple times during the college years, choosing a field of study serves as the first proxy of a much deeper question they are pursuing: "What is your Dream in life?" Parks describes this dimension in terms of a calling emanating from "a deep and satisfying sense of purpose" (2011, p. 190) and "a quality of vision... that orients meaning, purpose, and aspiration" (Parks, 2000, p. 146). It is

> a relational sensibility in which I recognize that what I do with my time, talents, and treasure is most meaningfully conceived not as a matter of personal passion and preference but in relationship to the whole of life.... Vocation is the place where the heart's deep gladness meets the world's deep hunger.
>
> *(2011, p. 192)*

It is probably rare that the articulation of one's "Dream" is fully realized during the college years, but as Parks states, it then becomes "the central work of emerging adulthood." In fact, it is probably the defining task of this period of life for most—to have a larger sense of purpose in the world while affirming one's place in it. Colleges and universities are essentially places of purpose, with readily available advice and mentoring, a catalog of resources for personal assessments, and charted pathways of success to guide emerging adults while they explore their options. Questions from family and friends, such as "What attracted you to that field?" or "What will you do with that major?", become daily motivators to seek clarification and pursue experiences. Career planning centers, advising offices, cooperative education assignments, field based practica and internships, study abroad excursions, and various other immersion opportunities, all stand ready to support and challenge emerging adults in real world contexts that test their skills, commitments and resolve. What appears to them initially as a vague interest over time may evolve into a deeper desire to be what one is intended to become. Ultimately, it is this sense of purpose that anchors emerging adults and points to the horizon of their journey. Postsecondary institutions are ideal places from which to launch such a journey and to explore its possibilities. To do so in the company of peers and trusted others is one of the greatest benefits of formal education and one at which colleges and universities excel. As communities of practice, they are uniquely designed to nurture and celebrate the challenges and achievements of this emerging period of adulthood.

Communities of Practice

A guided tour through most any college campus leaves little wonder that such institutions are communities of practice. The buzz of a student union at noon or late in the evening; harmonies of ritual inductions; the loud cheers of a closely contested game; the anticipated excitement of an annual student organization event; the resolute strains of reaching unexpected performance levels at the fitness center; the collaborative spirit of a learning commons; the low-keyed conversation of a residence lounge; and the serenity of a campus reflecting pool all suggest that students and their institutions understand well the power of engaging in hearth, table, and commons. Hearth includes spaces where individuals are "warmed in both body and soul, are made comfortable, and tend to linger." Such places "invite pause, reflection, and conversation" (Parks, 2011, p. 198). The practice of table works in similar ways: "In every culture, human beings have eaten together... The practice of the table prepares us for civitas... we learn to share, to wait, to accommodate, and to be grateful... we learn delayed gratification, belonging, commitment, and ritual" (pp. 199–200). Above all though, the table, like the hearth, is a place of dialogue and conversation, where dreams are shared and images are explored among peers and mentors. Lastly, the commons "affords practices of interrelatedness, belonging, and learning how to stand - and stand with - each other over time." Such places "confirm a common, connected life, and in common with various forms of story and ritual, it can become the center of shared faith and grounded hope" (p. 201). These practices of hearth, table, and commons affirm the sense of belonging and encourage encounters of otherness; they are places for considering big questions and images of goodness and truth, and for exercising evolving habits of mind. Ultimately, they are venues where Dreams are shared and shaped in the presence of others. Over time they seal the invitation of members into the experience called higher education, and the basic conditions of environmental design are achieved, as students are included, secured, engaged, and become full participants in the learning community.

Conclusion

The emerging adult years have been identified as a dynamic period of life for most, as decisions are explored and considered in preparation for assuming full status in the adult world. Although many options are available as suitable contexts for pursuing the challenges of this phase, it has been proposed here that colleges and universities are among the best environments for doing so, as long as they are designed intentionally to include, secure, engage, and invite individuals into their communities of learning (Strange & Banning, 2015). Furthermore, as they achieve such ends, it is also proposed that doing so through the dimensions of mentoring communities (Parks, 2011) can enhance the possibilities that emerging adults will succeed in their quest for meaning and purpose.

References

Arnett, J. J. (2015). *Emerging adulthood: The winding road from the late teens through the twenties* (2nd ed.). New York, NY: Oxford.

Astin, A. W. (1985). *Achieving educational excellence: A critical assessment of priorities and practices in higher education.* San Francisco, CA: Jossey-Bass.

Brown, K. W. (2013). *Adulting: How to become a grown-up in 468 easy (ish) steps*. New York, NY: Grand Central.

Chambliss, D. F., & Takacs, C. G. (2014). *How college works*. Cambridge, MA: Harvard University Press.

Chickering, A. W., & Reisser, L. (1993). *Education and identity* (2nd ed.). San Francisco, CA: Jossey-Bass.

Hassler, C. (2008). *20 something manifesto: Quarter-lifers speak out about who they are, what they want, and how to get it*. Novato, CA: New World Library.

Hassler, C. (2010). *20 something, 20 everything: a quarter-life woman's guide to balance and direction*. Novato, CA: New World Library.

Heath, S., & Cleaver, E. (2003). *Young, free and single? Twenty-somethings and household change*. New York, NY: Palgrave Macmillan.

Keniston, K. (1960). Alienation and the decline of utopia. *The American Scholar, 29*(2), 161–200.

Keniston, K. (1971). *Youth and dissent: The rise of the opposition*. New York, NY: Harcourt.

Levinson, D. (1997). *The seasons of a woman's life*. New York, NY: Ballantine.

Levinson, D. J. (1978). *The seasons of a man's life*. New York, NY: Ballantine.

Mayhew, M., Rockenbach, A., Bowman, N., Seiffert, T., & Wolniak, G. (2016). *How college affects students (Vol. 3): 21st century evidence that higher education works*. San Francisco, CA: Jossey-Bass.

Nash, R. J., Bradley, D. L., & Chickering, A. W. (2008). *How to talk about hot topics on campus: From polarization to moral conversation*. San Francisco, CA: Jossey-Bass.

Nash, R. J., & Murray, M. C. (2010). *Helping college students find purpose: The campus guide to meaning-making*. San Francisco, CA: Jossey-Bass.

Pace, C. R. (1984). *Measuring the quality of college student experiences: An account of the development and use of the college student experiences questionnaire*. Los Angeles, CA: UCLA Higher Education Research Institute. ERIC document no. ED 255099.

Palmer, P. J. (1987). Community, conflict, and ways of knowing: Ways to deepen our educational agenda. *Change, 19*(5), 20–25.

Parks, S. D. (2000). *Big questions, worthy dreams: Mentoring young adults in their search for meaning, purpose, and faith*. San Francisco, CA: Jossey-Bass.

Parks, S. D. (2011). *Big questions, worthy dreams: Mentoring emerging adults in their search for meaning, purpose, and faith* (2nd ed.). San Francisco, CA: Jossey-Bass.

Pascarella, E. T., & Terenzini, P. T. (1991). *How college affects students: Findings and insights from twenty years of research*. San Francisco, CA: Jossey-Bass.

Pascarella, E. T., & Terenzini, P. T. (2005). *How college affects students (Vol. 2): A third decade of research*. San Francisco, CA: Jossey-Bass.

Pooley, E. (2005). Generation Y: How twenty somethings are changing the workplace. *Canadian Business, 78*(12), 67–68.

Robbins, A., & Wilner, A. (2001). *Quarterlife crisis: The unique challenges of life in your twenties*. New York, NY: Tarcher/Putnam.

Strange, C., & Banning, J. (2015). *Designing for learning: Creating campus environments for student success*. San Francisco, CA: Jossey-Bass.

Strayhorn, T. L. (2012). *College students' sense of belonging: A key to educational success for all students*. New York, NY: Routledge.

11

STUDENT AFFAIRS PROGRAMS FOR EMERGING ADULTS

Maureen E. Wilson and Patrick G. Love

Student affairs work is continually evolving in response to the shifting sociopolitical, economic, legal, cultural, technological, and demographic contexts influencing higher education, and developing the whole student remains an important cornerstone of the work of student affairs. As Arnett (2015) argued, one of the results of this evolutionary dynamic is the emergence of a new identifiable developmental phase labeled emerging adulthood. Because this new phase coincides with the life stage of traditional-age college students, it behooves student affairs professionals to consider how their work needs to change so they can best meet the developmental needs of today's college students. In preceding chapters, authors have described emerging adulthood from a variety of perspectives. In this chapter, we consider the implications of emerging adulthood for campus life programs in student affairs and recommend how student affairs professionals might use this framework to inform their practice in a variety of functional areas.

Emerging Adulthood

Search #adulting on Twitter and you will find a long string of posts celebrating and bemoaning steps toward adulthood—moving out, killing spiders, pumping gas, managing a budget, having a job, negotiating relationships, and more. Arnett (2015) described five main features of emerging adulthood and these features map closely to the work of student affairs on college campuses. Other chapters have focused on these features: (1) *identity explorations*, answering the question "who am I?" and trying out various life options especially in love and work; (2) *instability* in love, work, and place of residence; (3) *self-focus*, as obligations to others reach a life-span low point; (4) *feeling in-between*, in transition, neither adolescent nor adult; and (5) *possibilities/optimism*, when hopes flourish and people have an unparalleled opportunity to transform their lives (p. 9).

The top three criteria for adulthood that emerged from Arnett's research are to (1) accept responsibility for oneself, (2) make independent decisions, and (3) become financially independent. Each of these milestones requires greater independence from parents, but emerging adults are still in between, many typically still relying on parents for money, advice, and emotional support. In one poll, 55% of 18–29-year olds reported having daily or near daily contact with their parents, a pattern facilitated by unlimited talk and text cellphone plans (Arnett, 2015).

Variations in the timing of traditional markers of adulthood, including marriage, children, additional education and training, and employment, as well as the social and economic pressures of each, cast doubt on those indicators of adulthood (Schneider, Klager, Chen, & Burns, 2016). For example, extending a "4-year" college degree to six years or more creates additional and substantial debt for students and/or their parents and delays the achievement of financial independence. When others (e.g., parents) have a large financial investment in one's life, they may also have a large say in decisions, thereby hampering one's ability to make independent decisions. The ability—or inability—to choose or secure stable employment also complicates the journey to adulthood.

Many traditional aged students arrive at college without much experience in having to accept responsibility for themselves, their actions, and their decisions. This is especially true for many students from affluent backgrounds and those whose parents have attended college (Lareau, 2015). More than their poorer and/or first-generation peers, many wealthier parents have shielded their children from the consequences of their behaviors and decisions. Middle- and upper-middle class parents are well positioned to be "cultural guides" (Lareau, 2015) and to deploy social "air bags" to aid and protect their children; these air bags come in myriad forms including tutors, attorneys, and therapy (Putnam, 2015). Twenge (2017) wrote about iGen, those born in 1995 and later. Raised with the Internet and cellphones, many became college students around 2013. As teens, they are "less likely to work at a job, have a driver's license, stay at home alone, or manage their own money" (p. 42). Twenge described this as a "slow life strategy," typical of those with smaller families and greater economic prosperity. Parents of such children have more time to cultivate and celebrate the success of each child. The social and familial context in which today's students make their way toward adulthood offers further insight on those criteria that emerging adults themselves have identified as significant milestones along this path.

Accept Responsibility for Oneself

Accepting responsibility for oneself entails a recognition that adults bear the consequences of their decisions and generally handle their own obligations without relying heavily on others. This aligns well with instrumental independence as described by Chickering and Reisser (1993). Being able to organize one's activities and be self-directed in solving problems are markers of instrumental independence. It requires some separation from parents and learning to care for oneself and one's needs. Schneider et al. (2016) remarked that in the current economy, many young adults cannot afford to live on their own, and thus, may have moved back in with parents or never left home. Those in low-wage or part-time positions may have difficulty perceiving themselves as adults. "Career success is not useful as a marker of adulthood, when young people have to wait until their late 20s or early 30s to achieve the labor-market outcomes that they envisioned when they began college" (p. 110).

Make Independent Decisions

Making one's own choices is another important criterion for adulthood. Participants in Arnett's (2015) research talked about getting input from others but recognizing final decisions were theirs to make. They also talked about this in light of their values. One said, "Once you can establish your own beliefs and control you own life, then you're an adult" (p. 315). Student affairs professionals have many opportunities to help students clarify their values and help them move toward more independent decision-making.

Become Financially Independent

Financial independence is the third element of adulthood. Paying one's own way is a big transition for many. Some emerging adults have never left home or have returned to live with parents because they cannot afford to live independently. Others live at home and consider themselves adults because they make their own decisions and have the financial means to live independently, even as they choose not to do so. One of Arnett's (2015) participants remarked that he could pay to live on his own, although he could not afford to buy all he does now. He saw his parents' home simply as a place to sleep. The discussion later in the chapter about college debt and employment prospects complicates the journey to financial independence for many.

Traditional Markers of Adulthood

Traditional markers of adulthood such as having a job or perhaps a career, living independent of parents, getting married, and having children have been postponed, or have become elusive or unappealing to many emerging adults. "Many adolescents are unsure of what others expect of them and unsure of what they expect of themselves as they try to envision what markers they need to be regarded as adults" (Schneider et al., 2016, p. 107).

These markers of adulthood have changed dramatically in the past several decades. Specifically, there has been a gender shift in employment, wages, and

TABLE 11.1 Living Arrangements of 18- 34-Year-Olds

	In a Parent(s)' Home		With Spouse or Significant Other	
	Men	Women	Men	Women
2014	35%	29%	28%	35%
1960	23%	17%	56%	68%

Data Source: Fry, 2016.

living arrangements for 18–34-year-olds since 1960. For men, employment rates and wages have fallen and greater numbers are living with parents. For women, rates of employment and wages have risen since 1960, yet more young adults are living with parents than in prior years (Fry, 2016). Analysis of U.S. Census data by the Pew Research Center (Fry, 2016) revealed that in 2014, more 18–34-year-old men were living with a parent(s) (35%) than with a spouse or significant other (28%). In contrast, more women of this age group lived with a spouse or significant other (35%) than with a parent(s) (29%). By comparison, in 1960, 23% of men and 17% of women lived with parents and 56% of men and 68% of women lived with a partner or significant other (Table 11.1).

Arnett (2015) argued that marriage is not the traditional marker of adulthood as it was in the past. More adults are cohabiting, marrying later in life, and raising children outside of marriage. The percentage of adults aged 25 and older who have never married is at an all-time high. In 2012, 17% of women and 23% of men had never married; in 1960, those rates were 8% and 10%, respectively. Now, the median age for first marriage is 27 for women and 29 for men; in 1960, the age was 20 and 23, respectively. Pew researchers have projected that a quarter of today's young adults will have never been married by their mid-40s to mid-50s (Wang & Parker, 2014).

More women than men are single parents living with their children (Fry, 2016). In the U.S., the percentage of births to unwed mothers has increased by 60% since the 1990s (Lamidi, 2016); 40.3% of births in 2015 were to unmarried mothers (Martin, Hamilton, Osterman, Driscoll, & Mathews, 2017). However, an increasing number of babies born to unmarried mothers are living with their mother and a cohabiting partner. The rate of unmarried births decreases as education increases (Payne, Manning, & Brown, 2012).

Emerging adulthood, with its focus on ages 18–29, clearly overlaps with a majority of "traditional aged" college students, especially those most likely to be engaged in typical student affairs functions, including residence life, student conduct, orientation, campus activities, and alcohol education. Schneider, Klager, Chen, and Burns (2016) argued that colleges and universities should be more active in aiding emerging adults to develop and implement a successful plan for the next decades of their lives. To understand better how student affairs professionals can support students to focus intentionally on the transition to adulthood, it is helpful to consider students' notions of adulthood.

Emerging Adults' Perceptions of Adulthood

Asking young people who are making that transition what it means to be an adult is illuminating. A rudimentary empirical way we did this was to analyze 200 responses of young adults (age determination based on photos and self-descriptions in Twitter profiles) to the Twitter hashtag #adultinginfivewords. An analysis of their responses revealed the following categories:

- Changing Priorities—Emerging adults revealed changes in how they spent their time and money; activities that are more "adult" took precedence.
- Adopting New Responsibilities—These responsibilities included paying off credit cards, setting up personal finance processes, doing car and home maintenance, and taking ownership of their healthcare.
- Participating in "Adult" Milestones—Some of these young people mentioned specific activities that signaled for them a step into adulthood. These milestones tended to focus on markers of financial independence and management of other basic life functions.
- Experiencing Additional Stress and Pressure and Feeling Tired—These Twitter users mentioned a significant increase in the pace of life that was associated with adulthood. For some the pace was having a negative effect on their lives and many spoke of being exhausted.
- Changing Perception of Money—Tweets tended to reflect the recognition that they were financially responsible for more expenses than had been the case in the past and learning more about the true cost of goods and services.
- Feeling Financial Pressure—Not only was the perception of money changing for some of these young people, they also associated financial pressure with their transition to adulthood.
- Adopting "Adult" Tastes—These emerging adults seemed to accept grudgingly that their tastes were changing in an "adult" direction. For example, a number mentioned excitement over appliance purchases, enhancements to their living space, or non-designer clothing purchases.
- New Versions of Autonomy—People also tweeted about realizing they could make decisions and do things that they could not have done in prior contexts, such as "Doritos and wine for dinner" or "Ice cream for breakfast isn't wrong."

The responses of these young people tracked strongly with two of the criteria for adulthood: accepting responsibility for oneself and becoming financially independent. The third criterion for adulthood was implied in several of the categories and responses, and highlighted in the "new versions of autonomy" category. These emerging adults were actively making independent decisions on matters large and small. The findings for this particular group of young people indicated their notions of entering adulthood closely match Arnett's findings.

Emerging Adults in College

Professionals in student affairs and other institutional units can frame their efforts to help traditional-aged students tackle the challenges of emerging adulthood during three phases: entering college, experiencing college, and exiting college and beyond. These phases interact and build upon previous developmental work the individual has done but bring forth particular tasks and challenges.

Entering College

The focus of the entering college phase is beginning to socialize and orient both prospective and entering students. From the time students first indicate interest in a college or university until they enroll, a process of anticipatory socialization begins to alert them to the necessary values, norms, knowledge, attitudes, and skills to operate in the new environment (Kuh, Schuh, Whitt, & Associates, 1991). Communications and marketing (or public relations) professionals shape many of these messages (Volkmann, 1998) and so it is crucial to collaborate with them effectively. It is also important to help shape the perspectives of students' parents and guardians, especially those who belong to social strata from which most so-called helicopter parents emerge: middle and upper middle class. These parents are more likely to have also attended and graduated from college. Students of these parents tend to be less autonomous and benefit from the advice and guidance of their parents (Lareau, 2015). First-generation students often lack this guidance, so campus administrators must help them and their families learn how to navigate college successfully (Ward, Siegel, & Davenport, 2012). Examining and then narrowing the gaps between the expectations of students, parents, faculty, and staff can contribute to students' successful transitions to college (Schilling & Schilling, 2005).

The units within and beyond student affairs with the most responsibility in this phase are admissions, new student orientation, first-year programs, and communications and marketing. Administrators in other programs such as residence life, campus activities, and career services also need to consider such anticipatory socialization communications. As prospective students (and often their parents) explore the institution, the messages conveyed in institutional publications and marketing materials such as email, postal mail, social media, and the institution's website should focus on making clear the intention that faculty and staff at the institution are committed to assisting these young people in establishing their identity as adults, moving through periods of instability toward stability in all phases of life, expanding students' focus to better include others and the community, helping them transition to full adulthood, and creating possibilities for their futures. Campus administrators should incorporate these same messages throughout the new student orientation and first-year programs process. Institutions try to promote themselves to prospective students throughout the admissions and orientation processes by spotlighting academic programs, cocurricular activities, and a wide assortment of amenities; however, they should also incorporate messages that speak to the institution's expectations and intentions regarding learning and development beyond the classroom and consider those messages as another form of marketing. These messages communicate to target audiences what the institution is promising to its constituents. They may also need to help dispel misperceptions and false impressions of college fueled by social media, movies, teachers, peers, parents, siblings, alumni, and so on to help students prepare for the reality of reading loads and academic expectations, sharing rooms and bathrooms with peers, and bearing the consequences of behavioral choices (Ward et al., 2012).

Some institutions use instruments like student success agreements to share their explicit expectations with students or encourage students to take actions or exhibit behaviors that will contribute to the likelihood of their success as students. For example, the University of the Incarnate Word (n.d.) includes in its student success agreement such behaviors as attending 95% of their classes, visiting professors during office hours, purchasing textbooks, and checking email daily. Program administrators expect these behaviors to lead to student persistence and success. First-year seminars are another tool for sharing and reinforcing expectations of students (Schilling & Schilling, 2005). Regarding emerging adulthood, we urge institutions to be transparent about their intention to encourage and expect students to practice the behaviors and actions of adulthood. In doing so, the institutional leaders make clear that they designed the curriculum, programs, and services to help students take more responsibility for themselves, make more independent decisions, and grow in understanding what it means to become financially independent. Rather than presenting a curriculum to develop these attributes without labeling them, administrators and faculty should be explicit with students and their parents and guardians that this is one of the expected outcomes of a college degree earned at the institution—preparation for full adulthood.

Administrators should also communicate clearly that the features of emerging adulthood are normal and expected, including exploring and delineating identity; experiencing instability in love, work, and place of residence; having a greater focus on self than on others; feeling in-between or transitional; and having the opportunity to transform their lives. Student affairs divisions and units need to communicate clearly in orientation and in first-year programs that the units comprising student affairs and related offices are committed to assisting students in navigating the journey to adulthood. They must construct this form of developmental transparency carefully because it may well run counter to typical messaging. First, many students have already navigated the transition to adulthood successfully; this may be especially true for nontraditional students and those who have already been operating independently by choice or circumstance. Second, many college students do not view themselves as adults and do not yet wish to have adult responsibilities. Others may perceive themselves as adults (and most are, legally), but have not yet assumed a full range of adult responsibilities such as caring for themselves, making independent decisions, and being financially independent.

Experiencing College

Many interacting, competing, and reinforcing frameworks underlie the work of student affairs including student learning, student development, retention and persistence, and student success. We contend that the framework of emerging adulthood should be included intentionally in the planned curriculum of student affairs work. In such a curriculum, professionals can promote an apprenticeship model of adulthood in which students are able to practice facing the challenges, expectations, and behaviors of adulthood. Staff model, scaffold, and coach these behaviors expected of adults. Staff then gradually removes the support and coaching while students are encouraged to enact the behaviors on their own, and eventually, generalize these behaviors to other contexts (Brandt, Farmer, & Buckmaster, 1993). Advisors of student organizations, while working with leaders of the organizations, can scaffold experiences related to independent decision-making and accepting responsibility for successes and failures. It will be important to highlight the relationship between these behaviors and future adult expectations. Such practices and high expectations paired with appropriate guidance and support contribute to student success and the developmental journey to adulthood.

In the experiencing college phase, the work of most student affairs units already engages students in activities and encounters that encourage them to take responsibility for themselves and their behaviors and that urge them to make more independent decisions. Administrators expect students to follow the student code of conduct and sanction those found responsible for violating it. Roommates in residence halls are encouraged to work through their problems together with staff assisting rather than dictating what should or should not be the answer to the concerns they may have with each other. Student clubs and organizations are expected to follow the policies and practices for social events and face consequences if they do not. However, each unit in student affairs should consider how they already help students take responsibility for themselves and encourage them to make independent decisions, and then seek ways in which they can more intentionally and strategically increase the opportunities for this to occur. Furthermore, they should also explore how to best support those students who are supporting others including children, parents, and siblings. For example, nearly one million of the four million women attending two-year public colleges are mothers. Many also have substantial work, family, and caregiving responsibilities. Lack of access to reliable and affordable childcare is a significant barrier to degree completion (St. Rose & Hill, 2013). When students begin college as parents, become parents while enrolled, or face caregiving duties for others, they will need institutional support to persist.

We also advise student affairs professionals to be intentional in their efforts to prepare juniors and seniors for the transition to adulthood. Utilizing the experiences of other young people in the midst of emerging adulthood is one strategy for doing so. For example, returning to the #adultinginfivewords analysis, they could provide specific examples of what these young people actually say they experience in the categories of changing priorities (e.g., "up late researching Roth IRA," "sleeping by 10 or 11p.m."), adopting new responsibilities (e.g., "going to the doctor alone"), or participating in "adult" milestones (e.g., "Shopping for my first apartment," "Applied for a credit card," or "Got a health savings account"). This involves urging students to reflect on the experiences they will face after graduation and beyond simple notions of getting a job and moving to a new place (if not back to parents); this is an active, intentional anticipatory socialization process.

Beyond the work of any particular student affairs unit in addressing the developmental tasks of young adults is the role of student employment. Student employment is a broad and diverse category of experience and consists of on-campus employment (including work-study), off-campus employment, paraprofessional roles (e.g., resident assistant, orientation leader), internships, and semester-long or yearlong co-op experiences. Approximately 80% of all undergraduate college students work, and this number has remained virtually unchanged since researchers began tracking it in the early 1990s (King, 2006). These different experiences vary in terms of the opportunity to learn how to make independent decisions, take responsibility for oneself, and move toward financial independence. In the work experiences supervised (i.e., work-study, paraprofessionals) or coordinated (i.e., internships, co-op) by college staff, they can intentionally build into training, supervision, and performance review specific expectations related to responsibility, personal decision-making, and financial responsibility. They can develop learning outcomes to assist in the development of knowledge and skills useful for employment upon graduation and design training to help prepare students for those jobs (Perozzi, Kappes, & Santucci, 2009) and help prepare them for an increasingly global society (Scrogham & McGuire, 2009).

An emphasis on customer service is a potential countervailing force in today's student affairs practice (Davis, 2011). Administrators should consider this in any discussion about preparing students for adulthood. A typical customer service model declares the customer [student] is always right, and providers try to lessen the impact of the consequences for actions or failure to take appropriate actions, especially if they upset the student to the point of leaving the institution. Instead, while remaining open to critical feedback regarding service, the institution's units need to maintain consistency of expectations regarding student behavior and hold students accountable when they fail to meet those expectations (e.g., missing deadlines, failing to complete paperwork).

The third criterion of adulthood, becoming financially independent, is not often addressed in colleges and universities beyond the financial aid office and accounts payable/bursar office, and even there, parents or guardians of many students assume that responsibility. Several themes highlighted above in the #adultinginfivewords analysis addressed financial concerns. Some institutions provide programs on personal fiscal management or offer personal finance courses but many need to do more. In order to be able to become financially independent at some point beyond college, students must have a greater understanding of the components necessary for financial independence. Certainly, the foundation is securing (or creating) a job that provides enough money to cover life's necessities—housing, food, clothing, transportation, and so on. Managing one's personal resources is a vital skill of adulthood and this includes becoming financially literate, setting financial goals, avoiding credit card debt, spending no more than earned (and knowing how to track that), creating a budget and spending plan, saving for major purchases, understanding basic investment strategies, understanding long-term investment strategies for retirement, and learning to protect one's investments and personal financial resources (e.g., disability insurance, diversification, liability coverage). Major life decisions such as having children or marrying will also affect financial plans. A variety of functional areas including residence life, student activities, and career services can play a role in increasing students' financial literacy. Among many available resources, the Federal Deposit Insurance Corporation offers *Money Smart*, a financial education program, free for download (https://www. fdic.gov/consumers/consumer/moneysmart/overview_program.html#yoh). The materials include PowerPoint presentations, presenter guides, participant handouts, and activities. Current offerings for adults include modules on credit, credit history, saving, renting and owning a home, and more. These prepackaged resources provide a strong foundation for programming aimed at helping students gain financial literacy as a foundation of financial independence.

Programming offered through career services can help students prepare for financial independence with educational sessions on understanding health insurance plans and other benefits, retirement savings, payroll taxes, tax planning, and budgeting. Researchers at the Institute for College Access and Success (2016) estimated that in 2015, 68% of public and private nonprofit college graduates had student loan debt. (Almost no for-profit colleges report graduates' load debt so figures for those graduates are unavailable.) Student loan debt ranged from $3,000 to $53,000 or $30,100 on average. Many emerging adults, therefore, must also include student loan payments in their monthly budgets. Of course, many leave college with student loan debt and no degree. Their average earnings are lower than those with a degree and they are at greater risk for loan default. Of those who did not earn a degree or certificate but who had federal student loans entering repayment in 2011–2012, 24% defaulted on those loans within two years, compared to a 9% default rate for degree completers (College Board, 2016). As noted above, more emerging adults are living with parents than in prior generations. One likely reason for this is their inability to afford to live on their own or with friends or partners.

In summary, campus life and student affairs professionals should review their programmatic offerings and priorities in light of emerging adulthood theory. They can do much more to help students learn to take responsibility for themselves, make independent decisions, and lay the foundation for financial independence.

Exiting College and Beyond

One goal of colleges and universities is to prepare students for employment upon graduation, sometimes after additional schooling. Schneider et al. (2016) articulated the challenge that many recent graduates face:

> Transitioning from college into the world of work takes time, but more young people, stuck in low-wage or part-time work, have difficulty viewing themselves as independent adults with a sustainable occupation. Career success is not useful as a marker of adulthood, when young people have to wait until their late 20s or early 30s to achieve the labor-market outcomes that they envisioned when they began college.
>
> *(p. 110)*

Given the nature of college work and experience, it is impossible for colleges to create the conditions to immerse traditional aged college students in a very "adult" environment. However, in the exiting college and beyond phase, all student affairs and related units should conduct business with the expectations in mind. As Gardner and Van der Veer (1998) pointed out, we need to do a much better job of preparing seniors for transition into the world of adults and adult expectations. Many campuses do this through capstone experiences and senior seminars focused on preparing students for life after college. They invite recent alumni to talk with students about their experiences and the challenges of transitioning out of college and into the working world. Some alumni programs have a particular emphasis on young alumni and provide them with career services even after they have graduated. Likewise, some career services offices continue to be available to alumni of all ages. We recommend that this become a standard expectation for career services offices.

Campus professionals should better prepare students for the world of work through internships and other experiential learning opportunities. Career services offices tend to do an especially effective job with business-oriented internships, and some professional academic programs (e.g., nursing, health professions, and engineering) require clinical or practical experiences in the academic curriculum. They should develop more such experiential learning opportunities for liberal arts and social science majors. All undergraduates need to understand the substantial differences between life as a college student and life as an employed person. It is through such apprenticeship experiences that students can assume more responsibility for themselves and learn to make decisions. It can also better foreshadow what skills and perspectives students need to develop financial independence. Part of the transition needs to help students understand that many entry-level jobs are low status, not very well paying, and involve routine tasks. Moving up in the organization requires succeeding in current duties. Professionals should be cognizant of what messages they send to students about the types of jobs and careers available immediately upon graduation. Perhaps a more long-range discussion needs to occur about the difference between where a career begins and where it can lead over time. The needs of particular students and student populations will vary from institution to institution and depend upon the make-up of the student population as well.

Summary

The scholarship on emerging adulthood raises a plethora of compelling issues and questions for the priorities of campus life programs. The current developmental priorities of many student affairs programs center on some of the traditional, and perhaps, newer student development theories and associated research. Through their work, student affairs professionals try to help students become more complex thinkers, have a more complex understanding of their identities (and the identities of others), have greater moral complexity, and develop self-authorship. Theorists may also want to do more work to understand autonomy and interdependence in the current environment, especially in what it means to become an adult while staying more closely tethered to parents than many in prior generations. And while students' social context including families, peer groups, communities, and personal characteristics affect their pathways to adulthood, planning and programming should still be framed around the three criteria for adulthood: (1) accepting responsibility for oneself, (2) making independent decisions, and (3) becoming financially independent (Arnett, 2015). These goals should supplement rather than displace the current developmental priorities.

References

Arnett, J. J. (2015). *Emerging adulthood: The winding road from the late teens through the twenties* (2nd ed.). New York, NY: Oxford.

Brandt, B. L., Farmer, J. A., & Buckmaster, A. (1993). Cognitive apprenticeship approach to helping adults learn. In D. D. Flannery (Ed.), *New directions for adult and continuing education: No. 59. Applying cognitive learning theory to adult learning* (pp. 69–78). San Francisco, CA: Jossey-Bass.

Chickering, A. W., & Reisser, L. (1993) *Education and identity* (2nd ed.). San Francisco, CA: Jossey-Bass.

College Board. (2016). *Trends in student aid 2016*. Trends in higher education series. Retrieved from https://trends.collegeboard.org/sites/default/files/2016-trends-student-aid_0.pdf

Davis, T. (2011). In this age of consumerism, what are the implications of giving students what they want?: Have it your way U. In P. M. Magolda & M. B. Baxter Magolda (Eds.), *Contested issues in student affairs: Diverse perspectives and respectful dialogue* (pp. 85–96). Sterling, VA: Stylus.

Fry, R. (2016, May 24). *For first time in modern era, living with parents edges out other living arrangements for 18- to 34-year-olds*. Washington, DC: Pew Research Center. Retrieved from www.pewsocialtrends.org/2016/05/24/for-first-time-in-modern-era-living-with-parents-edges-out-other-living-arrangements-for-18-to-34-year-olds/

Gardner, J. N., & Van der Veer, G. (1998). *The senior year experience: Facilitating integration, reflection, closure, and transition*. San Francisco, CA: Jossey-Bass.

Institute for College Access and Success. (2016, October). *Student debt and the class of 2015: 11th Annual Report*. Oakland, CA: Author. Retrieved from https://ticas.org/sites/default/files/pub_files/classof2015.pdf

King, J. (2006). Working their way through college: Student employment and its impact on the college experience. *ACE Issue Brief, ACE Center for Policy Analysis, American Council on Education*.

Kuh, G. D., Schuh, J. H., Whitt, E. J., & Associates. (1991). *Involving colleges: Successful approaches to fostering student learning and development outside the classroom*. San Francisco, CA: Jossey-Bass.

Lamidi. E. (2016). A quarter century of change in nonmarital births: Differences by education attainment. *Family Profiles, FP-16-05*. Bowling Green, OH: National Center for Family & Marriage Research. Retrieved from www.bgsu.edu/ncfmr/resources/data/family-profiles/lamidi-nonmarital-births-educational-attainment-fp-16-05.html

Lareau, A. (2015). Cultural knowledge and social inequality. *American Sociological Review, 80*(1), 1–27.

Martin, J. A., Hamilton B. E., Osterman, M. J. K., Driscoll, A. K., & Mathews, T. J. (2017). Births: Final data for 2015. *National Vital Statistics Report, 66*(1). Hyattsville, MD: National Center for Health Statistics.

Payne, K. K., Manning, W. D., & Brown, S. L. (2012). *Unmarried births to cohabiting and single mothers, 2005–2010* (FP-12–06). National Center for Family & Marriage Research. Retrieved from http://ncfmr.bgsu.edu/pdf/family_profiles/file109171.pdf

Perozzi, B., Kappes, J., & Santucci, D. (2009). Learning outcomes and student employment programs. In B. Perozzi (Ed.), *Enhancing student learning through college employment* (pp. 67–84). Bloomington, IN: ACUI.

Putnam, R. D. (2015). *Our kids: The American dream in crisis*. New York, NY: Simon & Schuster.

Schilling, K. M., & Schilling, K. L. (2005). Expectations and performance. In M. L. Upcraft, J. N. Gardner, B. O. Barefoot (Eds.), *Challenging and supporting the first-year student: A handbook for improving the first year of college* (pp. 108–120). San Francisco, CA: Jossey-Bass.

Schneider, B., Klager, C., Chen, I., & Burns, J. (2016). Transitioning into adulthood: Striking a balance between support and independence. *Policy Insights from the Behavioral and Brain Sciences, 3*(1) 106–113.

Scrogham, E., & McGuire, S. P. (2009). Orientation, training, and development. In B. Perozzi (Ed.), *Enhancing student learning through college employment* (pp. 199–220). Bloomington, IN: ACUI.

St. Rose, A., & Hill, C. (2013). *Women in community colleges: Access to success.* Washington, DC: American Association of University Women. Retrieved from www.aauw.org/files/2013/05/women-in-community-colleges.pdf

Twenge, J. M. (2017). *iGen: Why today's super-connected kids are growing up less rebellious, more tolerant, less happy—and completely unprepared for adulthood—and what that means for the rest of us.* New York, NY: Atria.

University of the Incarnate Word. (n.d.). *Student success agreement.* Retrieved September 19, 2017 from www.uiw.edu/firstyear/studentsuccessagreement.html

Volkmann, W. W. (1998). *Excellence in advancement: Applications for higher education and nonprofit organizations.* Gaithersburg, MD: Aspen.

Wang, W., & Parker, K. (2014, September 24). *Record share of Americans have never married: As values, economics and gender patterns change.* Washington, DC: Pew Research Center's Social & Demographic Trends project.

Ward, L., Siegel, M. J., & Davenport, Z. (2012). *First-generation college students: Understanding and improving the experience from recruitment to commencement.* San Francisco, CA: Jossey-Bass.

12

CULTIVATING RELATIONSHIPS BETWEEN THE INSTITUTION AND ITS EMERGING ADULT ALUMNI

Shelby K. Radcliffe

If truly embraced by alumni engagement professionals and student affairs professionals, Arnett's (2015) theory of emerging adulthood has the potential to completely revolutionize not just alumni engagement work, but how colleges and universities serve and support students *and* alumni. First, applying Arnett's theory and related research to the practice of alumni engagement could improve services alumni offices provide to young alumni. By embracing the responsibility to help students *and alumni* successfully navigate the entire period of emerging adulthood, colleges and universities would provide important challenge and support to young alumni populations, helping institutions deliver on the promise of the college investment. Second, utilizing older alumni to provide meaningful challenge and support for younger alumni would not just serve younger alumni well but also increase alumni engagement across multiple generations. Finally, Arnett's theory provides an intellectual and practical framework for reimagining the role of administrators in both student and alumni affairs around educational outcomes far more important than a credential. At a time when consumer confidence in higher education is at an all-time low and demographic and economic disruptions are challenging the fundamentals of the American higher education model, Arnett's theory poses, and perhaps answers, important questions about how colleges should evolve to better serve their students and alumni.

It has been 20 years since Gardner and Van der Veer (1998) first explored the importance of the senior year and asserted that colleges and universities played an important role in the college-to-career transition. The authors asserted that from the early 1990s forward "a growing number of educators and prospective employers are suggesting that colleges need to do more for seniors than simply hand them a diploma" (p. xi). Gardner and Van der Veer suggested that student affairs professionals could play a leading role in responding to these expectations with comprehensive career services during all four years of college, but especially during senior year.

Many colleges and universities have responded to this call to action in the last two decades, and the services provided to students by campus career centers have increased dramatically. During this time, however, we know that job changes and career transitions have often continued well beyond graduation, that 40% of college graduates are now likely to move back in with their parents at least once during their emerging adult years (Arnett, 2015, p. 57), and that even the basic premise of graduation in four chronological years is no longer the norm, with 40% of college students taking more than six years to graduate (Arnett, 2015, p. 147). In fact, within 15 years after Gardner and Van der Veer (1998) published their work, Skipper (2012) acknowledged these trends and cited Arnett's work in particular. Recognizing the new demographics of seniors and the theoretical framework of emerging adulthood, Skipper suggested that King and Kitchener's reflective judgment model might be a more useful tool for measuring the achievement of adulthood than completion of a four-year degree. The challenge, according to Skipper (2012), is that "few, if any, students leave college as reflective thinkers" (p. 33) even while they recognize "reflective thinking as an important component of achieving adulthood" (p. 33).

It should be no surprise, then, that according to the Pew Research Center Report, *Is College Worth It?* (Taylor et al., 2011), "only four-in-ten [Americans] say the higher education system does an excellent (5%) or good (35%) job providing value to students given the amount of money they and their families are paying for college" (p. 31). If the expected return on the investment in college is not just a credential, but a successful transition to adulthood, how can families and their students be satisfied when their transition to adulthood lasts well beyond graduation?

Chickering, a leading student development theorist, "saw the establishment of identity as the core developmental issue with which college students grapple" (Patton, Renn, Guido, & Quaye, 2016, p. 296), and the student affairs profession has expanded to support and catalyze this development in the cocurricular arena. Skipper (2012) noted, however, that "the time between graduation and attaining the external markers of adulthood has increased dramatically in the last three decades" (p. 26). Arnett (2015) warns against thinking of emerging adulthood as only "the transition to adulthood" (p. 22), reinforcing Chickering's focus on identity development, not just traditional adulthood achievements. The big difference between Chickering and Arnett is not the aim of this developmental period, but the length of it. That the identity development process continues well past traditional college age requires that we ask ourselves what role student affairs and alumni professionals have in supporting this development beyond graduation.

Higher education administrators and faculty can argue that the academic and cocurricular college experience provides the foundation for that development or that colleges and universities can only do so much in the four years a student is on campus. Whether students are taking a break for financial or other reasons, or have completed their degrees, support from their alma mater for this important development virtually evaporates when they leave campus. The more distance there is between the college experience and the achievement of adulthood markers, including the establishment of personal, professional, and relational identities, the less likely families and their emerging adults will credit the costly college experience with that success.

Imagine, instead, if student affairs and alumni relations professionals combined efforts and developed comprehensive programs for all students (graduated or not) and young alumni; programs designed to intentionally facilitate and support their development through the entire period of emerging adulthood. Looking at alumni engagement through the lens of emerging adulthood and simultaneously embracing the notion that student development continues well after degree completion, one begins to reimagine the work of the alumni office on many fronts.

This view requires that alumni offices think with their campus partners in student affairs about what emerging adults need and want during this period of their lives. It also requires that alumni and student affairs professionals think differently about how and when services are delivered to students and alumni. In all cases, delivering appropriate programming can engage both the emerging adult population and older alumni as those older alumni are recruited and engaged through meaningful volunteer work to support students and young alumni. Following are some practical applications of this thinking, organized around Arnett's themes of emerging adulthood including demographic variability, educational status, and a variety of identity explorations.

Demographics

Arnett (2015) outlines the high residential demographic variability of the emerging adult population. The unifying theme of this population is, in fact, that they are constantly on the move. Instead of simply updating alumni addresses more frequently to ensure delivery of event invitations and alumni magazines, this instability could be met by alumni offices with programming that supports young alumni during this period of constant change. Alumni offices could develop programs that introduce young alumni, not just the most recent graduates, to new regions and networks. Programming designed for the spring graduating classes should be expanded and adapted to address the needs of all emerging adults and to help them quickly find their college or university network in their new home. Programming could also be designed to help young alumni navigate the world of cohabitation or reentry into a childhood home. Far more than happy hours and alumni outings, cocurricular programming and support could significantly improve other important postgraduation outcomes like employment and graduate education attainment.

Educational Status

Arnett (2015) reports that while 60% of emerging adults go to college right after high school, only 35% have finished college by the end of this period. Even for those who do finish by the end of their twenties, nonlinear educational paths are far more common today than ever before. A wide variety of on-campus retention programs have evolved to address these issues (Berger, Ramirez, & Lyons, 2012), but alumni programs have stubbornly continued to focus their work on degreed alumni. While non-degreed alumni are invited to social alumni programming, alumni offices could embrace a role as part of the team that supports alumni through degree completion.

The emerging adult view of alumni relations calls upon alumni offices to truly embrace the nondegreed alumnus as an important part of the alumni community and a cohort of alumni that need and deserve a different set of engagement activities than degreed alumni. Partnering with student affairs (and likely academic affairs as well), alumni programs could share ownership for facilitating degree completion among these alumni, delivering on the promise of their years of investment and hard work. This perspective allows colleges to recognize the situation that nondegreed alumni are in and to remove some of the stigma they might feel; to say, "We see you, you matter to us and we're here for and with you." The present alternative is that even when colleges do engage non-degreed alumni, it's with a lack of recognition that they haven't completed their degrees, further isolating them and drawing out negative feelings about their alma mater.

In practical terms, this could mean that alumni relations teams would cultivate volunteers who can counsel and support nondegreed alumni to completion wherever they may live. Programming could include webinars and on-campus programs to help non-degreed alumni understand financial options for continuing in school or map out paths to graduation. Creative partnerships with other educational institutions in regions where many young alumni live could facilitate degree completion and retain connection to alma mater. Financial education and financial support could be made available for alumni for whom money is the largest barrier to finishing their degree. Support groups and mentoring programs with older alumni, faculty, or student affairs colleagues could be valuable for non-degreed alumni who are working through personal and family issues that make completion difficult. Whatever the programming, alumni relations teams could dramatically expand services to these alumni who are too often forgotten or left behind. When these alumni truly feel that the institution stayed with them until the end, their loyalty and engagement will be far higher than the current trends with non-degreed alumni who have been ignored or neglected by their alma maters.

Identity Explorations

Emerging adulthood is a period of intense identity exploration in many areas, including self-identity (around issues of gender, race, ethnicity, and more), love-identity (around issues of sexual relationships and partner selection), and work-identity (around issues of jobs and careers and issues of ambition and quality of life). In all of these areas, alumni programming could do so much more to engage and support the emerging adult population.

Self-Identity

Cocurricular programs have grown to include many resources to support the identity exploration that often begins in earnest, or dramatically increases, at the start of emerging adulthood. Centers organized around gender and sexuality exploration, racial and ethnicity identity exploration, first generation and immigrant identity exploration, and more are important parts of the challenge and support network while students are on campus. Some alumni programs have begun to help alumni connect with each other around these identity experiences in informal and formal ways. What few alumni programs have done, however, is provide continued educational and support programming for emerging adults that compliments what was provided on campus.

From online safe-spaces for alumni to mentoring from older alumni with similar identities to developmentally appropriate educational and social programming, alumni offices could do more to connect emerging adults to services and to each other. In addition, older alumni could provide a much needed support network for emerging adult alumni with similar identities.

Love and Relationship Identity

Like other self-identities mentioned above, sexual orientation exploration is likely to continue well beyond graduation, and emerging adult alumni would benefit from programming and support networks initiated by their alumni office. In addition, while no one would argue that match-making is the responsibility of a college or university, alumni programs can capitalize on this element of emerging adulthood with programming specifically for singles and couples.

Work and Professional Identity

While current standards of professional practice stipulate that college career centers should engage students in thinking about life after college long before their last semester on campus (Wells, 2015), Arnett's (2015) work helps us to understand that the career conversation will likely extend well beyond that final spring semester. Of the students who go to graduate school, for example, only 50% go right after graduation. Alumni need access to graduate advising as much as, if not more than, undergraduates as a result. Graduates will likely change jobs, two, three, or more times in the decade after graduation. The need for continued guidance, mentoring, and support around career discernment and placement is dramatically higher than current alumni programming capabilities support.

In the last decade, there has been a dramatic expansion of alumni programming around work and career identity. From profession-based alumni networking events to alumni webinars on resume writing and interview skills, alumni offices have recognized the opportunity of engaging alumni around professional interests. Much more is possible in this arena, however, if alumni offices embrace both this role and Arnett's theory. Moving from distinct student vs. alumni programming could enable a combined effort to support students and alumni where they are in their career development, as opposed to focusing on when they are in their relationship to their alma mater.

Some sophomores have no need for discernment counseling but want coaching to get an internship that will help them land the graduate program acceptance of their dreams. Some mid-twenties emerging adults will need the discernment counseling they overlooked while on campus as their identity exploration leads them to make different choices than they had imagined during school. Some colleges and universities are beginning to house career centers within advancement offices to encourage this kind of collaboration between pre- and postgraduation career services professionals. While merging these offices may not be appropriate on all campuses, tighter collaboration and program development and delivery would help colleges and universities provide one of the most important services that families want from their investment in tuition—launching their child successfully in a job or career.

Achieving Adulthood

What is perhaps most illuminating about Arnett's work for the student and alumni affairs collaboration, however, is the way emerging adults themselves define what adulthood means. In a variety of studies with young people in their teens and twenties, demographic transitions such as finishing education, settling into a career, marriage, and parenthood rank at the bottom in importance among possible criteria considered necessary for the attainment of adulthood (Arnett, 1997, 1998; Greene, Wheatley, & Aldava, 1992; Scheer, Unger, & Brown, 1996). The characteristics that matter most to emerging adults in their subjective sense of attaining adulthood are not demographic transitions but individualistic qualities of character (Arnett, 1998). Specifically, the two top criteria for the transition to adulthood in a variety of studies have been accepting responsibility for oneself and making independent decisions (Arnett, 1997, 1998; Greene et al., 1992; Scheer et al., 1996). Evaluating the impact of alumni engagement programs against these priorities would be a dramatic shift from tracking event attendance and giving behaviors, but one that could prove impact and make a more substantial case for additional resources in both student and alumni affairs.

Becoming financially independent is a third signal of reaching adulthood, also individualistic but more tangible, that emerging adults consistently rank high in importance (Arnett, 1997, 1998; Greene et al., 1992; Scheer et al., 1996). So even if an alumni office successfully developed substantial programming to support emerging adults through demographic changes, college completion, and the many types of identity exploration, that programming might miss the mark. Data from the Institute for College Access and Success (2016) reveal that 68% of bachelor degree recipients have debt at graduation and that debt averages about $30,000 per student. That is quite a financial burden for any emerging adult to bear.

Most students will be paying on that debt for the entirety of their emerging adult years. The average $200–400 loan payments could, in fact, present a substantial barrier to achieving financial independence, thus contributing to the delay of some important milestones to reaching adulthood. Making independent decisions becomes much more possible when finances don't require continued reliance, or even dependence, on parents or other family members.

Student affairs offices could utilize alumni to help prepare current students for the financial responsibilities of life after graduation. Alumni programs could provide financial management programming and mentoring by older alumni. A final, radical way that alumni programs could support emerging adults would be to partner with their development colleagues to raise money for student loan forgiveness funds, which would be available for young alumni as they make their way through emerging adulthood. While the challenges to a program like this could be many, the idea is also rich with opportunities for engaging both younger alumni and the older alumni who could mentor and support them.

Conclusion

The theory of emerging adulthood provides a framework for rethinking the work of alumni engagement *and* student affairs. An integrated approach to student and alumni support during emerging adulthood could increase retention and completion rates dramatically. Radical change could differentiate colleges that serve the students and alumni through their entire emerging adult years and deliver far more value for the high cost of tuition.

The logistics of comingling strategy and execution for the support and service to students and alumni around identity development during emerging adulthood may seem daunting. Facilitating healthy identity development has long been the specialty of student affairs professionals while advancement staff have not needed to understand cognitive or psychosocial development theories, racial/gender/ orientation/or other identity development theories, and more. To successfully understand this audience and develop appropriate programming, advancement professionals will need to immerse themselves in the theory and practice of student affairs and to partner with their student affairs colleagues to develop a through-line between on-campus programming during college and alumni programming after. On the other hand, advancement offices have mastered the art of measuring and tracking inputs and outcomes and reporting on return-on-investment. To benefit from this expertise, student affairs professionals will need to embrace a data-driven, relationship management model of service delivery.

The combined talents of these professions actually seem ripe for collaboration and success. Where student affairs professionals know developmental theory and can easily build programs to maximize student growth and achievement, alumni affairs professionals know how to plan and design, market, and implement programs across multiple locations and platforms. Advancement teams have made substantial strides in using data to inform strategy and advocate for resources, a talent that could be useful in the severely under-resourced world of student affairs. A strong understanding of the prevailing identity development theories and practices can dramatically improve the effectiveness of programming for students *and* alumni. It can provide a set of principles that facilitate decisions about modifying, growing, or even eliminating programming. It can catalyze the development of new and more effective uses of institutional resources. And in the end, delivering a higher return-on-investment to students and their families could positively influence recruitment of future students as well as alumni giving behavior. Embracing the notion that the alumni relations program is *part* of the team that supports the identity development of students and the student affairs program is *part* of the team that supports the identity development of alumni changes just about everything if you let it.

References

Arnett, J. J. (1997). Young people's conceptions of the transition to adulthood. *Youth & Society, 29*(1), 3–23.

Arnett, J. J. (1998). Learning to stand alone: The contemporary American transition to adulthood in cultural and historical context. *Human Development, 41*, 295–315.

Arnett, J. J. (2015). *Emerging adulthood: The winding road from the late teens through the twenties* (2nd ed.). New York, NY: Oxford.

Berger, J. B., Ramirez, G. B., & Lyons, S. (2012). Past to present: A historical look at retention. In A. Seidman (Ed.), *College student retention: Formula for success* (2nd ed., pp. 7–34). Lanham, MD: Rowman & Littlefield.

Gardner, J. N., & Van der Veer, G. (Eds.) (1998). *The senior year experience: Facilitating integration, reflection, closure, and transition.* San Francisco, CA: Jossey-Bass.

Greene, A. L., Wheatley, S. M., & Aldava, J. F., IV (1992). Stages on life's way: Adolescents' implicit theories of the life course. *Journal of Adolescent Research, 7*(3), 364–381.

Institute for College Access and Success. (2016, October). *Student debt and the class of 2015: 11th Annual Report.* Oakland, CA: Author. Retrieved from https://ticas.org/sites/default/files/pub_files/classof2015.pdf

Patton, L. D., Renn, K. A., Guido, F. M., & Quaye, S. J. (2016). *Student development in college: theory, research, and practice* (3rd ed.). San Francisco, CA: Jossey-Bass.

Scheer, S. D., Unger, D. G., & Brown, M. B. (1996). Adolescents becoming adults: Attributes for adulthood. *Adolescence, 31*(121), 127–131.

Skipper, T. L. (2012). The kids are alright: Emerging adulthood and the transition out of adulthood. In M. S. Hunter, J. R. Keup, J. Kinzie, & H. Maietta (Eds.), *The senior year: Culminating experiences and transitions* (pp. 25–48). Columbia, SC: National Resource Center for The [sic] First Year Experience and Students in Transition.

Taylor, P., Parker, K., Fry, R., Cohn, D., Wang, W., Velasco, G., & Dockterman, D. (2011). *Is college worth it? College presidents, public assess value, quality and mission of higher education.* Washington, DC: Pew Research Center.

Wells, J. B. (2015). *CAS professional standards for higher education* (9th ed.). Washington, DC: Council for the Advancement of Standards in Higher Education.

13

CONCLUSION AND FUTURE DIRECTIONS

Joseph L. Murray and Jeffrey Jensen Arnett

As explained in the opening chapter, the purpose of this book is to introduce emerging adulthood theory to a higher education and student affairs readership, with particular attention to its implications for administrative and student affairs practice, research on college students, and the advancement of student development theory. Given the rapid expansion of the literature on emerging adulthood over the past two decades, coupled with its more limited exposure within higher education and student affairs circles, this was no small task. Nevertheless, the contributing authors covered significant ground related to such varied topics as career development, social and emotional adjustment, family relationships, and student success. In this chapter, we synthesize key points embedded in their work and set forth an agenda for both theoretically based practice and future scholarship.

Integration of Emerging Adulthood Theory into the Literature of Student Affairs

In the first five chapters of this book, the various authors helped to establish the basic compatibility of Arnett's (2015) theory of emerging adulthood with the foundational literature of the student affairs field, elucidating its potential contributions to the future expansion of this body of work and cautioning against misapplication of its tenets. In our own introductory chapter, we highlighted the evolution of the student affairs profession's guiding philosophy from its initial focus on student services to its current emphasis on student learning. In so doing, we recognized the enduring influence of psychosocial theory on contemporary views of student affairs, even amidst a trend toward adoption of a broader range of disciplinary perspectives. Arnett then offered an overview of his theory of emerging adulthood, which addressed both the social conditions that have given rise to a longer pathway to adulthood and the main features of the emerging adult life stage. From there, Murray reviewed the body of psychosocial theory that has traditionally informed student affairs practice, along with more recent contributions to the theoretical literature of the field. Contextualizing college student development in a broader life stage framework, he elaborated on theories of identity development in college, both generally and in relation to race, ethnicity, gender, sexuality, disability status, and other aspects of social identity. He also highlighted the influence of the constructive developmentalist, environmental, critical, and poststructural perspectives that have increasingly shaped understandings of psychosocial development in college. Building upon this foundation, Perez and Landreman presented an in-depth analysis of social identity development in relation to Arnett's theory of emerging adulthood, raising critical questions as to how experiences of this life stage might vary across diverse student populations. Murray then turned his attention to the literature on generational change, focusing primarily on the characteristics of those entering higher education over the past two decades.

Based on this review of the relevant literature, we see a fundamental compatibility between the more familiar body of work on psychosocial development in college and Arnett's theory of emerging adulthood. Arnett's work aligns well with more established theoretical perspectives in its emphasis on identity development during the college years, and extends the basic concept of a stage-based model of psychosocial development across the lifespan. At the same time, with its multicultural and interdisciplinary footprint, the rapidly expanding body of research inspired by Arnett's concept of emerging adulthood mirrors the expansion of theoretical perspectives on college student development and the integration of existing perspectives, which together have served to promote the progress of thought within the field.

Emerging adulthood theory brings unity to the study of psychosocial development and generational change, both of which are topics of longstanding interest to the student affairs profession, but which heretofore have generally been treated separately within both the literature of the field and graduate preparation programs. The transition from the Millennial cohort to Generation Z, which has reinvigorated the study of generational theory, presents an opportune moment for those interested in higher education and student affairs to engage developmental psychologists and social theorists in interdisciplinary dialogue of the sort that is already occurring in the community of scholars that has formed to advance the study of emerging adulthood.

In light of growing concern for equity and inclusion in higher education, Perez and Landreman's critical analysis of emerging adulthood theory makes an important contribution to such dialogue. In their chapter, they addressed the far-reaching influences of power and privilege on access to opportunities for one's future, as well as cultural biases embedded in definitions of adulthood that center largely on the attainment of independence from one's family of origin.

They also probed more deeply into issues affecting student populations identified on the basis of race, ethnicity, social class, gender, sexual orientation, and disability status. Such topics have also been widely debated within the literature of emerging adulthood, and the breadth of disciplines that have been brought to bear on this dialogue has contributed to its richness and depth.

The influence of social class, in particular, on experiences of passage into adulthood has drawn considerable attention within the literature of emerging adulthood, owing in large measure to its inclusion of research on both student and non-student populations (Arnett, 2016; Arnett, Kloep, Hendry, & Tanner, 2011). We believe this point of differentiation within the traditional college-aged population represents one of the most significant contributions that Arnett's theory of emerging adulthood and related scholarship can bring to the literature of student affairs. Professionals in the field, and in higher education generally, have taken seriously the call for equity and inclusion on their campuses and have sought to better understand the social and economic conditions that create roadblocks to degree attainment for marginalized populations. Despite gains in understanding of such barriers, it remains unlikely that research solely on existing student populations can contribute fully to academics' understanding of the most formidable obstacles to higher learning. In contrast, research on both student and non-student populations, of the sort advanced in the literature on emerging adulthood, can help institutional officials to better understand both those young people whom they currently serve and those they have yet to reach.

Facets of Emerging Adult Development in College

In Arnett's overview of his theory of emerging adulthood, he elaborated on four societal conditions that largely account for the longer transition to adulthood today: (1) the Technology Revolution, (2) the Sexual Revolution, (3) the Women's Movement, and (4) the Youth Movement. Likewise, he expounded on five essential features of emerging adulthood: (1) identity explorations, (2) instability, (3) self-focus, (4) feeling in-between, and (5) possibilities/optimism. Building upon the theoretical foundation established by Arnett and others in the first five chapters of this book, the authors of the next three chapters examined specific aspects of student development in college, with attention to the themes articulated by Arnett and drawing upon both the relevant literature and their own professional experience. For the purpose of this analysis, developmental issues were organized in three major categories: (1) career development in emerging adulthood, (2) problems associated with emerging adulthood, and (3) the role of parents in emerging adulthood.

In addressing the topic of career development, Severy examined both the social and psychological dimensions of the challenge that it poses to current college students. First affirming the link between work and love and the centrality of both to personal identity, she quickly acknowledged the economic realities that inevitably temper even the most romantic idealism of emerging adults on campus. The rising cost of higher education compels attention to return-on-investment, as the college degree itself becomes increasingly an occupational necessity. The instability of emerging adulthood manifests itself in a process of career exploration that now typically extends well past graduation from college and encompasses multiple job changes, as well as a significant element of happenstance. Under such circumstances, management of expectations becomes a key factor in emerging adults' ability to satisfactorily navigate the process of career development. To complicate matters further, the in-between nature of the emerging adult life stage creates wide variation in individuals' ability to cope with the stress associated with career transitions. In her chapter, Severy noted the influences that account for such variation, including relationships with parents, the range of available options, and one's personal sense of self-determination.

The challenges of emerging adulthood were likewise cast into sharp relief by Adams and Sharkin, who examined various problems that are of particular concern to clinicians and others working with traditional aged college students. These issues were classified into two broad categories: (1) externalizing problems, which bring deleterious effects to one's interaction with the outside world and (2) internalizing problems, in which pain and suffering are turned inward upon oneself. Among the externalizing problems discussed in the chapter were risky driving, crime, substance abuse, and issues pertaining to parental involvement, romantic and sexual relationships, and academic distress. Internalizing problems included depression, anxiety disorders, eating disorders, post-traumatic stress disorder, nonsuicidal self-injury, suicide, and low self-esteem.

Traditional aged students' relationships with their parents were further explored by Mullendore, Daniel, and Toney, in relation to the five essential features of emerging adulthood set forth by Arnett. In examining the influence of parents on students' identity exploration, the authors highlighted the processes of college selection, the first-year transition, personal identity exploration, selection of a major, and career exploration. A novel aspect of this chapter was the inclusion of first-person accounts of emerging adulthood, as experienced by Daniel and Toney, both relatively new professionals in student affairs. Their personal anecdotes further underscored the significance of Arnett's work to student affairs practice, insofar as the field has long maintained a system of professional preparation and initial employment that contributes to an elongation of the transition to adulthood. Entrants into the field typically complete two years of full-time graduate enrollment, often supplementing part-time assistantship earnings with parental support, before assuming entry-level positions in which live-in responsibilities, frequent travel, irregular hours, relatively low pay, and various other occupational constraints can lead to further postponement of traditional adult commitments. Thus, emerging adulthood theory holds implications for both work with students and re-cruitment, preparation, supervision, and advancement of new professionals in student affairs.

To varying degrees, the relationship between traditional aged students and their parents figured prominently in each of the three chapters highlighted in this section. Like Mullendore et al., Severy recognized the potentially signifi-cant influence of parents on emerging adults' career choices. Likewise, Adams and Sharkin discussed the challenge of parental disengagement in the lives of troubled emerging adults, even while recognizing dysfunctional parent-child relationships as a significant problem for some emerging adults in college. With appropriate caveats noted, the authors of the three chapters generally recog-nized parents as an important source of support for student affairs professionals in their work with emerging adults, consistent with advancements in the pro-fession noted elsewhere in this volume. Mullendore et al., in particular, offered a useful set of guidelines for optimal engagement of parents in the lives of their emerging adult sons and daughters, which have broad applicability across mul-tiple areas of student affairs practice.

Implications for Practice

In the four chapters immediately preceding this closing chapter, the respec-tive authors directly examined the implications of Arnett's theory of emerging adulthood for administrative and student affairs practice in higher education. The subtopics addressed in their chapters were organized in four broad clusters that encompassed the work of multiple organizational units: (1) strategic enroll-ment management (SEM) for emerging adults, (2) creating campus environ-ments for emerging adults, (3) student affairs programs for emerging adults, and (4) cultivating relationships between the institution and its emerging adult alumni.

In the first of these chapters, Warshaw and Hearn addressed the topics of recruitment, retention, and academic support for emerging adults, focusing mainly on use of SEM to promote equitable access to the benefits of higher edu-cation. Informed by the prior literature on economically disadvantaged emerg-ing adults, the authors discussed various aspects of SEM, including financial aid policies, tuition discounting practices, testing requirements, and structuring of the admissions cycle, all of which can be used to increase opportunities for di-verse student populations. They also discussed the use of "academic coaching" as a means of promoting academic success and fostering independence in emerging adults. Recognizing the active role of parents in emerging adults' decisions concerning college enrollment and persistence to degree completion, they saw merit in outreach to parents of current and prospective students, as well as a more intentional transfer of certain aspects of the parental role to fac-ulty and staff "surrogates," informed by prior research on students' transitions toward greater autonomy in college.

In the next chapter, Strange examined the characteristics of optimally supportive campus environments for emerging adults, based on a hierarchical model of environmental design set forth previously by Strange and Banning (2015). This earlier model comprised three progressively ordered environmental characteristics, which cumulatively served to maximize student success: (1) inclusion and safety, (2) engagement, and (3) community. This model allowed for the purposeful design of growth-producing campus environments through attention to four categories of environmental elements: (1) physical, (2) human aggregate, (3) organizational, and (4) socially constructed. Tailoring this model to the needs of emerging adults, Strange drew upon the related scholarship of Parks (2011), whose seminal work on mentoring communities had previously been revised to reflect current understandings of emerging adulthood. Under his expanded hierarchical model, Strange linked Parks's seven characteristics of mentoring communities to the three environmental levels identified by Strange and Banning, thereby setting a foundation for further examination of campus-based programs and services for emerging adults.

In Wilson and Love's chapter on student affairs programs for emerging adults, they turned first to Arnett's (2015) research on emerging adults' own definitions of adulthood, in which three criteria were overwhelmingly favored: (1) acceptance of responsibility for oneself, (2) making independent decisions, and (3) becoming financially independent. In their own analysis of 200 responses to the Twitter hashtag #adultinginfivewords, by men and women within the emerging adult age range, Wilson and Love identified eight categories of response, which added texture to the aforementioned criteria: (1) changing priorities, (2) adopting new responsibilities, (3) participating in "adult" milestones, (4) experiencing additional stress and pressure and feeling tired, (5) changing perception of money, (6) feeling financial pressure, (7) adopting "adult" tastes, and (8) new versions of autonomy. Recognizing that recent college graduates have often felt unprepared for the challenges of adult life that await them, Wilson and Love recommended that student affairs professionals, together with their colleagues in other organizational units, act with greater intention to cultivate students' independence and sense of responsibility at three stages of their relationship with the institution: (1) entering college, (2) experiencing college, and (3) exiting college and beyond.

In the next chapter, Radcliffe elaborated further on the third stage of the student-institution relationship, examining implications of a longer pathway to adulthood for work with young alumni. Her musings led her to envision an institutional commitment to student success that would extend beyond the traditional four years of continuous enrollment. Under this model, alumni relations professionals, in partnership with their student affairs colleagues, would work to facilitate the continued identity exploration of nondegreed alumni, even after their departure from campus, and work to create pathways to degree completion where appropriate. Recognizing the high geographic mobility of emerging adults, Radcliffe described an approach to alumni networking that would also focus on supporting all recent alumni in their adjustment to new community environments through engagement with more established alumni in their areas. Other alumni programming would systematically address the three aforementioned criteria for adult status endorsed by emerging adults (accepting responsibility for oneself, making independent decisions, and attaining financial independence). Such an approach would form a seamless extension of the type of campus-based programs and services envisioned by Wilson and Love, thus bolstering the rationale for collaborative partnerships between alumni relations and student affairs personnel.

A common theme across all four chapters was mentorship, whether in the form of a one-on-one relationship or a mentoring community. In a commonly referenced work on the topic, Kram (1985) characterized the mentoring relationship as one that evolves over time, becoming more coequal as the protégé matures under the tutelage of the mentor. This understanding of mentorship would seem to support the longer view envisioned by Wilson and Love and by Radcliffe, just as their shared emphasis on partnerships across institutional divisions aligns well with the holistic environmental approach advocated by Strange. The transfer of certain mentoring functions from parents to academic and student affairs personnel, as envisioned by Warshaw and Hearn and by Wilson and Love, offers a prelude to the subsequent transfer of mentoring functions to senior alumni, as envisioned by Radcliffe. In each of these instances, the longer timeline for entry into adulthood creates continuation of mentoring further into emerging adults' developmental processes, but also sets the stage for long-term relationships that mature appropriately over time. This dynamic view of the mentoring relationship is also applicable to new professionals' enculturation into student affairs, as reflected in the prior literature of the field (Reesor, Bagunu, & Gregory, 2015), and likewise responds to the challenges of emerging adulthood, as recounted by Daniel and Toney in their chapter with Mullendore.

The collaborative approach to alumni relations envisioned by Radcliffe also aligns well with the student affairs profession's growing emphasis on collegial partnerships within its guiding philosophy, as reflected in the various statements reviewed in our opening chapter. Such an approach would likely require some rudimentary knowledge of student development theory on the part of alumni relations professionals, as well as a basic understanding of institutional advancement on the part of their student affairs colleagues. Penney and Rose (2001) authored a highly readable primer on the latter, which could serve as a template for creating other staff development resources suitable for use in building partnerships across divisional lines. Toward this end, we would also recommend the incorporation of standards and guidelines for alumni relations programs into future editions of the *CAS Professional Standards for Higher Education* (Wells, 2015). While the articulation of such standards and guidelines should be led by an established association for alumni relations professionals, such as the Council for Advancement and Support of Education (CASE), we believe the coordinating function of CAS would be instrumental in advancing mutual understanding between alumni relations and student affairs colleagues, who may not share a common history of collaboration on their campuses.

Recommendations for Further Research

While our immediate purpose in assembling this volume was to introduce emerging adulthood theory to scholars and practitioners specializing in higher education and student affairs, our further hope is that readers might be motivated as well to contribute to the scholarship of emerging adulthood. Over the past two decades, the body of research on emerging adulthood has continued to grow, facilitated in large part by the Society for the Study of Emerging Adulthood (SSEA), which from its inception has been multinational and multidisciplinary in scope. The membership of the organization includes scholars and practitioners across multiple academic and professional fields, who share a common concern for the growth and well-being of young people, as they discover their place in the adult world. By virtue of both their educational background and current work activities, student affairs professionals are well situated to contribute to the scholarship of emerging adulthood and in turn to benefit from it.

In particular, there is a need for more comparative research on student versus nonstudent populations. While the literature on emerging adulthood includes studies of both, direct comparisons within studies remain somewhat rare. This is an area in which higher education and student affairs scholars and practitioners might make a valued contribution to the advancement of research on emerging adulthood. Through their work, student affairs professionals often have access to potential research participants who are both students and emerging adults. Collaboration with faculty whose research involves emerging adults in other settings might yield fruitful lines of inquiry, while concurrently building an institutional ethos of collegiality.

Another line of research that is important to promote is the post-college development of emerging adults. The theory of emerging adulthood emphasizes that adulthood is not suddenly reached at age 18 or 21, nor upon college graduation. On the contrary, entry to adulthood occurs gradually through the twenties, and the roles that form the framework of adult life for most people— marriage or another stable partnership, parenthood, and stable work—are not entered until about age 30 in the United States and other economically developed countries. Thus, it is important for researchers to trace more definitively the path after college, particularly how a college education prepares emerging adults for the workplace—or not (Arnett, 2015). According to data from the U.S. Department of Labor, it takes young people who obtain a four-year college degree an average of four years before they obtain their first long-term job (defined as a job lasting at least five years) (Yates, 2005). We need to know more about why it takes so long to find a stable job after college. Student affairs professionals could be a vital link in collaborating with researchers to answer this question through their work with young alumni. It is also important to delineate more clearly the paths of those who do not obtain their degree even after six years. According to the National Center for Education Statistics (2018), this is the outcome for nearly half of the students who enter a four-year program. More needs to be done to raise the success rate, and research is the best path to developing effective strategies. Here again, student affairs professionals can collaborate with researchers in recruiting appropriate samples.

As more structured interventions are implemented to challenge and support emerging adults in college and beyond, assessment of outcomes associated with various approaches remains a critical element in advancing the literature on best practices. Building upon a long history in which educators have used action research to inform their own practice (Mills, 2003), the scholarship of teaching and learning (Hutchings, Huber, & Ciccone, 2011), rooted in the work of Boyer (1990), has generated broader interest in applied research within higher education settings. Concurrent emphasis on accountability in higher education (Burke, 2005) has prompted investment in institutional research and expansion of the literature on student affairs assessment (Keeling, Wall, Underhile, & Dungy, 2008; Upcraft & Schuh, 1996), which can, in turn, provide guidance and support for the scholarship of teaching and learning.

The chapters in this book can serve as an important resource in efforts to apply emerging adulthood theory to higher education and student affairs practice, as well as to advance the research of the field. As explained in our own opening chapter, the book was structured intentionally to draw upon the power of meaningful learning and conditionalized knowledge to promote transfer of theory to practice. In addressing their respective topics, the contributing authors rose to this challenge by drawing upon both their subject matter expertise and their own experience as scholars, practitioners, and in some instances, emerging adults. Moving forward, we invite readers to build upon this foundation through original applications of emerging adulthood theory to administrative and student affairs practice, as well as through contributions to the growing body of research on emerging adulthood itself. This book was born of a desire to open a conversation on implications of emerging adulthood theory for higher education and student affairs. It is very much our hope that it will not be the final word on the subject.

References

Arnett, J. J. (2015). *Emerging adulthood: The winding road from the late teens through the twenties* (2nd ed.). New York, NY: Oxford.

Arnett, J. J. (2016). Does emerging adulthood theory apply across social classes? National data on a persistent question. *Emerging Adulthood, 4*, 227–235.

Arnett, J. J., Kloep, M., Hendry, L. A., & Tanner, J. L. (2011). *Debating emerging adulthood: Stage or process?* New York, NY: Oxford.

Boyer, E. L. (1990). *Scholarship reconsidered: Priorities of the professoriate.* San Francisco, CA: Jossey-Bass.

Burke, J. C. (Ed.) (2005). *Achieving accountability in higher education: Balancing public, academic, and market demands.* San Francisco, CA: Jossey-Bass.

Hutchings, P., Huber, M. T., & Ciccone, A. (2011). *The scholarship of teaching and learning reconsidered: Institutional integrity and impact.* San Francisco, CA: Jossey-Bass.

Keeling, R. P., Wall, A. F., Underhile, R., & Dungy, G. J. (2008). *Assessment reconsidered: Institutional effectiveness for student success.* Washington, DC: NASPA.

Kram, K. E. (1985). *Mentoring at work: Developmental relationships in organizational life.* Glenview, IL: Scott, Foresman.

Mills, G. E. (2003). *Action research: A guide for the teacher researcher* (2nd ed.). Upper Saddle River, NJ: Merrill Prentice Hall.

National Center for Education Statistics (NCES). (2018). *The condition of education, 2013.* Washington, DC: U.S. Department of Education. Retrieved from www.nces.gov.

Parks, S. D. (2011). *Big questions, worthy dreams: Mentoring emerging adults in their search for meaning, purpose, and faith* (2nd ed.). San Francisco, CA: Jossey-Bass.

Penney, S. W., & Rose, B. B. (2001). *Dollars for dreams: Student affairs staff as fundraisers.* Washington, DC: NASPA.

Reesor, L. M., Bagunu, G. A., & Gregory, L. (2015). Making professional connections. In M. J. Amey & L. M. Reesor (Eds.), *Beginning your journey: A guide for new professionals in student affairs* (4th ed., pp. 177–201). Washington, DC: NASPA.

Strange, C. C., & Banning, J. H. (2015). *Designing for learning: Creating campus environments for student success* (2nd ed.). San Francisco, CA: Jossey-Bass.

Upcraft, M. L., & Schuh, J. H. (1996). *Assessment in student affairs: A guide for practitioners.* San Francisco, CA: Jossey-Bass.

Wells, J. B. (Ed.). (2015). *CAS professional standards for higher education* (9th ed.). Washington, DC: Council for the Advancement of Standards in Higher Education.

Yates, J. A. (2005). The transition from school to work: Education and work experiences. *Monthly Labor Review, 128*(2), 21–32.

APPENDIX

INFORMATION AND RESOURCES ON EMERGING ADULTHOOD

Society for the Study of Emerging Adulthood (SSEA)

"The Society for the Study of Emerging Adulthood (SSEA) is a multidisciplinary, international organization with a focus on theory and research related to emerging adulthood, which includes the age range of approximately 18 through 29 years. The primary goal of the Society is to advance the understanding of development in emerging adulthood through scholarship, education, training, policy and practice. This goal is promoted through Biennial Meetings, the flagship journal Emerging Adulthood, and a website that includes information on topics, events, and publications pertaining to emerging adults from diverse backgrounds, cultures, and countries. Membership is open to researchers, policy makers, educators and practitioners with special interests in development during this period of life." (SSEA website, 2018). Additional information is available at the SSEA website, ssea.org.

Emerging Adulthood, the Journal

Emerging Adulthood (EA) is the flagship journal of the Society for the Study of Emerging Adulthood (SSEA). It is an interdisciplinary and international journal for advancements in theory, methodology, and empirical research on development and adaptation during the late teens and twenties. The journal seeks manuscripts that advance basic and applied knowledge of normative and atypical development during emerging adulthood; studies that focus on the antecedents and/or consequences of experiences during this age-period are also welcome. The journal embraces the use of both qualitative and quantitative methodology. The journal also considers manuscripts that advance theory or measurement/methodology. *Emerging Adulthood* is an interdisciplinary forum covering clinical, developmental, and social psychology, and other social sciences such as anthropology, psychiatry, public policy, social work, sociology, public health, and postsecondary education. Editor: Moin Syed. For more information, see https://uk.sagepub.com/en-gb/eur/emerging-adulthood/journal202127.

SSEA Student Affairs and College Student Development Topic Network

The Student Affairs and College Student Development Topic Network is one of 23 groups that bring together SSEA members who have common interests in specific areas of emerging adulthood research or practice. This topic network focuses specifically on the ways in which today's traditional aged college students and young alumni differ from those of previous generations. Members of the network share an interest in learning and development in higher education. The purpose of the network is to explore how colleges and universities have been affected by today's longer pathway to adulthood and how they can become more effective in addressing the needs of their emerging adult constituents. Chair: Joe Murray; Co-Chair: Jarrett Warshaw. Additional information on this and other topic networks is available on the SSEA topic network webpage, http://ssea.org/membership/topic_networks.htm.

APA Division 7: Developmental Psychology

Division 7 of the American Psychological Association (APA) "promotes research in the field of developmental psychology and high standards in the application of scientific knowledge to educational, child care, policy, and related settings" (APA website, 2018). Contact information and additional details of the Division's services and resources can be found at its website, http://www.apadivisions.org/division-7/index.aspx?_ga=2.59429865.539189703.1521918214-1028161052.1519179284.

Oxford University Press Emerging Adulthood Series

In 2014, Oxford University Press initiated a line of books addressing specific aspects of emerging adult development. Additional information about the series can be found at the publisher's website, https://global.oup.com/academic/content/series/e/emerging-adulthood-series-eas/?lang=en&cc=us.

Inventory of the Dimensions of Emerging Adulthood (IDEA)

The *Inventory of the Dimensions of Emerging Adulthood (IDEA)* is an instrument developed by Alan Reifman, which is used to assess individuals' identification with key themes associated with the transition to adulthood. Additional information about the instrument is available at the Measurement Instrument Database for the Social Sciences website, http://www.midss.org/content/idea-inventory-dimensions-emerging-adulthood.

Becoming Adult: How Young People Are Making It in Today's World

Jennifer Tanner, an applied developmental psychologist at Rutgers University, maintains a blog on the *Psychology Today* website, where she addresses various aspects of the transition to adulthood. The main blog page can be found at https://www.psychologytoday.com/us/blog/becoming-adult.

Alan Reifman's Emerging Adulthood Page

Alan Reifman, Professor of Human Development and Family Studies at Texas Tech University, has created a website that serves as a gateway to various resources related to emerging adulthood and the transition to adulthood generally. The main page for the website can be found at http://emergingadulthood.blogspot.com/.

CONTRIBUTOR BIOGRAPHIES

Editors

Joseph L. Murray is Associate Professor of Education and Director of the Graduate Program in College Student Personnel at Bucknell University. He has previously held student affairs positions at Ohio University, Saint Martin's College (now Saint Martin's University), Michigan State University, and Thomas M. Cooley Law School, and has developed management training for Arthur Andersen & Company. He earned his Ph.D. in College and University Administration from Michigan State University and his M.Ed. in Student Personnel Services from Ohio University, and completed his undergraduate work in Social Work, Sociology, and Special Education at Quincy College (now Quincy University). He is the author of *Training for Student Leaders* (1994, 1998) and *Undergraduate Research for Student Engagement and Learning* (2018). His work has also appeared in the *Journal of College Student Development*, *NASPA Journal*, *About Campus*, *Journal of College Student Retention*, *Journal of College and Character*, and *Council on Undergraduate Research Quarterly*. He currently chairs the Society for the Study of Emerging Adulthood's Student Affairs and College Student Development Topic Network and is a past recipient of ACPA's Annuit Coeptis Award for emerging professionals in student affairs.

Jeffrey Jensen Arnett is a Research Professor in the Department of Psychology at Clark University in Worcester, Massachusetts. He has also taught at the University of Missouri. During 2005, he was a Fulbright Scholar at the University of Copenhagen, Denmark. He is the author of the book *Emerging Adulthood: The Winding Road from the Late Teens through the Twenties*, now in its 2nd edition, published in 2015 by Oxford University Press. He is also the Founding President and Executive Director of the Society for the Study of Emerging Adulthood (www.ssea.org). His book (with Elizabeth Fishel) for parents of emerging adults, *Getting to 30: A Parent's Guide to the Twentysomething Years*, was published in May 2014. For more information, see www.jeffreyarnett.com.

Contributors

Aimee C. Adams is Associate Professor and Faculty Counselor in the Department of Counseling and Psychological Services at Kutztown University of Pennsylvania. She also holds an adjunct faculty appointment at Lehigh University in the Counseling Psychology Department and College of Education. Dr. Adams earned her Ph.D. in Counseling Psychology from Lehigh University. Her research interests include professional practice issues; legal, ethical, and policy issues; counselor multicultural competence; and college counseling issues. She has presented at numerous regional, state, and national conferences on topics including policies on mandated assessment in college counseling, ethical issues in college counseling, nutrition's impact on mental health, and college students' expectations for counselor multicultural competence. She has published on the topics of animal assisted counseling interventions, racial identity, mandated continuing education, and sexual violence education policy, and has served as a peer reviewer for the American Counseling Association (ACA).

Christina Daniel is Associate Director of Orientation, Transition and Parent Programs at the University at Buffalo, where she oversees the planning and implementation of orientation programs for all domestic undergraduate students. Prior to joining the University, she served on the New Student and Sophomore Programs staff at Georgia Institute of Technology. She earned her M.Ed. in College Student Affairs Administration from the University of Georgia and completed her undergraduate degree in Business Administration at Bowling Green State University. She is an active member of NODA: the Association for Orientation, Transition, and Retention. She has served the organization's membership through conference committee work and presentations focused on graduate student development, student leadership, the first-year student experience, and the pedagogy of orientation programs. In 2011, she was honored as a recipient of the Ohio College Personnel Association's (OCPA) Undergraduate Student Leadership Award.

James C. Hearn is Professor of Higher Education and Associate Director of the Institute of Higher Education at the University of Georgia. He holds a Ph.D. in Sociology of Education and an M.A. in Sociology from Stanford University, as well as an M.B.A. in Finance from the University of Pennsylvania's Wharton School of Business. He completed his undergraduate work at Duke University. His teaching and research focus on postsecondary education organization, policy, and finance. Most recently, he has studied strategic institutional change and state postsecondary policy development. Dr. Hearn is currently a member of the Editorial Advisory

Board for the *Journal of Higher Education* and a consulting editor for *Research in Higher Education*. In the past, he has served as an associate editor of the *Educational Researcher* and *Research in Higher Education* and on the editorial boards of the *Review of Higher Education*, *Teachers College Record*, and *Sociology of Education*. He has also served as a section editor for the annual volume *Higher Education: Handbook of Theory and Research*. He is a past recipient of the Distinguished Research Award of Division J (Postsecondary Education) of the American Educational Research Association (AERA) and has been named a TIAA-CREF Institute Fellow.

Lisa Landreman is Assistant Vice President and Dean of Student Life at Roger Williams University. Her higher education career has spanned over 25 years and has included student affairs administration in the areas of residence life, disability services, social justice education, Title IX, study abroad, disability services, and crisis management. She has also taught courses in intergroup dialogue facilitation, Women's Studies, and Higher Education Administration. Dr. Landreman earned her Ph.D. in Higher Education from the University of Michigan, her M.S. in Higher Education and Student Affairs from Indiana University, and her B.S. in Social Work from the University of Wisconsin-LaCrosse. Her research interests include critical multicultural education practice, intercultural development, and liberal arts learning. She is editor of the book, *The Art of Effective Facilitation: Reflections from Social Justice Educators* (2013). Her work has also appeared in the *Journal of College Student Development*, *Research in Higher Education*, and *About Campus*. She has served on the governing board of ACPA and was recognized in 2011 as an ACPA Diamond Honoree.

Patrick G. Love is Vice President for Student Affairs and Director of the Student Personnel Administration graduate program at Springfield College. Prior to joining Springfield, he was Executive-in-Residence for the Higher Education and Student Affairs graduate program at Bowling Green State University. He was also Vice President for Student Affairs at New York Institute of Technology and has held high-level administrative positions at Rutgers University, Pace University, and Le Moyne College and tenured faculty appointments at Kent State University and New York University. He earned his Ph.D. in higher education and student affairs from Indiana University and his M.S. in counseling psychology and student development and B.A. in political science from The State University of New York at Albany. He has published five books and over 35 articles and book chapters on various aspects of higher education and student affairs, and has consulted with or spoken before more than 40 institutions and organizations. He has held leadership positions in ACPA, NASPA, and the Association of College and University Housing Officers—International (ACUHO-I), and was recognized by the NASPA Foundation in 2017 as a Pillar of the Profession. He is also a past recipient of ACPA's Diamond Honoree and Annuit Coeptis awards.

Richard Mullendore retired in 2014 as Professor Emeritus of College Student Affairs Administration at the University of Georgia, where he earlier served as Vice President for Student Affairs and Associate Provost. He also served as Vice Chancellor for Student Life at the University of Mississippi and worked at the University of North Carolina at Wilmington, the University of Charleston, and Tusculum College. He is currently a Fellow of the National Resource Center for the First-Year Experience and Students in Transition. Dr. Mullendore received his B.A. from Bradley University, his M.S. from Southern Illinois University at Carbondale, and his Ph.D. from Michigan State University. He is a frequent speaker and consultant on student affairs administration, student learning, orientation, parent programs, housing and residence life, and transfer students. He is the author of approximately 50 publications. He has served as President of NODA and as a member of the NASPA Board of Directors, the NASPA Region III Advisory Board, the Editorial Board of the *Journal of Student Affairs Research and Practice*, and the Directorates of Commissions I & II of ACPA. He has received several awards including the Pillar of the Profession (NASPA), the Bob Leach Award for Outstanding Service to Students (NASPA, Region III), the Outstanding Contributions to the Orientation Profession Award (NODA), the Outstanding Professional Contribution Award (North Carolina College Personnel Association), and the President's Award (NODA).

Rosemary J. Perez is Assistant Professor in the School of Education at Iowa State University, where she teaches in the Student Affairs master's and Higher Education doctoral programs. She is also a Faculty Affiliate in Women and Gender Studies and serves as the Director of the Education for Social Justice Graduate Certificate. She has previously held professional positions in student affairs at the University of San Francisco and American University. She earned her Ph.D. in Higher Education from the University of Michigan, her M.Ed. in Higher Education and Student Affairs from the University of Vermont, and her B.S. in Biological Sciences and Psychology from Carnegie Mellon University. Her research interests include student development theory, intercultural learning, social justice education, and professional socialization in student affairs. Her work has appeared in *Equity & Excellence in Education*, the *Journal of Diversity in Higher Education*, the *Journal of College Student Development,* and the *Journal of Higher Education*. She also currently serves on the editorial boards of the *Journal of College Student Development* and the *Journal for the Study of Postsecondary and Tertiary Education*. She is a 2017–2019 ACPA Emerging Scholar and was previously an ACPA Coalition for Women's Identities Emerging Scholar in Residence.

Shelby K. Radcliffe is Vice President for Advancement at Willamette University. Prior to assuming her current position, she served as Vice President for Institutional Advancement at Occidental College for four years and held various positions in advancement at Bucknell University for 15 years. She holds a BA in English from Pennsylvania State University and an MSED in College Student Personnel from Bucknell University. She regularly speaks at the national and international conferences of the Association of Professional Researchers in Advancement (APRA), the Council for the Advancement and Support of Education (CASE), the Association of Fund Raising Professionals (AFP), and Academic Impressions. Her work has been featured in the *Chronicle of Philanthropy* and *CASE Currents*. In 2008, she received the APRA Award for Distinguished Service to the Profession, and in 2017, she received the CASE Crystal Apple Award for Teaching Excellence.

Lisa Severy is currently Director of Career Services at the University of Colorado Boulder. Before joining the team in Colorado, she worked at the University of Florida's Career Resource Center for seven years. Dr. Severy earned her bachelor's degree from Indiana University and three graduate degrees, including a PhD in Counselor Education, from the University of Florida. Additionally, she is a Licensed Professional Counselor in Colorado. Dr. Severy is a past president of the National Career Development Association (NCDA) and currently serves on the Governing Council of ACA. She is a national leader in the fields of career development and counseling, the new collegiate job market, experiential education, international student employment, student affairs, and the intersection of education and employment. She has co-authored two books, *Making Career Decisions that Count* and *Turning Points,* and has made contributions to the *Encyclopedia of Counseling,* the *Counselor's Guide to Career Assessment Instruments, Rentz's Student Affairs Practice in Higher Education,* the *Career Development Quarterly,* the *Journal of College Student Development,* and the *Journal of College Counseling.*

Bruce Sharkin is Faculty Psychologist and Professor in the Department of Counseling and Psychological Services at Kutztown University of Pennsylvania. He has 30 years of experience in college counseling and has chaired his department. He earned his Ph.D. in Counseling Psychology from the University of Maryland. Dr. Sharkin is the author or co-author of over 25 journal articles and the author of two books, *College Students in Distress: A Resource Guide for Faculty, Staff, and Campus Community* (2006) and *Being a College Counselor on Today's Campus: Roles, Contributions, and Special Challenges* (2012). He has served as an editorial reviewer for the *Journal of College Counseling, Journal of Counseling Psychology,* and *Journal of Counseling and Development.* Dr. Sharkin currently serves as a reviewer for the ACA Publications Office.

C. Carney Strange is Professor Emeritus of Higher Education and Student Affairs at Bowling Green State University where, from 1978 to 2013, he taught graduate courses on student development and the design and impact of campus environments. Dr. Strange earned both his Ph.D. in Student Development in

Higher Education and his M.A. in College Student Personnel from the University of Iowa. He completed his undergraduate work at Saint Meinrad College of Liberal Arts, where he studied French Literature, Philosophy, and Classical Languages. He has published widely in the field of higher education and student affairs, serving as co-editor and author of *Achieving Student Success: Effective Student Services in Canadian Higher Education* (2010) and *Serving Diverse Students in Canadian Higher Education* (2016) and senior co-author of *Designing for Learning: Creating Campus Environments for Student Success* (2015). An ACPA Senior Scholar and NASPA Faculty Fellow, he was selected as a Diamond Honoree (1999) and Pillar of the Profession (2006), and was the recipient of ACPA's 2010 Contribution to Knowledge Award.

Michael Toney is Director of Orientation at Emory University, where he oversees the planning and implementation of orientation programs for new undergraduate students. He earned his M.Ed. in College Student Affairs Administration from the University of Georgia and completed his undergraduate work at the Georgia Institute of Technology. He is actively involved in NODA: The Association for Orientation, Transition, and Retention and has presented on supporting underrepresented populations, student staff education, and new professional development. His professional and academic interests include the first year experience, students in transition, institutional governance, and identity development.

Jarrett B. Warshaw is Assistant Professor of Higher Education in the Department of Educational Leadership and Research Methodology at Florida Atlantic University. Prior to joining the faculty at Florida Atlantic, he was a research consultant for The Council of Independent Colleges' project on the financial futures of small, private colleges and for the Office of Strategy and Policy at The University of Texas at Austin. He has also worked in undergraduate admissions. He earned his Ph.D. in Higher Education from the Institute of Higher Education at the University of Georgia, where he was a Presidential Fellow of the Graduate School. He holds an MSED in College Student Personnel from Bucknell University and a BA in English from Skidmore College. His research interests include postsecondary organization, finance, and policy, with a focus on how colleges and universities change and adapt in relation to their external environments. His work has appeared in the *Journal of Higher Education*, *Journal of Education and Work*, and *Journal of Higher Education Policy and Management*. In 2015, he was selected as Outstanding Doctoral Student by ACPA's Standing Committee for Graduate Students and New Professionals.

Maureen E. Wilson is Professor and Chair of the Department of Higher Education and Student Affairs at Bowling Green State University. She holds a Ph.D. in Higher Education and Student Affairs from Ohio State University, an MA in College and University Administration from Michigan State University, and a BSBA in Business Administration and Communication Arts from Aquinas College of Michigan. She has previously held student and academic affairs positions at Mississippi State University, Ohio State University, the University of South Carolina, and the College of William and Mary. Her research interests are focused on college students, professional practice in student affairs, and college teaching. Her most recent work has dealt with professional identity and socialization in student affairs and behavioral norms of student affairs. Her work has appeared in the *Journal of College Student Development, Journal of Student Affairs Research and Practice, College Student Affairs Journal, Journal of College and University Student Housing*, and *Peabody Journal of Education*. She has also written 15 peer reviewed book chapters and edited or co-edited two anthologies on college student development, as part of the *ASHE Reader Series*. She is an ACPA Senior Scholar, past recipient of ACPA's Emerging Scholar, Annuit Coeptis, and Diamond Honoree awards, as well as ACUHO-I's Research and Publication and Betty L. Harrah Manuscript of the Year awards, OCPA's Phillip A. Tripp Distinguished Service Award, and ACPA Mid-Level Community of Practice's Outstanding Research, Contribution, and/or Scholarship Award.

INDEX

Note: Page numbers in bold and italics indicate tables and figures, respectively

Printed in the USA
CPSIA information can be obtained
at www.ICGtesting.com
LVHW022030101223
766158LV00005B/268